CONFLICT REFUGEES

Based on a systematic and empirical comparative study of six European Union (EU) countries, Christel Querton explores judicial decision-making in the context of persons fleeing armed conflicts in the EU. Addressing and redressing misconceptions about the relevance of the Refugee Convention, this book demonstrates how appellate authorities across the EU approach situations of armed conflict predominantly through outdated understandings of warfare and territoriality. Thus, they apply a higher standard of proof than is warranted by international refugee law. Adopting a gender perspective, Querton also shows how appellate authorities fail to acknowledge the gender-differentiated impact of armed conflicts. Drawing from gender and security studies, this book proposes an original conceptual framework that, supported by existing international legal standards, reframes the definition of 'refugee' and better reflects the reality of violence in modern-day conflicts. In doing so, it reasserts the Refugee Convention as the cornerstone of international protection.

CHRISTEL QUERTON is a Wallscourt Fellow in Law at the University of the West of England, Bristol. She researches international refugee law, focusing on the protection of persons fleeing contemporary armed conflicts and refugee women. Prior to academia, she practised as an immigration and human rights barrister in London.

Cambridge Asylum and Migration Studies

At no time in modern history have so many people been on the move as at present. Migration facilitates critical social, economic, and humanitarian linkages. But it may also challenge prevailing notions of bounded political communities, of security, and of international law.

The political and legal systems that regulate the transborder movement of persons were largely devised in the mid-twentieth century, and are showing their strains. New challenges have arisen for policymakers, advocates, and decision-makers that require the adaptation and evolution of traditional models to meet emerging imperatives.

Edited by a world leader in refugee law, this new series aims to be a forum for innovative writing on all aspects of the transnational movement of people. It publishes single or co-authored works that may be legal, political, or cross-disciplinary in nature, and will be essential reading for anyone looking to understand one of the most important issues of the twenty-first century

Books in the Series

The Child in International Refugee Law
Jason M. Pobjoy

Refuge Lost: Asylum Law in an Interdependent World
Daniel Ghezelbash

Demanding Rights: Europe's Supranational Courts and the Dilemma of Migrant Vulnerability
Moritz Baumgärtel

Climate Change, Disasters, and the Refugee Convention
Matthew Scott

CONFLICT REFUGEES

European Union Law and Practice

CHRISTEL QUERTON
University of the West of England, Bristol

CAMBRIDGE
UNIVERSITY PRESS

CAMBRIDGE
UNIVERSITY PRESS

Shaftesbury Road, Cambridge CB2 8EA, United Kingdom

One Liberty Plaza, 20th Floor, New York, NY 10006, USA

477 Williamstown Road, Port Melbourne, VIC 3207, Australia

314–321, 3rd Floor, Plot 3, Splendor Forum, Jasola District Centre, New Delhi – 110025, India

103 Penang Road, #05–06/07, Visioncrest Commercial, Singapore 238467

Cambridge University Press is part of Cambridge University Press & Assessment, a department of the University of Cambridge.

We share the University's mission to contribute to society through the pursuit of education, learning and research at the highest international levels of excellence.

www.cambridge.org
Information on this title: www.cambridge.org/9781009359399

DOI: 10.1017/9781009359429

First published 2023

A catalogue record for this publication is available from the British Library.

Library of Congress Cataloging-in-Publication Data
Names: Querton, Christel, author.
Title: Conflict refugees : European Union law and practice / Christel Querton, University of the West of England, Bristol.
Description: Cambridge, United Kingdom ; New York, NY : Cambridge University Press, 2023. | Series: Cambridge asylum and migration studies | Based on author's thesis (doctoral – University of Newcastle upon Tyne, 2019) issued under title: Gender, Political Violence and Refugees : The International Protection of Persons Fleeing Armed Conflicts in the European Union. | Includes bibliographical references and index.
Identifiers: LCCN 2022062056 | ISBN 9781009359399 (hardback) | ISBN 9781009359405 (paperback) | ISBN 9781009359429 (ebook)
Subjects: LCSH: Refugees – Legal status, laws, etc. – European Union countries
Classification: LCC KJE6057 .Q84 2023 | DDC 342.408/3–dc23/eng/20230519
LC record available at https://lccn.loc.gov/2022062056

ISBN 978-1-009-35939-9 Hardback
ISBN 978-1-009-35940-5 Paperback

CONTENTS

TABLES

SERIES EDITOR'S PREFACE

The dissonance between Europe's generous reception of refugees from the war in Ukraine and its reluctance to welcome refugees fleeing conflicts in Afghanistan, Iraq and Syria is striking. Whereas Ukrainian refugees have benefited from a special regional regime that welcomes them with open arms and minimal red tape, refugees from other contemporary conflicts have been forced to navigate the more traditional systems to secure recognition of their protected status. These refugees have too often been wrongly denied Convention refugee status on the basis of a misconception that the Refugee Convention distinguishes between refugees fleeing conflict and others – and in particular that formal refugee status is not to be recognised in the case of those who are fleeing the 'indiscriminate' risks that arise during armed conflict.

Christel Querton's important book makes clear why this approach is mistaken. Drawing on insights from both feminist and security studies, she shows that violence in situations of armed conflict is not in fact indiscriminate. Rather, Querton argues, violence during conflict is actually imbued with strategic logic and is often highly gendered. And because the nature of violence experienced by persons in situations of contemporary armed conflict is motivated, tactical and, most important, political, its victims should be understood usually to meet the requirements for recognition of refugee status. Those denied that status – including those shunted off into less generous complementary or subsidiary protection regimes – have been wrongly deprived of their rights as refugees under international law.

Querton grounds her arguments not just in extensive security studies and feminist literature, but on a systematic and empirical comparative study of appellate jurisprudence in six European Union states. She shows why her arguments are not simply conceptually important, but are needed in practice to counter the common and unlawful disfranchisement of refugees from conflict. Querton argues that by not coming to grips with the true nature of violence experienced during modern conflict, courts have failed in their duty to ensure the continued relevance of the Refugee Convention.

Conceived with clarity and intellectual rigour, and consistently tested against empirical realities, the arguments presented in *Conflict Refugees* are both powerful and timely.

Editor, Cambridge Asylum and Migration Studies

ACKNOWLEDGEMENTS

This book would not have been possible without the expertise and support of many friends and colleagues. In particular, I am grateful to my principal PhD supervisor María-Teresa Gil-Bazo for her support in completing my dissertation, which formed the basis of this book. My thanks also go to my other supervisors, Richard Collier and Colin Harvey. Significantly, a special thank you to Hélène Lambert for her examination of my thesis and continued interest since then.

This research was made possible by a tuition and maintenance grant from the Arts and Humanities Research Council and the Northern Bridge Doctoral Training Partnership between September 2016 and September 2019. With respect to the studentship, particular thanks go to Sarah Rylance and Michael Rossington for their support in the early years of the project.

I am indebted to the following for enabling access to essential data underlying this research project: Bettina Chu from the Danish Refugee Council, Laurent Dufour from the Centre for Research and Documentation of the French National Asylum Court and the Data Access Panel and staff at HM Courts and Tribunals Service in the UK.

My venture from legal practice into academia was encouraged by many along the way. I have had the benefit of academic and professional support and exchanges with many, but I would like to acknowledge the following in particular. At Newcastle University Law School: Francesco De Cecco, Ilke Turkmendag, Kathryn Hollingsworth, Conall Mallory, Hélène Tyrrell, Ruth Houghton, Jenny Johnstone, Nikki Godden-Rasul, Catherine Dale, Philippa Carter and last but not least Raffaella D'Antonio. From the Refugee Law Initiative, School of Advanced Study at the University of London: David Cantor, Sarah Singer, Nick Maple, Susan Reardon-Smith, Reuven (Ruvi) Ziegler, Jean-François Durieux, Brian Gorlick and Matthew Scott. From Bristol Law School at the University of the West of England: Noëlle Quénivet, Nicholas Ryder, Shilan Shah-Davis, Demelza Hall, Jessica Elliott, James Green and Sarah Leonard. Finally, colleagues across institutions, including Jesper Lindholm from Aalborg University, James C. Simeon from York University in Toronto and Moira Dustin from Sussex University, with whom I founded the Women in Refugee Law network.

Of course, this long-term project would not have been possible without the support of my family, across countries and during Brexit plus a pandemic, in particular my mum Gertrud Querton and my partner Daniel Campano Florido. This book is dedicated to our imminent new addition to the family, I look forward to starting this new chapter.

TABLE OF CASES

Court of Justice of the European Union

European Court of Human Rights

International Court of Justice

International Tribunal for the former Yugoslavia

International Tribunal for Rwanda

Australia

France

The Netherlands

New Zealand

United Kingdom

TABLE OF TREATIES AND OTHER INTERNATIONAL AND REGIONAL INSTRUMENTS

ABBREVIATIONS

AN	Spanish National High Court (Audiencia Nacional)
BE	Belgium
CCE/RvV	Belgian Council for Alien Law Litigation (Conseil du Contentieux des Étrangers/Raad voor Vreemdelingenbetwistingen)
CE	Council of State (Conseil d'État)
CEAS	Common European Asylum System
CEDAW	Convention for the Elimination of All Forms of Discrimination against Women
CENDOJ	General Council of the Judiciary (Consejo General del Poder Judicial)
CERD	International Convention on the Elimination of All Forms of Discrimination
CESEDA	Code de l'Entrée et du Séjour des Étrangers et du Droit d'Asile
CJEU	Court of Justice of the European Union
CNDA	French National Asylum Court (Cour Nationale du Droit d'Asile)
DK	Denmark
DRAB	Danish Refugee Appeals Board (Flygtningenævnet)
DRC	Danish Refugee Council
EASO	European Asylum Support Office
ECHR	European Convention on Human Rights
ECRE	European Council on Refugees and Exiles
ECtHR	European Court of Human Rights
ELENA	The European Legal Network on Asylum
ES	Spain
EU	European Union
EUAA	European Union Agency for Asylum
FR	France
FTT	First-Tier Tribunal
HMCTS	Her Majesty's Courts and Tribunals Service
IAC	Immigration and Asylum Chamber
ICC	International Criminal Court
ICCPR	International Covenant on Civil and Political Rights
ICJ	International Court of Justice
ICL	International Criminal Law
ICRC	International Committee of the Red Cross
ICTR	International Criminal Tribunal for Rwanda
ICTY	International Criminal Tribunal for the former Yugoslavia

IED	improvised explosive device
IHL	International Humanitarian Law
IHRL	International Human Rights Law
IRO	International Refugee Organisation
IS/ISIS/ISIL	Islamic State/Islamic State of Iraq and Syria/Islamic State of Iraq and the Levant
MS	Member States
NGO	non-government organisation
NL	The Netherlands
OAR	Spanish Office for Asylum and Refuge (Oficina de Asilo y Refugio)
OAU	Organisation of African Unity
OCHA	Office for the Coordination of Humanitarian Affairs
OSAGI	Office of the Special Adviser to the Secretary-General on Gender Issues and Advancement of Women
PSG	Particular Social Group
PYD	Democratic Union Party (Partîya Yekîtî ya Dêmokrat)
QD	Qualification Directive
Rb	Dutch District Court (Rechtbank)
RvS	Council of State (Raad van State)
SRSG-SVC	UN Special Representative to the Secretary-General on Sexual Violence in Conflict
TFEU	Treaty on the Functioning of the European Union
TS	Spanish Supreme Court (Tribunal Supremo)
UDHR	Universal Declaration of Human Rights
UK	United Kingdom
UN	United Nations
UNAMA	United Nations Assistance Mission in Afghanistan
UNGA	United Nations General Assembly
UNHCR	United Nations High Commissioner for Refugees
UNSC	United Nations Security Council
USAID	United States Agency for International Development
UT	Upper Tribunal
VCLT	Vienna Convention on the Law of Treaties

1

Introduction

1.1 Introduction

The number of forcibly displaced persons in the world today is the highest ever recorded, and in the last decade alone, their number has doubled.[1] Violence associated with armed conflict has become the main cause of forced displacement in the twenty-first century,[2] and most refugees originate from countries experiencing protracted armed conflicts such as Syria, Afghanistan, South Sudan, Myanmar, Somalia, Democratic Republic of Congo, Sudan and Iraq. Global trends are reflected in the number and origins of persons seeking asylum in the European Union (EU). However, there are many misconceptions and disagreements as to whether persons fleeing armed conflicts are refugees as defined by the Refugee Convention. This book is thus an enquiry into the continued relevance of the 1951 Convention relating to the Status of Refugees (Refugee Convention) for the growing number of persons fleeing contemporary armed conflicts.

The book takes as a starting point the claim made in security studies that the nature and characteristics of armed conflicts across the world today have changed, and have important gendered dimensions that affect the reasons why persons flee their homes.[3] More specifically, this scholarship identifies the fundamental characteristics of contemporary armed conflicts as including the rise of non-state actors and their relative control over the conduct of hostilities, weakening of state institutions, identity politics as drivers of violence and the gendered strategies and tactics of fighting parties. Scholars in this field thus highlight that one of the main strategies of fighting parties is to exercise political control over territory by forcibly displacing and terrorising populations through highly visible forms of human rights violations. Further, it has been claimed that the role of violence cannot be understood without reference to gender.[4] Drawing on this knowledge, the book conceptualises violence exercised in situations of contemporary armed conflict as being imbued

[1] A total of 89.3 million by the end of 2021, United Nations High Commissioner for Refugees (UNHCR), 'Global Trends 2021' (16 June 2022) <www.unhcr.org/62a9d1494/global-trends-report-2021> accessed 26 July 2022, 2; UNHCR, 'Global Trends: Forced Displacement in 2020' (18 June 2021) <www.unhcr.org/uk/statistics/unhcrstats/60b638e37/global-trends-forced-displacement-2020.html> accessed 12 July 2021, 6.

[2] Volker Türk, Alice Edwards and Cornelis Wouters, 'Introduction' in Volker Türk, Alice Edwards and Cornelis Wouters (eds), *In Flight from Conflict and Violence: UNHCR's Consultations on Refugee Status and Other Forms of International Protection* (CUP 2017) 1.

[3] Mary Kaldor, *New and Old Wars: Organized Violence in a Global Era* (3rd edn, Polity Press 2012); Laura Sjoberg, *Gendering Global Conflict: Toward a Feminist Theory of War* (Columbia University Press 2013).

[4] Laura Sjoberg, 'Gender/Violence in a Gendered/Violent World' (2014) 42 *Millennium: Journal of International Studies* 532.

with strategic logic and highly gendered. Viewed in this manner, the nature of violence experienced by persons in situations of armed conflict presents itself as motivated, tactical and, most importantly, political. Accordingly, the book challenges the perception that violence in situations of armed conflict is indiscriminate,[5] and the perceived dichotomy between direct violence resulting from armed fighting and indirect violence resulting from the breakdown of law and order.[6]

The book examines the extent to which asylum appellate authorities in the EU take into account the changing nature of contemporary armed conflicts. It focuses on judicial practice in the EU owing to the regional codification of a distinct international protection status for persons fleeing armed conflicts. The book also explores how the Refugee Convention may be interpreted in a manner that better responds to the changed nature of contemporary armed conflicts from a gender perspective, thus reconceptualising the concept of the refugee. To answer these questions, the book provides an empirical analysis of how appellate authorities in six EU Member States (MS) interpret the Refugee Convention definition in Afghan, Iraqi and Syrian asylum appeals between 2013 and 2016.[7] Hence, this research contributes to existing debates regarding the continued relevance of the Refugee Convention some seventy years after it was adopted, and supports existing views that the Refugee Convention can be interpreted in a way that includes groups of individuals perceived as falling outside its scope.[8] Accordingly, the book rejects widely held opinions that the Refugee Convention requires reform in order to respond to contemporary forms of forced displacement.[9]

The introduction starts by setting the scene of international protection in the EU. It provides an overview of the international and regional refugee and human rights obligations of its MS and identifies some of the pitfalls of the creation of a new form of subsidiary protection for persons fleeing indiscriminate violence in situations of armed conflict. It then introduces the concepts at the core of this book, including violence, contemporary armed conflicts and the gender-differentiated impact of violence in conflict. The second part of the introduction explains the methodology designed for this empirical study. Finally, the structure of the book is set out.

[5] As noted in UNHCR, *Guidelines on International Protection No. 12: Claims for Refugee Status Related to Situations of Armed Conflict and Violence under Article 1A(2) of the 1951 Convention and/or 1967 Protocol Relating to the Status of Refugees and the Regional Refugee Definitions* (HCR/GIP/16/12, 2 December 2016) para 33; see also Cornelis (Kees) Wouters, 'Conflict Refugees' in Cathryn Costello, Michelle Foster and Jane McAdam (eds), *The Oxford Handbook of International Refugee Law* (OUP 2021) 817.

[6] As conceptualised in Hélène Lambert and Theo Farrell, 'The Changing Character of Armed Conflict and the Implications for Refugee Protection Jurisprudence' (2010) 22 *International Journal of Refugee Law* 237; Hélène Lambert, 'The Next Frontier: Expanding Protection in Europe for Victims of Armed Conflict and Indiscriminate Violence' (2013) 25 *International Journal of Refugee Law* 207.

[7] Belgium, Denmark, France, Spain, the Netherlands and the UK. Although the UK left the EU on 31 January 2020, it was a member of the EU during the study reference period.

[8] Michelle Foster, *International Refugee Law and Socio-Economic Rights: Refuge from Deprivation* (CUP 2007); Jane McAdam, *Complementary Protection in International Refugee Law* (OUP 2007); María-Teresa Gil-Bazo, 'Refugee Protection under International Human Rights Law: From Non-Refoulement to Residence and Citizenship' (2015) 34 *Refugee Survey Quarterly* 11; Jane McAdam, 'The Enduring Relevance of the 1951 Refugee Convention' (2017) 29 *International Journal of Refugee Law* 1.

[9] See for example Alexander Betts, 'Survival Migration: A New Protection Framework' (2010) 16 *Global Governance* 361; Colin Harvey, 'Time for Reform? Refugees, Asylum-Seekers, and Protection under International Human Rights Law' (2015) 34 *Refugee Survey Quarterly* 43.

1.1.1 International Protection in the EU

The principal international legal instrument for the protection of refugees is the Refugee Convention, which defines a refugee as a person who 'owing to well-founded fear of being persecuted for reasons of race, religion, nationality, membership of a particular social group or political opinion, is outside the country of his nationality and is unable or, owing to such fear, is unwilling to avail himself of the protection of that country'.[10] However, various regions such as the EU have created distinct protection statuses for persons fleeing 'indiscriminate violence' in situations of armed conflict. A beneficiary of subsidiary protection in EU law is a 'person who does not qualify as a refugee but in respect of whom substantial grounds have been shown for believing that the person concerned, if returned to his or her country of origin [...] would face a real risk of suffering serious harm [...] and is unable, or, owing to such risk, unwilling to avail himself or herself of the protection of that country'.[11] Serious harm is defined in Article 15(c) of the Qualification Directive as a 'serious and individual threat to a civilian's life or person by reason of indiscriminate violence in situations of international or internal armed conflict'. A third protection status in the EU provides for temporary protection 'in the event of a mass influx' of persons unable to return to their country of origin owing to the prevailing situation, in particular 'persons who have fled areas of armed conflict or endemic violence' and 'persons at serious risk of, or who have been the victims of, systematic or generalised violations of their human rights'.[12] The Common European Asylum System (CEAS) thus establishes different legal categories of international protection, creating a distinction between refugees and complementary protection beneficiaries whose rights and entitlements differ.[13] Current practice by EU MS is to grant different length of residence permits and substantive rights to Convention refugees and beneficiaries of subsidiary protection. For example, Belgium grants five-year residence permits to refugees and one year to subsidiary protection beneficiaries, whereas France issues ten-year residence permits to refugees and four years to subsidiary protection beneficiaries.[14] Residence permits for persons with temporary protection is harmonised at EU level, and they are granted an initial one-year residence permit that can be extended up to three years.[15] Moreover, the European Commission's proposal for a Regulation to replace the EU Qualification Directive would mandate different residence permit lengths,[16] and access to

[10] Article 1A(2) Convention Relating to the Status of Refugees (adopted 28 July 1951, entered into force 22 April 1954) 189 UNTS 137 (Refugee Convention) (hereinafter the 'refugee definition').

[11] Article 2(f) Directive 2011/95/EU of the European Parliament and of the Council of 13 December 2011 on standards for the qualification of third-country nationals or stateless persons as beneficiaries of international protection, for a uniform status for refugees or for persons eligible for subsidiary protection, and for the content of the protection granted (recast) [2011] OJ L337/9 (Qualification Directive).

[12] Articles 1 and 2(c) Council Directive 2001/55/EC of 20 July 2001 on minimum standards for giving temporary protection in the event of a mass influx of displaced persons and on measures promoting a balance of efforts between Member States in receiving such persons and bearing the consequences thereof (Temporary Protection Directive).

[13] In addition, some MS provide various forms of humanitarian protection based on domestic law.

[14] See Appendix A for further details.

[15] Article 4 Temporary Protection Directive.

[16] European Commission, Proposal for a Regulation of the European Parliament and of the Council on standards for the qualification of third-country nationals or stateless persons as beneficiaries of international protection, for a uniform status for refugees or for persons eligible for subsidiary protection and for the content of the protection granted and amending Council Directive 2003/109/EC of 25 November 2003 concerning the status of third-country nationals who are long-term residents (COM(2016) 466 final, 2016) Article 26.

travel documents,[17] and enable MS to limit social assistance for beneficiaries of subsidiary protection compared with refugees.[18]

Globally, state practice in interpreting the Refugee Convention has been inconsistent when the asylum claims of persons fleeing armed conflicts are assessed.[19] Many require claimants to be 'singled out' for persecution,[20] thereby excluding from refugee protection persons who have fled situations of armed conflict and widespread violence.[21] In her research, Holzer considers that one of the main issues that courts struggle with is the assessment of whether a person has a well-founded fear of being persecuted *for reasons of* the Refugee Convention grounds in the context of armed conflicts.[22] This difficulty may reflect UNHCR's traditional approach of treating 'war refugees' as 'special cases',[23] with the UNHCR Handbook stating that 'persons compelled to leave their country of origin as a result of international or national armed conflicts are not normally considered refugees'.[24] However, it goes on to note that 'foreign invasion or occupation of all or part of a country can result – and occasionally has resulted – in persecution for one or more of the reasons enumerated in the 1951 Convention'.[25] UNHCR has since recognised that persons fleeing conflicts may have a well-founded fear of being persecuted for a Convention reason in many situations.[26] In recognition of this important issue and restrictive trends in state practice, UNHCR issued Guidelines on International Protection on claims for refugee status related to situations of armed conflict and violence in 2016,[27] recognising that the majority of these situations lead

17 Ibid., Article 27. 18 Ibid., Article 34(2).

19 Türk, Edwards and Wouters, 'Introduction' (n 2) 2.

20 James Hathaway and Michelle Foster, *The Law of Refugee Status* (2nd edn, CUP 2014) 174; James Hathaway, 'Refugee Status Arising from Generalized Oppression' in Gudmundur Alfredsson and Peter Macalister-Smith (eds), *The Living Law of Nations: Essays on Refugees, Minorities, Indigenous Peoples and the Human Rights of Other Vulnerable Groups* (N. P. Engel 1996) 61; Volker Türk, 'Protection Gaps in Europe? Persons fleeing the Indiscriminate Effects of Generalized Violence' (UNHCR 2011) <www.refworld.org/publisher,UNHCR,4d37d8402,0.html> accessed 12 July 2021, 6.

21 Guy Goodwin-Gill and Jane McAdam, *The Refugee in International Law* (3rd edn, OUP 2007) 126–127; Cornelis Wouters, 'Protecting People Fleeing Conflict and Generalized Violence' in UNHCR and Council of Europe (eds), *Joint UNHCR/Council of Europe Colloquium on the Role of Regional Human Rights Courts in Interpreting and Enforcing Legal Standards for the Protection of Forcibly Displaced Persons: Conference Report* (Council of Europe 2011) 65.

22 Vanessa Holzer, *Refugees from Armed Conflict: The 1951 Refugee Convention and International Humanitarian Law* (Intersentia 2015) 183.

23 Elena Fiddian-Qasmiyeh, 'Gender and Forced Migration' in Elena Fiddian-Qasmiyeh et al. (eds), *The Oxford Handbook of Refugee and Forced Migration Studies* (OUP 2014) 399–400.

24 UNHCR, *Handbook and Guidelines on Procedures and Criteria for Determining Refugee Status under the 1951 Convention and the 1967 Protocol Relating to the Status of Refugees* (UNHCR 2019 (reissue)) para 164.

25 Ibid., para 165.

26 United Nations General Assembly (UNGA), Note on International Protection: International Protection in Mass Influx (submitted by the High Commissioner) (A/AC.96/850, 1 September 1995) para 11; UNHCR, *Summary Conclusions on International Protection of Persons Fleeing Armed Conflict and Other Situations of Violence; Roundtable 13 and 14 September 2012, Cape Town, South Africa* (UNHCR 2012) para 9, 19; UNHCR, *Expert Meeting on Complementarities between International Refugee Law, International Criminal Law and International Human Rights Law* (UNHCR 2011) para 25; UNHCR, *Guidelines on International Protection No. 11: Prima Facie Recognition of Refugee Status* (HCR/GIP/15/11, 24 June 2015); Vanessa Holzer, The 1951 Refugee Convention and the Protection of People Fleeing Armed Conflict and Other Situations of Violence (UNHCR, PPLA/2012/05, September 2012) 12.

27 UNHCR, *Guidelines on International Protection No. 12* (n 5).

to gender persecution.[28] Despite state parties highlighting the continued significance of the Refugee Convention,[29] important differences remain in the manner in which they implement their international obligations under the Refugee Convention, including in terms of who qualifies as a refugee. Divergent state practice and sometimes restrictive interpretation in the application of the refugee definition to persons fleeing armed conflicts and widespread violence has created an 'implementation gap'.[30]

In the EU, the European Commission for example has noted that diversity in national legal frameworks and decision-making practices and different levels of rights awarded by various MS continued to lead to the secondary movement of asylum seekers,[31] and concluded that the objective of creating a level playing field in the qualification of beneficiaries of international protection in the EU had not been achieved.[32] This practice has resulted in varying rates of recognition of refugee and subsidiary protection status despite attempts at harmonising the practice of EU MS in the context of the CEAS.[33]

The uneven application and interpretation of the law in respect of asylum applicants originating from the same countries of origin characterised by protracted armed conflicts is particularly stark, as the risk of violence is likely to impact a greater number of persons in a similar way. The empirical study discussed in this book focuses on Syria, Iraq and Afghanistan because the majority of persons granted international protection in the EU in 2016 came from those three countries.[34] However, the percentage of persons granted refugee status at first instance across the EU decreased from over 38 per cent in 2015 to just 21 per cent in 2021.[35] Moreover, statistics demonstrate that within nationality groups, the outcome of first-instance decisions and appeals varied significantly. For example, whereas the proportion of positive first-instance decisions for Iraqi asylum applicants across the EU in 2016 was 63 per

[28] Ibid., para 1.

[29] Ministerial Meetings of State Parties to the Refugee Convention in December 2011 reiterated 'the continuing relevance and resilience of this international regime of rights and principles' and confirmed that the Refugee Convention and the Protocol 'are the foundation of the international refugee protection regime and have enduring value and relevance in the twenty-first century', see Guy Goodwin-Gill, 'The International Law of Refugee Protection' in Fiddian-Qasmiyeh et al. (eds), *The Oxford Handbook of Refugee and Forced Migration Studies* 45.

[30] Volker Türk and Rebecca Dowd, 'Protection Gaps' in Fiddian-Qasmiyeh et al. (eds), *The Oxford Handbook of Refugee and Forced Migration Studies* 280.

[31] European Commission, Proposal for a Directive of the European Parliament and of the Council on minimum standards for the qualification and status of third country nationals or stateless persons as beneficiaries of international protection and the content of the protection granted (COM(2009) 551 final, 21 October 2009) 6.

[32] European Commission, Report from the Commission to the European Parliament and the Council on the Application of Directive 2004/83/EC of 29 April 2004 on the Minimum Standards for the Qualification and Status of Third Country Nationals or Stateless Persons as Refugees or as Persons who Otherwise Need International Protection and the Content of the Protection (COM(2010) 314 final, 2010) 15.

[33] Ibid., 281.

[34] Eurostat, 'Asylum Decisions in the EU – EU Member States Granted Protection to More than 700 000 Asylum Seekers in 2016: Over Half of the Beneficiaries were Syrians' (26 April 2017) <www.europeanmigrationlaw.eu/documents/Eurostat-AsylumDecisions-2016.pdf> accessed 12 July 2021.

[35] Eurostat defines first-instance decision as 'a decision made in response to an asylum application at the first instance level of the asylum procedure'. Statistics compiled from Eurostat, 'First Instance Decisions on Applications by Citizenship, Age and Sex – Annual Aggregated Data (Rounded)', <https://ec.europa.eu/eurostat/databrowser/view/MIGR_ASYDCFSTA__custom_3117264/default/table?lang=en> last updated 15 July 2022, accessed 26 July 2022. Figures from 2020 exclude the UK.

cent, this figure varied from 12 per cent in Denmark and the UK to 81 per cent in France and 100 per cent in Spain.[36] The proportion of positive first-instance decisions for Afghan nationals across the EU in 2016 averaged 57 per cent. However, the figure varied from about 35 per cent in the Netherlands and the UK to 60 per cent in Belgium and 82 per cent in France.[37]

Although the proportion of positive first-instance decisions for Syrian nationals was more consistent across the EU in 2016, the outcome of those decisions varied greatly across EU MS. Thus, whereas 85 per cent of Syrian applicants were awarded refugee status in the UK, less than 1 per cent were recognised as refugees in Spain. Conversely, less than 1 per cent of Syrian applicants were granted subsidiary protection by first-instance decision makers in the UK compared with 97 per cent in Spain.[38] Outcome of appeals across the EU for Afghan, Iraqi and Syrian appellants also varied widely.[39]

The question of how the Refugee Convention is and should be interpreted in the cases of persons fleeing contemporary armed conflicts is highly relevant, as the type of international protection granted, namely refugee or subsidiary protection status, has important consequences for the rights and entitlements awarded to beneficiaries of international protection. Most noteworthy is the length of the residence permit, which gives effective access to the socio-economic rights attached to international protection and impacts on prospects of integration in the host country.[40] The enquiry is particularly pressing in light of the significant increase in persons fleeing armed conflicts worldwide and ongoing reforms of a CEAS, which despite creating a hierarchy of protection status nonetheless reiterates the foundation of the Refugee Convention as the international legal regime for the protection of refugees. This book is the first systematic, comparative and interdisciplinary enquiry into judicial interpretation of the Refugee Convention definition in the cases of persons fleeing armed conflicts in Europe.

1.1.2 Violence in Contemporary Armed Conflicts

The book is premised on an analytical distinction between the notions of armed conflicts and violence. As Kalyvas argues, the distinction is essential because the severity of an armed conflict and the level of violence in a country characterised by an armed conflict are not necessarily causally related.[41] The onset of armed conflicts and the exercise of violence in situations of armed conflict display different dynamics, and it is argued here that the latter should be the frame of analysis for the purpose of refugee protection. The book thus avoids the term 'generalised violence' because it is often misconceived as meaning 'indiscriminate violence', and ultimately the type of violence covered by subsidiary protection under Article 15(c) Qualification Directive.[42] Although UNHCR originally widely used the term 'generalised violence' in

36 Eurostat, 'First Instance Decisions on Applications by Citizenship, Age and Sex Annual Aggregated Data (Rounded) [migr_asydcfsta]' <https://ec.europa.eu/eurostat/web/asylum-and-managed-migration/data/database> accessed 1 April 2019; see also Section 2.4.1 in Chapter 2 and Appendix B.

37 Ibid. 38 Ibid.

39 This is discussed in further detail in Section 2.4.1 in Chapter 2 and Appendix B.

40 Céline Bauloz and Géraldine Ruiz, 'Refugee Status and Subsidiary Protection: Towards a Uniform Content of International Protection?' in Vincent Chetail, Philippe De Bruycker and Francesco Maiani (eds), *Reforming the Common European Asylum System: The New European Refugee Law* (Brill Nijhoff 2016) 264.

41 Stathis N. Kalyvas, *The Logic of Violence in Civil War* (CUP 2006) 20.

42 Jean-François Durieux, 'Of War, Flows, Laws and Flaws: A Reply to Hugo Storey' (2012) 31 *Refugee Survey Quarterly* 161, 165.

the context of persons fleeing armed conflicts, it eventually opted to drop the adjective from its International Guidelines.[43] Instead, the book uses the adjective 'widespread' to infer that violence is distributed over a large area and/or impacts a large number of persons.

In discussing the changing nature of contemporary armed conflicts, the book draws on Kalyvas and Balcells' typology of armed conflicts. Thus, the term 'nature' of armed conflicts is used to indicate the particular type of armed conflicts such as conventional or asymmetric.[44] Further, the book refers to the 'characteristics' of armed conflicts to mean the individual features that together characterise contemporary armed conflicts such as the rise of non-state actors and their relative control over the conduct of hostilities, weak states, identity politics as drivers of violence, and gendered strategies and tactics of fighting parties.[45] The term 'situations of (contemporary) armed conflict' is used throughout to refer to situations in the country of origin of persons seeking international protection characterised by high levels or spread of violence that impact on civilians.[46] The term is utilised to avoid the limitations of the definitions of international or non-international armed conflicts as found in international humanitarian law, and may include different combinations of state and non-state fighting parties.[47]

1.1.3 Gender-Differentiated Impact of Armed Conflicts

There has been a wealth of research looking not only at the experiences of women in conflict but also at how women and men are 'differentially involved in, and affected by, conflict situations which lead to mass displacement'.[48] Importantly, research into the experiences of men and women during conflict now recognises that men and boys may be the victims of gender-based violence and persecution and that women may directly participate in or instigate acts of violence.[49]

Nevertheless, it is now generally accepted within the international community that women are disproportionately affected by armed conflicts,[50] and that perpetrators enjoy

43 UNHCR, *Guidelines on International Protection No. 12* (n 5); compare with for example Türk, 'Protection Gaps in Europe?' (n 20).

44 Stathis N. Kalyvas and Laia Balcells, 'International System and Technologies of Rebellion: How the End of the Cold War Shaped Internal Conflict' (2010) 104 *American Political Science Review* 415.

45 Those are discussed in turn in Chapter 3.

46 The term was also used by UNHCR in its Guidelines on Situations of Armed Conflict, UNHCR, *Guidelines on International Protection No. 12* (n 5) para 5.

47 See further Section 2.2.1 in Chapter 2.

48 Fiddian-Qasmiyeh, 'Gender and Forced Migration' (n 23) 401.

49 Ibid.

50 UN Secretary-General, Report to the Security Council on the Protection of Civilians in Armed Conflict, UN Doc S/1999/957, 8 September 1999, para 18; UN Security Council (UNSC) Resolution 1265 (17 September 1999) UN Doc S/RES/1265, preamble; UNSC Res 1296 (12 April 2000) UN Doc S/RES/1296, para 9; UNSC Res 1325 (31 October 2000) UN Doc S/RES/1325; UN Secretary-General, Women, Peace and Security: Study submitted by the Secretary-General pursuant to Security Council Resolution 1325 (2000) (UN 2002) ix; UNSC Res 1820 (19 June 2008) UN Doc S/RES/1820; UNSC Res 1888 (30 September 2009) UN Doc S/RES/1888; UNSC Res 1894 (11 November 2009) UN Doc S/RES/1894, preamble; UN Committee on the Elimination of All Forms of Discrimination Against Women, Concept Note: General Discussion on the Protection of Women's Human Rights in Conflict and Post-Conflict Contexts (UN 2011) 7; Committee on the Elimination of All Forms of Discrimination Against Women (CEDAW Committee), 'General Recommendation No 19' in 'Note by the Secretariat, Compilation of General Comments and General Recommendations Adopted by Human Rights Treaty Bodies' (29 July 1994) UN Doc HRI/GEN/1/Rev.1, para 16.

widespread impunity in this context.[51] This has been attributed to their sex and status in society.[52] It has been documented that civilian women face different risks and threats than civilian men owing to prescribed gender roles and social attitudes.[53] Martin, for example, noted that there is a fine line between discrimination and persecution, and concluded that women who are the targets of military attacks may find it difficult to convince decision makers that they are the victims of persecution rather than random violence. She refers to Bosnia, Eritrea, Guatemala, Mozambique, Rwanda and Somalia as examples where attacking women has been a deliberate tactic.[54] The United Nations (UN) Secretary-General stated that women are the 'targets of specific forms of violence and abuse, including sexual violence and exploitation'.[55] Women are disproportionately affected by conflict through the use of rape and sexual violence as wartime strategy,[56] although men and boys are also victims of rape and sexual violence and have been described as the unrecognised minority.[57] In addition to these deliberate tactics, in situations where violence against women and discrimination is already prevalent, armed conflict further exacerbates this trend.[58]

Feminist perspectives in international refugee law have also explained how asylum decision makers consider state-sanctioned violence more serious than violence within the family or the community by the emphasis on state sovereignty in international refugee law.[59] This emphasis on state sovereignty has resulted in an interpretation of the concept of persecution by non-state actors as comprising two distinct elements requiring separate legal assessment, namely the existence of a risk of serious harm coupled with the absence of state protection.[60] Initially, this approach was welcomed for its recognition of non-state actors as agents of persecution with the potential to better cater for asylum claims on the basis of gender-based violence.[61] Nevertheless, the breaking down of the elements of the refugee definition in this

51 UNSC Res 1674 on Protection of Civilians in Armed Conflict (UN 2006) paras 7, 8, 11.

52 UN Fourth World Conference on Women, Platform for Action: Women and Armed Conflict (UN 1995) para 135; UN Secretary-General, Women, Peace and Security: Study (n 50) para 6.

53 UN Secretary-General, Women, Peace and Security: Study (n 50) paras 51–57.

54 Susan Forbes Martin, *Refugee Women* (2nd edn, Lexington Books 2004) 31–32.

55 UN Secretary-General, Women, Peace and Security: Study (n 50) ix, paras 58–63.

56 UN Special Rapporteur on Violence against Women Its Causes and Consequences, 15 Years of the United Nations Special Rapporteur on Violence against Women Its Causes and Consequences (UN 2009) 15.

57 Sandesh Sivakumaran, 'Sexual Violence against Men in Armed Conflict' (2007) 18 *European Journal of International Law* 253; Médecins Sans Frontières, 'Shattered Lives: Immediate Medical Care Vital for Sexual Violence Victims' (MSF, June 2009) 11.

58 UN Secretary-General, Women, Peace and Security: Study (n 50) para 6.

59 Heaven Crawley, 'Engendering the State in Refugee Women's Claims for Asylum' in Susie Jacobs, Ruth Jacobson and Jennifer Marchbank (eds), *States of Conflict: Gender, Violence and Resistance* (Zed Books 2000) 92.

60 See for example Lord Hoffmann in *Islam v Secretary of State for the Home Department Immigration Appeal Tribunal and Another, Ex Parte Shah, R v* [1999] UKHL 20: 'These two elements have to be combined to constitute persecution within the meaning of the Convention. As the *Gender Guidelines for the Determination of Asylum Claims in the UK* (published by the Refugee Women's Legal Group in July 1988) succinctly puts it (at p. 5): "Persecution = Serious Harm + The Failure of State Protection".'

61 Rachel Bacon and Kate Booth, 'Persecution by Omission: Violence by Non-State Actors and the Role of the State under the Refugees Convention in Minister for Immigration and Multicultural Affairs v Khawar' (2002) 24 *Sydney Law Review* 584, 602.

manner has been said to create a stricter test for meeting the requirements of that definition because it focuses the assessment on whether the state of origin has done enough to protect the person rather than the risk of serious harm.[62] Feminist scholarship has concluded that as a result, women (although not exclusively) are insufficiently or unequally protected under international refugee law because violence by non-state actors is the most prevalent form of ill-treatment against women.[63] What is more, the issue of state protection is further compounded in the context of armed conflicts and failed states.[64]

In light of this, the book is also concerned with how violence in contemporary armed conflicts impacts on men and women differently, and the extent to which this is taken into account when the Refugee Convention is applied and interpreted. It thus aims 'to question the assumptions of neutrality and universal applicability of norms of international law'.[65] Feminist scholars have argued that the apparent neutral, universal and general application of international law has hidden the manner in which gender may play an essential role in how refugees are created,[66] and revealed that the lived experiences of women were not adequately represented by the legal framework both in its substance and application.[67]

The gender lens adopted in this book thus challenges law as a 'neutral', 'objective' and universal source of authority,[68] and instead demonstrates that international refugee law is interpreted in a manner that fails to recognise the gender-differentiated impact of violence in situations of armed conflict. This critical approach seeks to counter mainstream legal scholarship whose ideas have remained so resistant to the inclusion of a gender analysis.[69] The book adopts the concept of 'gender' as a social phenomenon in which identities are socially constructed.[70] Adopting a gender lens thus involves an enquiry into 'a set of cultural institutions and practices that constitute the norms and standards of masculinity and femininity'.[71] The book also engages with the notion of 'gender subordination', a process whereby relations of power and dominance are characterised by the valorisation of masculinities over

62 Daniel Wilsher, 'Non-State Actors and the Definition of a Refugee in the United Kingdom: Protection, Accountability or Culpability?' (2003) 15 *International Journal of Refugee Law* 68, 83; see all the questions raised by Anker in attempts to define the required level of protection by the state in cases of non-state actors of persecution, Deborah Anker, 'Refugee Law, Gender, and the Human Rights Paradigm' (2002) 15 *Harvard Human Rights Journal* 133, 147.

63 Siobhán Mullally, 'Domestic Violence Asylum Claims and Recent Developments in International Human Rights Law: A Progress Narrative?' (2011) 60 *International and Comparative Law Quarterly* 459.

64 Tara Magner, 'Does a Failed State Country of Origin Result in a Failure of International Protection? A Review of Policies toward Asylum-Seekers in Leading Asylum Nations' (2001) 15 *Georgetown Immigration Law Journal* 703.

65 Hilary Charlesworth, Christine Chinkin and Shelley Wright, 'Feminist Approaches to International Law' (1991) 85 *American Journal of International Law* 613, 644.

66 Doreen Indra, 'Gender: A Key Dimension of the Refugee Experience' (1987) 6 *Refuge* 3, 3.

67 Colin Harvey, 'Engendering Asylum Law: Feminism, Process and Practice' in Susan Millns and Noel Whitty (eds), *Feminist Perspectives on Public Law* (Cavendish 1999) 223.

68 Jo Shaw, 'Importing Gender: The Challenge of Feminism and the Analysis of the EU Legal Order' (2000) 7 *Journal of European Public Policy* 406, 412.

69 Joanne Conaghan, *Law and Gender* (OUP 2013) 16; Carol Smart, *Feminism and the Power of Law* (Routledge 1989).

70 Sally Engle Merry, *Gender Violence: A Cultural Perspective* (Wiley-Blackwell 2009) 180.

71 Christine Chinkin and Mary Kaldor, 'Gender and New Wars' (2013) 67 *Journal of International Affairs* 167, 167.

femininities.[72] Gender dynamics are influenced by situations of armed conflict and violence as these impact on traditional gender roles, norms and expectations within a given society.[73] As will be discussed, international human rights norms are particularly significant for the interpretation of international refugee law as they identify unequal gender relations as a cause and continuation of violence.[74]

1.2 Methodology

The book explores how the Refugee Convention is applied and interpreted in situations of armed conflict by reviewing a large stratified and systematic probability sampling of asylum appeals of persons fleeing Afghanistan, Iraq and Syria determined between 2013 and 2016 in six EU MS. The methodology adopted enables the identification of current practice and trends in the EU in respect of the determination of approximately one-third of asylum claims made in the EU.

1.2.1 Comparative Legal Research

The focus of this book is on appellate decision-making because the role of the judiciary in interpreting the Refugee Convention is fundamental. Lambert argues that refugee law 'has evolved mostly under the influence of judges' and that this area of law has become 'fundamentally judicialised'.[75] In the absence of an international court empowered to provide a common interpretation to the Refugee Convention,[76] courts have developed a key role as 'agents of normative change'.[77] In the EU, the way in which MS conceive of refugee protection can be gleaned by enquiring into judicial interpretation of international protection provisions in EU law. The Qualification Directive has been transposed into each EU MS and is currently being interpreted by domestic appellate authorities. As appellate authorities' role is to review the decisions of the executive, they play an essential role in safeguarding the rule of law.[78] Analysis of judicial interpretation thus provides significant

[72] Characteristics generally associated with masculinity include domination, strength, protection, aggression, public life, leadership and rationality, whereas characteristics generally associated with femininity include submission, weakness, vulnerability, passivity, private life, care and emotion; see V. Spike Peterson and Anne Sisson Runyan, *Global Gender Issues* (Westview Press 1993) 5–8.

[73] Alexis Henshaw, 'Masculinity and New War: The Gendered Dynamics of Contemporary Armed Conflict' (2017) 25 *Gender & Development* 343; Rosemary Grey and Laura J. Shepherd, '"Stop Rape Now?" Masculinity, Responsibility, and Conflict-Related Sexual Violence' (2013) 16 *Men and Masculinities* 115; Fidelma Ashe, *The New Politics of Masculinity: Men, Power and Resistance* (Routledge 2011).

[74] For a detailed exposition of these norms, see Christel Querton, 'Gender and the Boundaries of International Refugee Law: Beyond the Category of "Gender-Related Asylum Claims"' (2019) 37 *Netherlands Quarterly of Human Rights* 379, 392–395; see Section 2.2.2 in Chapter 2.

[75] Hélène Lambert, 'Transnational Law, Judges and Refugees in the European Union' in Hélène Lambert and Guy S. Goodwin-Gill (eds), *The Limits of Transnational Law: Refugee Law, Policy Harmonization and Judicial Dialogue in the European Union* (CUP 2010) 4.

[76] Although the International Court of Justice (ICJ) has jurisdiction to determine any dispute between states regarding the interpretation of the Refugee Convention, it has never been invoked; Article 38 Refugee Convention.

[77] Lambert, 'Transnational Law, Judges and Refugees in the European Union' (n 75).

[78] See for example Article 2 Consolidated versions of the Treaty on European Union and the Treaty on the Functioning of the European Union 2012/C 326/01, Official Journal C 326, 26/10/2012 P. 0001–0390.

insight into practice and trends as to how the EU and its MS interpret the Refugee Convention definition.

More specifically, the empirical study is based on decisions of first-instance appeal authorities. Existing empirical research on judicial practice in international refugee law tends to focus on decisions of the higher courts.[79] The current approach supports a richer analysis, as first-instance appeals generally include questions of facts and law – compared with higher courts whose jurisdiction may be limited to errors of law. A more limited number of (but potentially informative) judgments from higher instances are also examined because lower courts are required to or may follow the jurisprudence of higher courts. Accordingly, reference to some judgments from higher courts supports the analysis by providing a more comprehensive data set and subsequent conclusions. Thus, the enquiry involves a comparative analysis of the extent to which issues of gender and violence in the context of contemporary armed conflicts are addressed in judicial determinations.

1.2.2 Sampling

The judgments for this study were collected using a stratified and systematic probability sampling method that allows for the making of generalisations about judicial practice in the EU in a manner that an analysis of published asylum judgments collected in a purposive or ad hoc manner could not. Probability sampling is associated with the minimum level of sampling bias and is sometimes referred to as representative sampling because each unit of analysis in the population from which the sample is drawn has an equal and independent chance of being included in the sample. Statistical inferences can thus be drawn.[80]

The sample was selected by reference to appellants' country of origin, namely Afghanistan, Iraq and Syria. These countries were selected because they represented the top three nationalities of asylum applicants in the EU between 2015 and 2018 and they are characterised by armed conflicts and widespread violence.[81] Moreover, in 2017 and 2018 applicants from those three countries constituted 30 per cent of all first-time asylum

[79] See for example Lambert, 'The Next Frontier' (n 6); Valerie Oosterveld, 'Women and Girls Fleeing Conflict: Gender and the Interpretation and Application of the 1951 Refugee Convention' in Türk, Edwards and Wouters (eds), *In Flight from Conflict and Violence*; although note some exceptions in Goodwin-Gill and Lambert (eds), *The Limits of Transnational Law*; see also Appendix A for an overview of the appellate procedure in the relevant EU MS.

[80] R. B. Jain, 'Sampling Method in Legal Research' in Shashi Kant Verma and Mohammad Afzal Wani (eds), *Legal Research and Methodology* (Indian Law Institute 2001) 322.

[81] Although the number of first-time asylum applicants from Venezuela and Colombia overtook those from Iraq in 2019 and 2020, Syria, Afghanistan and Iraq remained in the top five countries of origin in the EU; Eurostat, 'Asylum Applicants by Type of Applicant, Citizenship, Age and Sex – Annual Aggregated Data (Rounded)' <https://ec.europa.eu/eurostat/databrowser/view/MIGR_ASYAPPCTZA__custom_1616346/default/bar?lang=en> last updated 18 November 2021, accessed 21 November 2021. Significant changes in the geopolitical situation in Afghanistan occurred in August 2021 when the Taliban seized power. For an analysis of international protection needs following these changes, see Christel Querton, 'The Fall of Kabul: International Protection in the Context of the Armed Conflict and Violence in Afghanistan' (Refugee Law Initiative, 1 September 2021) <https://rli.blogs.sas.ac.uk/2021/09/01/the-fall-of-kabul-international-protection-in-the-context-of-the-armed-conflict-and-violence-in-afghanistan/> accessed 26 July 2022.

applicants in the EU.[82] A sample constituted of appellants from those countries is thus representative of a significant number of claims being lodged in the EU. Furthermore, as these three countries are characterised by protracted armed conflicts, this selection is fitting for an examination of judicial decisions in the appeals of persons fleeing armed conflicts over time.

The judgments selected were determined between 1 January 2013 and 31 December 2016. The selected time period allows the identification of trends from 2013 to 2016. This period experienced a significant shift in asylum applications in the EU and the sample thus comprises a time frame when the number of asylum claims in the EU rose sharply from 431,100 applications in 2013 to 1,322,850 applications in 2015.[83]

Judgments were collected from six EU MS (Belgium, Denmark, France, the Netherlands, Spain and the UK).[84] These MS were selected because there are sufficient similarities between them to make meaningful comparisons whilst simultaneously some differences exist thereby constituting a representative sample of MS in the EU. Although all six of those MS are signatory parties to the Refugee Convention and the European Convention on Human Rights (ECHR), they have some different obligations in the context of the CEAS. Thus, whereas Belgium, France, the Netherlands and Spain are bound by the recast Qualification Directive 2011, the UK was bound by the earlier 2004 version of the Qualification Directive[85] and Denmark has opted out of the CEAS altogether.[86] Furthermore, the locations of those six MS provide a geographical variation of Southern and Northern states.

Finally, there are differences in the asylum appeal processes within the six MS, which may have an impact on the outcome of decisions. The principal differences in the asylum appellate procedures include the type of appellate system, the grounds of appeal and the characteristics of the hearing.[87] Thus, whereas asylum appeals in Belgium, Denmark, France and the UK are determined by specialist asylum appellate bodies, they are determined by general administrative law courts in Spain and the Netherlands. Appeals against the grant

[82] Eurostat, 'Asylum in the EU Member States – 650 000 First-Time Asylum Seekers Registered in 2017: Syrians, Iraqis and Afghans Continued to Be Top Citizenships' (20 March 2018) <http://ec.europa.eu/eurostat/documents/2995521/8754388/3-20032018-AP-EN.pdf/50c2b5a5-3e6a-4732-82d0-1caf244549e3> accessed 12 July 2021; Eurostat, 'Asylum in the EU Member States – 580 800 First-Time Asylum Seekers Registered in 2018, Down By 11% Compared with 2017: Syrians, Afghans and Iraqis Continued to Be the Top Citizenships' (14 March 2019) <https://ec.europa.eu/eurostat/documents/2995521/9665546/3-14032019-AP-EN.pdf/eca81dc5-89c7-4a9d-97ad-444b6bd32790> accessed 12 July 2021.

[83] Eurostat, 'Asylum and First Time Asylum Applicants – Annual Aggregated Data (Rounded) (tps00191)' (6 February 2020) <https://ec.europa.eu/eurostat/databrowser/view/tps00191/default/table?lang=en> accessed 9 February 2020; the total number of applicants in 2014 was 626,965 and 1,260,920 in 2016.

[84] As noted, although the UK is no longer an EU MS, it left the EU on 31 January 2020. The discussion that follows summarises the UK's legal obligations whilst it was an EU member.

[85] The UK withdrew from the EU on 31 January 2020 but continued to be bound by EU law until the end of the implementation period on 31 December 2020, European Union (Withdrawal Agreement) Act 2020. Since that time, the UK is no longer bound by the Qualification Directive, although the Refugee or Person in Need of International Protection (Qualification) Regulations 2006 SI No. 2525 that were adopted to transpose the Qualification Directive into domestic law constituted EU-derived domestic legislation, European Union (Withdrawal) Act 2018, s 2, until 28 June 2022 when they were revoked. The definition of a refugee is now found in the Nationality and Borders Act 2022, ss 30–35.

[86] Protocol (No) 22 on the Position of Denmark annexed to the Treaty on the Functioning of the European Union (TFEU).

[87] See Appendix A.

of subsidiary protection on Refugee Convention grounds may be brought in all the EU MS surveyed except the Netherlands, where the District Courts do not have jurisdiction to hear 'upgrade appeals'.[88] Finally, although all asylum appeals in Belgium, France, the Netherlands and the UK envisage an oral hearing, asylum appellants in Denmark may be routed into the written procedure,[89] and in Spain no hearing of asylum appellants is explicitly required unless requested by the parties.[90] Accordingly, whereas there are essential similarities between the selected countries, particularly in relation to their legal obligations, there are also slight variations such as the legal frameworks, processes and geographical locations, which may shed light on any differences in legal interpretation, if any. The aim was to collect sixty judgments in total from each of the six EU MS, comprising twenty judgments from each of the three countries of origin. Some of the differences in their national asylum systems, however, meant this was not possible for each, as will be discussed.[91]

The sample of judgments contains asylum appeals filed by men and women. The reason for this is two-fold. Firstly, understanding and analysing how appellate authorities in the EU take into consideration gender requires that the research data includes the cases of both men and women in order to make meaningful and robust comparative findings. According to Yuval-Davis, a proper understanding of gender requires examination of both masculinity and femininity. Thus conclusions on the gender sensitivity of judicial determinations are likely to be more comprehensive by considering issues of gender generally. Secondly, this methodology addresses criticism of equating gender with women and treating women's claims for international protection as 'special' cases, calling for exceptional or 'outside the norm' application of the international refugee law framework.[92] Thus, the methods are rooted in a theoretical framework aiming to move away from researching and analysing women's asylum claim as 'special cases' and aiming to adopt a gendered approach to the identification, analysis and interpretation of international refugee law. This approach is embedded in the understanding that gender is an essential lens for the proper application of international refugee law in general and indispensable to an adequate understanding of the nature of violence in contemporary armed conflicts more specifically.

The analysis presented in this book is predominantly qualitative in nature. This is because if gender is understood as the construction of social relations between men and women, the manner in which international refugee law is interpreted and applied does not lend itself well to a quantitative analysis. As Cockburn highlights, although the relative position of men versus women suggests statistics, they always reveal exceptions.[93] Thus, pointing to a higher rate of refugee protection granted to women seeking asylum does not necessarily

[88] The Netherlands (NL): RvS N° 20010591481 28.03.2002.

[89] For example, where the appeal is deemed unfounded or the appellant is seeking a status upgrade, see s. 56(4)(1)–(2) Udlændingeloven: Lov nr. 226 af 8 juni 1983, Lovtidende A 1983, as amended by Lov om ændring af udlændingeloven: Lov nr. 239 af 10 marts 2019, Lovtidende A 2019.

[90] Art. 62 of the Ley 29/1998, de 13 de julio, reguladora de la Jurisdicción Contencioso-administrativa; Article 29(1) Ley 12/2009, de 30 de octubre, reguladora del derecho de asilo y de la protección subsidiaria BOE núm. 263, de 31 de octubre.

[91] See Section 1.2.3.

[92] Querton, 'Gender and the Boundaries of International Refugee Law' (n 74).

[93] Cynthia Cockburn, 'The Gendered Dynamics of Armed Conflict and Political Violence' in Caroline O. N. Moser and Fiona C. Clark (eds), *Victims, Perpetrators or Actors? Gender, Armed Conflict and Political Violence* (Zed Books 2001) 15.

demonstrate that there is no discrimination in the application of international refugee law.[94] Such findings cannot be made on the basis of statistics alone. For example, the success of an asylum claim may be related to the reasons for fleeing. Furthermore, although women represent 50 per cent of the refugee population worldwide, only 30 per cent of asylum applications in the EU are made by women. It is therefore considered necessary to analyse the basis of asylum claims and applicants' individual circumstances against the decisions to determine the existence of any disparity in decision-making. Overall, although the data collected has yielded some quantitative findings, the substantive analysis of the book is qualitative.

Despite the advantages of large stratified and systematic probability sampling methods there are a few limitations due to the individual characteristics of each EU MS. Firstly, although an almost equal number of appeals were selected for each of the EU MS surveyed, the total number of appeals decided for appellants from Afghanistan, Iraq and Syria vary considerably across MS. Thus, the sample from MS with higher numbers of decided appeals from a given country of origin will be less representative than another with fewer decided appeals. Secondly, although Afghans, Iraqis and Syrians are the main asylum applicants since 2015 in the EU, each MS has different 'top three' countries of origin. Finally, judgments themselves may not reveal the entirety of judges' reasoning because the extent and transparency of reasoning within judgments is highly dependent on the legal traditions and cultures within different MS. In the future, further research based on different methods, such as interviews with judges, may provide an additional dimension to the findings of this study.

1.2.3 Application of the Sampling Method

As public access to asylum appeal judgments varies significantly across the EU MS selected for this study, the application of the sampling method required adaptation in some cases. It is summarised for each jurisdiction.

The sample from the Belgian Council for Alien Law Litigation (Conseil du Contentieux des Étrangers/Raad voor Vreemdelingenbetwistingen, CCE/RvV) was collected using its online database.[95] The CCE/RvV's publication of judgments policy is that that all decisions are published online since 1 November 2010.[96] Accordingly, the sample was generated entirely randomly as each appeal had an equal chance of being included in the sample and was evenly spread across the relevant period.

The Danish Refugee Appeals Board (Flygtningenævnet, DRAB) regularly publishes anonymised summaries of selected decisions described as a representative sample of the DRAB's practice regarding certain countries.[97] The summaries contain the full reasoning of the DRAB in the particular case.[98] The selection criteria for publication are not clear however, and it is only since May 2015 that the DRAB publishes summaries of all its decisions online.

[94] Thomas Spijkerboer, *Gender and Refugee Status* (Ashgate 2000) 26.

[95] CCE/RvV, 'Arrêts' <www.rvv-cce.be/fr/arr> accessed 12 July 2021.

[96] Except where the Commissioner General for Refugees and Stateless Persons' decisions are withdrawn, appellants are absent, adjournments happen, or in the case of unfounded or inadmissible appeals, although a selection of those cases are nonetheless included, see CCE/RvV, 'Politique de Publication' (1 November 2010) <www.rvv-cce.be/fr/arr/politique-publication> accessed 12 July 2021.

[97] DRAB, 'Praksis' <https://fln.dk/da/Praksis> accessed 12 July 2021.

[98] DRAB, 'Information om nævnets offentliggørelse af praksis på fln.dk' (27 May 2010) <https://fln.dk/da/Information_til/Advokater/Naevnets_praksis> accessed 12 July 2021.

However, the DRAB sends all of its decisions and accompanying interview transcripts to the Danish Refugee Council (DRC) that stores the information in its own database. Accordingly, a data collection visit was undertaken to the DRC in Copenhagen in September 2017 to access their database of DRAB decisions. The random systematic sampling method was applied to the DRC database.

The French National Asylum Court (Cour Nationale du Droit d'Asile, CNDA) publishes thematic and yearly reports with extracts of its jurisprudence,[99] but no other data is available publicly. Therefore, a data collection visit was undertaken to the Centre for Research and Documentation of the CNDA in Paris in September 2017 to access the Court's database of judgments. The random systematic sampling method was applied to the CNDA database. During the data collection visit, asylum appeal hearings at the CNDA were observed during a full day, enabling a better understanding of the context in which the CNDA judges made their decisions.

Not all decisions by the Dutch District Court (Rechtbank, Rb) are published on the official database of judicial decisions in the Netherlands.[100] The judiciary has adopted a Decree that sets out the criteria for publication of judgments in the database.[101] The database thus is not exhaustive and contains only judgments that the courts have selected on the basis that they are particularly interesting and may influence other courts sitting elsewhere. The lists of Afghan, Iraqi and Syrian appeals for the period 1 January 2013 to 31 December 2016 were created by cross-referencing the public database with two other private databases, namely Migratieweb and VluchtWeb, the latter being managed by the Dutch Refugee Council. The random systematic sampling method was thus applied to the most exhaustive lists of Rb asylum decisions that could be created. However, these three databases contain different types of appeals ranging from substantive asylum appeals to applications for injunctive relief against removal and unlawful detention claims and therefore the random probability sampling method when applied did not result in the full sample of sixty asylum appeals judgments.

The total number of asylum appeals by Afghan, Iraqi and Syrian nationals in Spain between 2013 and 2016 was significantly smaller than in the other EU MS surveyed and even fewer than the sixty judgments which were to be selected for the sample of each jurisdiction. Accordingly, the totality of Afghan, Iraqi and Syrian appeals determined by both the Spanish National High Court (Audiencia Nacional, AN) and the Supreme Court (Tribunal Supremo, TS) between 2013 and 2016 were collected using the public database of judicial decisions (General Council of the Judiciary – Consejo General del Poder Judicial, CENDOJ).[102] The final sample of Spanish appellate decisions concerning appellants from Afghanistan, Iraq and Syria thus includes thirty-six judgments from both the AN and the TS.

As none of the decisions of the UK First-Tier Tribunal (FTT) are published online, access to FTT decisions was obtained through the Data Access Panel of Her Majesty's Courts and

99 CNDA, 'Recueils de Jurisprudence' <www.cnda.fr/Ressources-juridiques-et-geopolitiques/Recueils-de-jurisprudence> accessed 12 July 2021.

100 Rechtspraak, 'Uitspraken' <https://uitspraken.rechtspraak.nl/> accessed 12 July 2021.

101 Rechtspraak, 'Selectiecriteria' (26 March 2012) <www.rechtspraak.nl/Uitspraken/Paginas/Selectiecriteria.aspx> accessed 12 July 2021.

102 CENDOJ, 'Centro de Documentación Judicial' <www.poderjudicial.es/search/indexAN.jsp> accessed 12 July 2021.

Table 1.1 *Sample of asylum appeals*

Sample	Afghanistan	Iraq	Syria	Total
BE	20	20	20	60
DK	20	20	20	60
ES	4	3	29	36
FR	18	20	20	58
NL	16	18	12	46
UK	20	20	20	60
Total	98	101	121	320

Table 1.2 *Outcome of sample appeals by country of origin and EU Member State*

Country of Origin	Outcome	BE	DK	ES	FR	NL	UK	Total	%
Afghanistan	Allowed	1	6	2	15	8	10	42	42.86
	Dismissed	19	14	2	3	8	10	56	57.14
Iraq	Allowed	3	3	1	8	7	6	28	27.72
	Dismissed	17	17	2	12	11	14	73	72.28
Syria	Allowed	9	6	4	5	2	6	32	26.45
	Dismissed	11	14	25	15	10	14	89	73.55

Tribunals Service (HMCTS). Accessing decisions of the FTT is particularly difficult,[103] and to the author's knowledge there is only one other study based on FTT asylum decisions obtained through HMCTS, although the focus of the research was the quality of administrative justice.[104] For this study, HMCTS applied the random systematic sampling method to their database themselves and access to the sample was provided at a secure location in September 2018.

Thus, the total sample collected for this study over the course of twenty-one months, between January 2017 and September 2018, amounted to 320 asylum appeal decisions as detailed in Table 1.1.

The total sample size is adequate to make inferences about the manner in which the judiciary in EU MS determine asylum appeals of persons fleeing armed conflicts. Overall, 32 per cent of all the appeals in the sample were allowed and 68 per cent were dismissed.[105] The outcome of appeals by country of origin and EU MS is set out in more detail in Table 1.2.

[103] See for example challenges identified in Asylum Aid, Migrants Resource Centre and NatCen Social Research, 'Through Her Eyes: Enabling Women's Best Evidence in UK Asylum Appeals' (November 2017) 12–13 <www.natcen.ac.uk/media/1499615/through-her-eyes_full-report_nov17.pdf> accessed 12 July 2021.

[104] Robert Thomas, *Administrative Justice and Asylum Appeals: A Study of Tribunal Adjudication* (Hart 2011) 29.

[105] Totalling 102 appeals and 218 appeals respectively.

1.3 Structure of the Book

Having set out the broad subject of the book, the conceptual notions and empirical study that underpin this contribution, Chapter 2 reviews the legal frameworks that apply to the international protection of persons fleeing contemporary armed conflicts from a gender perspective. It critically engages with international and EU refugee and human rights law, international humanitarian law and international criminal law and argues that the effective protection of persons fleeing situations of armed conflict requires consideration of present-day realities, including the nature and dynamics of violence in contemporary armed conflicts. In turn, understanding the nature and dynamics of violence in contemporary armed conflicts requires engagement with knowledge in security and feminist studies. Accordingly, Chapter 3 proposes a conceptual framework drawing on gender and security studies to reframe the interpretation of the Refugee Convention definition. Chapters 4 to 6 discuss the findings of the empirical enquiry. Chapter 4 explores how appellate authorities in the EU understand and approach situations of armed conflict. Chapters 5 and 6 examine how two essential elements of the Refugee Convention definition, namely the 'well-founded fear of being persecuted' and reasons for persecution respectively, are applied and interpreted by appellate authorities when individuals flee contemporary armed conflicts. Finally, Chapter 7 draws the findings together and makes some recommendations for interpreting the Refugee Convention in a manner that better responds to the characteristics of contemporary armed conflicts.

2

The Legal Framework

The International Protection of Persons Fleeing Armed Conflicts

2.1 Introduction

Chapter 1 highlighted that the issue of whether persons fleeing armed conflicts can be defined as refugees under the Refugee Convention has been the subject of some debates in the past. Hence, there is disagreement regarding the application and interpretation of the Refugee Convention definition to the asylum claims of persons fleeing armed conflicts. Moreover, Hathaway and Foster claim that courts are reluctant to recognise as refugees persons whose fear of harm is shared by many others, as is often the case in situations of widespread violence.[106]

As noted, the application and interpretation of the Refugee Convention in the cases of persons fleeing armed conflicts is further compounded by changes in the nature of armed conflicts themselves.[107] Contemporary armed conflicts are said to be fundamentally different to earlier conflicts in respect of their length, the nature of parties involved, the relative power of non-state actors, their gendered strategies and, by implication, the impact of violence on individuals.[108] As Goodwin-Gill argued, one of the challenges to international refugee law is its ability to respond to 'new factual situations'.[109] For example, Hathaway and Foster raised the question of how refugee law should address 'the situation in which the war is not a one-sided effort by the state to inflict violence on a particular minority, but rather a generalised conflict in which many, if not all, groups within the state are at risk because of their religious, ethnic, or other protected form of identity'.[110] For this reason, this chapter is concerned not only with whether the Refugee Convention definition applies to persons who fear returning to their countries of origin due to armed conflicts, but also more broadly whether international refugee law is able to fulfil its purpose of international protection in light of the changing characteristics of contemporary armed conflicts.

As will be discussed further in Chapter 3, contemporary armed conflicts can be distinguished from previous forms of conflicts. The latter were characterised by warfare between sovereign nations exercised through armed confrontations conducted by their respective national armies. Recent conflicts are instead typified by protracted fighting,[111] the rise in the number of non-state actors,[112] their relative power over the conduct of fighting,[113]

[106] Hathaway and Foster, *The Law of Refugee Status* (n 20) 174.

[107] See in general Kaldor, *New and Old Wars* (n 3).

[108] This is discussed in detail in Chapter 3.

[109] Guy S. Goodwin-Gill, 'The Dynamic of International Refugee Law' (2013) 25 *International Journal of Refugee Law* 651, 656.

[110] Hathaway and Foster, *The Law of Refugee Status* (n 20) 178.

[111] See Section 3.2 in Chapter 3.

[112] See Section 3.3 in Chapter 3.

[113] See Section 3.5 in Chapter 3.

and weak states.[114] As Chinkin and Kaldor claim that the characteristics of contemporary armed conflicts challenge the main concepts underpinning international law,[115] it is necessary firstly to discuss this more generally,[116] before considering international refugee law more specifically.[117] The central claim of this chapter will then be made, namely that interpreting the Refugee Convention definition to ensure the effective protection of persons fleeing contemporary armed conflicts requires the incorporation of existing knowledge on the characteristics of contemporary armed conflicts and the dynamics of violence in situations of armed conflicts found in the conflict and gender literature. This interpretative obligation is then discussed in the context of European Union (EU) Member States (MS) acting within the EU legal order.[118]

2.2 International Law and Contemporary Armed Conflicts

This section explores claims that the foundational concepts of international law increasingly fail to reflect contemporary realities.[119] A positivist approach posits that international law is based on the centrality of the state as the principal and sole subject of international law.[120] This view provides that the fundamental cornerstone of international law is the principle of the sovereign equality of states. Some of the basic tenets that flow from this principle are that each state is sovereign in its own territory and that other states will not interfere in matters within their jurisdiction, in particular in areas concerned with national security and conflict.[121]

The organisation of the international system along the lines of absolute state sovereignty is often described as the 'Westphalian system' by reference to the Peace of Westphalia in 1648 which marked the end of the Thirty Years' War in Germany.[122] However, Neff highlights that developments in the international legal system, which placed the state at its centre, occurred in the nineteenth century rather than the seventeenth century. At most, Neff notes, the Peace of Westphalia provided an outline for the creation of separate domestic and international spheres of power that developed in later periods.[123]

In any event, the organisation of the international system on the basis of the concept of state sovereignty occurred at a time when frequent warfare took place between sovereign states, mostly conducted by professionally trained national armies. The problems caused by wars between individual states led to international efforts to regulate this state of affairs and restrict states' freedom to resort to warfare.[124] The principles of the sovereign equality of states and non-interference were later codified in the United Nations (UN) Charter.[125]

114 See Section 3.4 in Chapter 3.

115 C. M. Chinkin and Mary Kaldor, *International Law and New Wars* (CUP 2017), in particular Chapter 6.

116 See Section 2.2. 117 See Section 2.3. 118 See Section 2.4.

119 See for example Chinkin and Kaldor, *International Law and New Wars* (n 115); Winston S. Williams and Christopher M. Ford (eds), *Complex Battlespaces: The Law of Armed Conflict and the Dynamics of Modern Warfare* (OUP 2018).

120 Stephen C. Neff, 'A Short History of International Law' in Malcolm D. Evans (ed), *International Law* (5th edn, OUP 2018) 14.

121 Ibid., 15. 122 Anthony Aust, *Handbook of International Law* (2nd edn, CUP 2010) 3.

123 Neff, 'A Short History of International Law' (n 120) 11.

124 Giovanni Distefano, 'Use of Force' in Andrew Clapham et al. (eds), *The Oxford Handbook of International Law in Armed Conflict* (OUP 2015) 545.

125 Charter of the United Nations (adopted 26 June 1945, entered into force 24 October 1945) 1 UNTS XVI (UN Charter).

Article 2(1) of the UN Charter provides that the UN itself and all its members shall act in accordance with the fundamental principle that 'the Organization is based on the principle of the sovereign equality of all its Members'. In addition, Article 2(4) enshrines the central rule of the international system, namely that 'all Members shall refrain in their international relations from the threat or use of force against the territorial integrity or political independence of any state, or in any other manner inconsistent with the purposes of the United Nations'. It was thus a concern with regulating the conduct of states and the relationship between them that spurred the development of concepts underpinning international law. In this state-centric system of international law, sovereign states are the main actors of the international legal order whose jurisdiction is defined primarily by territorial borders.

The principles of international law discussed illustrate the relationship between state sovereignty, territory and war. Accordingly, the ban on the use of force is a strict prohibition on 'any forcible trespassing of State boundaries'[126] and is only lawful as a means of self-defence when a state's sovereignty has been breached through an armed attack, provided it is necessary and proportionate.[127] Spheres of sovereignty are defined by nation-states' physical borders wherein they exercise exclusive jurisdiction. Thus, even if a state's jurisdiction is not solely territorial, the main criterion for establishing jurisdiction is the territoriality principle.[128] Overall, the way international law has developed historically and continues to operate to date highlights that the notions underpinning state sovereignty, territoriality and the conduct of war are closely related. As a consequence, foundational concepts of the use of force in international law are heavily based on the way warfare was traditionally conducted, namely between sovereign states through the use of national armies funded by taxation.

Although states remain the principal subjects of international law and the principles of sovereignty and territoriality continue to regulate the international legal system today, limitations are increasingly being identified.[129] There is a rising concern that the way the world operates today has created challenges to the traditional perspective of international law based on sovereignty and territoriality.[130] In particular, the changed characteristics of contemporary armed conflicts have raised questions about the continued ability of international law on the use of force to restrain the exercise of warfare.[131] Indeed, although the conduct of war is a quintessential concern of international law, conflicts todays are rarely fought between sovereign states and engage parties with very different military capacity.[132]

[126] Distefano, 'Use of Force' (n 124) 548.

[127] Article 51 of the UN Charter provides that 'Nothing in the present Charter shall impair the inherent right of individual or collective self-defence if an armed attack occurs against a Member of the United Nations, until the Security Council has taken measures necessary to maintain international peace and security [...]'. For further analysis of the legal requirement under Article 51 UN Charter see Distefano, 'Use of Force' (n 124) 552–557.

[128] Bruno Simma and Andreas Th. Müller, 'Exercise and Limits of Jurisdiction' in James Crawford, Martti Koskenniemi and Surabhi Ranganathan (eds), *The Cambridge Companion to International Law* (CUP 2012) 137.

[129] Ibid., 135, 156 (in relation to the law of jurisdiction).

[130] Daniel Bethlehem, 'The End of Geography: The Changing Nature of the International System and the Challenge to International Law' (2014) 25 *European Journal of International Law* 9.

[131] Chinkin and Kaldor, *International Law and New Wars* (n 115).

[132] David Kennedy, 'Lawfare and Warfare' in Crawford, Koskenniemi and Ranganathan (eds), *The Cambridge Companion to International Law* 163.

Most conflicts today are internal armed conflicts characterised by weak states and the rise in the number and relative power of armed groups. The role of states as the main actors in international relations is thus increasingly restricted as they no longer have the monopoly on the use of force or even dictate the conduct of war. As a result, scholars have queried whether international law, as a system for the regulation of relations between states, is adequate in its traditional form to regulate the conduct of contemporary armed conflicts.[133]

This book claims that the interpretation of international refugee law in the EU is similarly challenged by the question of forced displacement in contemporary times and in particular by refugee movements caused by situations of armed conflict and widespread violence. Gilbert and Rüsch claim that international refugee law highlights the 'pervading Westphalian character of international law'.[134] Likewise, Goodwin-Gill and McAdam note how international refugee law is partly based on the principle of 'State sovereignty and the related principles of territorial supremacy and self-preservation'.[135] The fact that, by definition, refugees must cross sovereign borders is in itself an expression of sovereignty and territory. The application of the principles of state sovereignty and territoriality means that host states can only exercise protection when refugees become subject to their jurisdiction as derived from territorial sovereignty. The empirical study analysed in this book will show how notions of sovereignty – states as the dominant entities in international relations and territoriality – not only underpin the Refugee Convention definition itself, but also extensively inform judicial authorities' interpretation of the Refugee Convention definition when persons flee armed conflicts. Hence, this book brings to the fore the contradictions between the state-centric interpretation of international refugee law through the notions of sovereignty and territoriality and the changed nature of contemporary armed conflicts.

Despite the identification of valid challenges to the effectiveness of international law in light of the changing nature of contemporary armed conflicts, there are disagreements, however, regarding the continued relevance of international law to regulate armed conflicts and the use of force.[136] As noted in Chapter 1, there have long been similar debates within international refugee law scholarship as to whether the Refugee Convention definition encompasses persons fleeing wars. Therefore, this book asks whether the existing framework for international protection is capable of ensuring the effective protection of persons fleeing contemporary forms of armed conflicts that are characterised by protracted and large-scale violence, weak states, the rise in number and power of non-state actors and the use of highly visible forms of gendered human rights violations based on identity politics as fighting tactics, which contest notions of sovereignty and territoriality. In response, this chapter contends that the general rule of treaty interpretation requires an interpretation of the Refugee Convention definition that gives effect to the purpose of the

[133] Chinkin and Kaldor, *International Law and New Wars* (n 115); Williams and Ford (eds), *Complex Battlespaces* (n 119).

[134] Geoff Gilbert and Anna Magdalena Rüsch, 'International Refugee and Migration Law' in Evans (ed), *International Law* 812, 837.

[135] Goodwin-Gill and McAdam, *The Refugee in International Law* (n 21) 1.

[136] For an example of authors rejecting the adequacy of international law, see Chinkin and Kaldor, *International Law and New Wars* (n 115). For examples of arguments that international law is sufficient to regulate modern warfare, see Georges Abi-Saab, 'The Proper Role of International Law in Combatting Terrorism' in Andrea Bianchi (ed), *Enforcing International Law Norms against Terrorism* (Hart Publishing 2004) xv; Williams and Ford (eds), *Complex Battlespaces* (n 119).

treaty. Accordingly, the effective protection of persons fleeing armed conflicts can only be achieved by applying and interpreting the Refugee Convention in light of existing knowledge of contemporary armed conflicts from a gender perspective. This would contribute to a revision of the state-centric and territorial perspective of warfare currently adopted by EU appellate authorities.[137]

One of the key challenges of international refugee law is to ensure a consistent and inclusive interpretation and application of the Refugee Convention amongst state parties.[138] Although the International Court of Justice (ICJ) has jurisdiction to determine disputes between state parties to the Refugee Convention,[139] the provision has never been invoked.[140] Thus, in the absence of a single authoritative entity actually resolving questions of interpretation, the task falls on domestic authorities.[141] In discharging their obligations under the Refugee Convention, these authorities must comply with the general rule of interpretation set out in the Vienna Convention on the Law of Treaties (VCLT).[142] Hathaway and Foster suggest this rule enables the 'conception of objective interpretive principle'.[143] The starting point here is that state parties to the Refugee Convention must ensure the implementation of their obligations in good faith.[144]

Despite the mandatory interpretative direction of the VCLT, fragmentation in interpretation of the Refugee Convention definition may occur as a result of inconsistent interpretation of the constituent elements of the Refugee Convention definition among domestic authorities. Hathaway and Foster suggest this is caused by differences in the legal systems and social traditions between state parties to the Refugee Convention.[145] Moreover, in the particular cases of persons fleeing armed conflicts, inconsistent interpretation of the Refugee Convention definition may also be due to different views across domestic authorities and the literature regarding the relationship between international refugee law and other areas of international law such as international humanitarian law and international criminal law. This is discussed in Section 2.2.1.

2.2.1 The Interaction between International Refugee Law, International Humanitarian Law and International Criminal Law

Although it has regularly been reiterated that the Refugee Convention directly applies to persons fleeing armed conflicts,[146] there has been extensive debate within refugee law scholarship whether international humanitarian law should serve as an aid to interpretation in

137 See Chapter 4.

138 Philippo Grandi, 'Foreword' in Türk, Edwards and Wouters (eds), *In Flight from Conflict and Violence* xiii.

139 Article 38 Refugee Convention provides that 'Any dispute between Parties to this Convention relating to its interpretation or application, which cannot be settled by other means, shall be referred to the International Court of Justice at the request of any one of the parties to the dispute.'

140 Geoff Gilbert, 'UNHCR and Courts: Amicus Curiae … Sed Curia Amica Est?' (2016) 28 *International Journal of Refugee Law* 623, 625.

141 Hathaway and Foster, *The Law of Refugee Status* (n 20) 3–4; on the role played by domestic appellate authorities in the development of international refugee law, see also Section 1.2 in Chapter 1.

142 VCLT (adopted 22 May 1969, entered into force 27 January 1980) 1155 UNTS 331.

143 Hathaway and Foster, *The Law of Refugee Status* (n 20) 5.

144 Article 26 VCLT.

145 Hathaway and Foster, *The Law of Refugee Status* (n 20) 3.

146 See most recently UNHCR, *Guidelines on International Protection No. 12* (n 5) para 1.

the asylum claims of persons fleeing armed conflicts.[147] United Nations High Commissioner for Refugees (UNHCR) Consultations revealed there were conflicting views among participants at the roundtable convened by UNHCR regarding the adoption of specialist terms found in international humanitarian law, such as 'international armed conflict' and 'armed conflict not of an international character', within international refugee law.[148] This subsection sets out the reasons for rejecting reliance on the norms of international humanitarian law to interpret the Refugee Convention definition.

Scholars supporting the use of international humanitarian law as a tool or complement for interpretation highlight that international humanitarian law is the *lex specialis* in cases of war and armed conflict.[149] Storey claims that as some human rights norms are derogable in times of emergency/armed conflict,[150] international humanitarian law is therefore better suited as a starting point to the determination of claims from persons fleeing armed conflict.[151] Whereas the ICJ in the *Wall Advisory Opinion* found that international humanitarian law would retain its status as *lex specialis* in situations of armed conflict, it also found that international human rights law continued to apply in situations of armed conflict unless they had been lawfully derogated from.[152] Furthermore, the definition of an armed conflict for the purpose of international protection in EU law is not subject to the same threshold that applies to a 'public emergency which threatens the life of the nation'.[153] Accordingly, from the perspective of interpreting the Refugee Convention, international human rights law applies as relevant rules of international law irrespective of whether the country of origin is at peace or at war. Moreover, human rights such as the prohibition of torture and degrading and inhuman treatment and punishment are non-derogable and the fear of such treatment is most often the basis of asylum claims. The *lex specialis* argument may be more persuasive in situations involving cumulative breaches of derogable human rights where the persecution feared is an accumulation of measures or treatment that by themselves would not amount to persecution.[154]

147 See for example Holzer, *Refugees from Armed Conflict* (n 22); David James Cantor and Jean-François Durieux, 'Refuge from Inhumanity? Canvassing the Issues' in David James Cantor and Jean-François Durieux (eds), *Refuge from Inhumanity? War Refugees and International Humanitarian Law* (Brill Nijhoff 2014); Stephane Jaquemet, 'Expanding Refugee Protection through International Humanitarian Law: Driving on a Highway or Walking near the Edge of the Abyss?' in Cantor and Durieux (eds), *Refugee from Inhumanity?*; Hugo Storey, 'Armed Conflict in Asylum Law: The "War-Flaw"' (2012) 31 *Refugee Survey Quarterly* 1; Hugo Storey and Rebecca Wallace, 'War and Peace in Refugee Law Jurisprudence' (2001) 95 *American Journal of International Law* 349.

148 UNHCR, *Summary Conclusions* (n 26) para 12.

149 Holzer, *Refugees from Armed Conflict* (n 22) 8, 76–77; Jaquemet, 'Expanding Refugee Protection through International Humanitarian Law' (n 147) 97; Storey, 'Armed Conflict in Asylum Law' (n 147) 14.

150 On derogation from the International Covenant on Civil and Political Rights (ICCPR), see UNHRC, 'General Comment No 29 – Article 4: Derogations during a State of Emergency' (31 August 2001) UN Doc CCPR/C/21/Rev.1/Add.11.

151 Storey, 'Armed Conflict in Asylum Law' (n 147) 12–13.

152 *Legal Consequences of the Construction of a Wall in the Occupied Palestinian Territory* (Advisory Opinion) [2004] ICJ Rep 136, para 106; see also Leah Friedman, 'Legal Consequences of the Construction of a Wall in the Occupied Palestinian Territory (Advisory Opinion), International Court of Justice, 9 July 2004' (2005) 27 *Sydney Law Review* 715.

153 UNHRC, 'General Comment No 29 – Article 4: Derogations during a State of Emergency', para 3.

154 As provided for example in Article 9(1)(b) Qualification Directive 2011.

The Court of Justice of the European Union (CJEU) rejected the use of international humanitarian law as the legal framework to interpret the subsidiary protection provisions found in EU law.[155] It noted that the EU terms were not identical to those found in international humanitarian law,[156] and it suggested subsidiary protection was designed to protect categories of persons in types of situations *in addition to* those envisaged by international humanitarian law.[157]

Another difficulty with relying on international humanitarian law as a starting point for determining asylum claims from persons fleeing armed conflicts is the threshold requirement under this body of law. Reliance on international humanitarian law as 'relevant rules of international law'[158] would thus require prior evidence that the threshold necessary for its application had been met, for example by demonstrating the existence of an 'armed conflict not of an international character' as a condition for international protection.[159] Wouters notes this would distract asylum decision makers from focusing on the harm faced by refugees.[160]

In addition to the different purposes served by both legal frameworks and the high threshold for application of international humanitarian law, scholars have challenged the continued relevance of international humanitarian law norms within their own field. Thus, international humanitarian law has been significantly criticised for its failure to adequately reflect more recent understandings of contemporary armed conflict[161] and the gender-differentiated impact of armed conflict.[162] More specifically, Farrell and Schmitt claim that the concepts generally relied on in social science theory and international law, such as the civilian/combatant dichotomy, do not adequately encompass the complexities of armed conflicts in the global system.[163] They therefore conclude that existing international law concepts fail to properly reflect the realities of armed conflicts. Similarly, Chinkin and Kaldor have claimed that 'the laws of war are inadequate in the new global context'.[164] They claim that international humanitarian law is based on a conceptualisation of conflict based on 'old wars' that does not adequately reflect contemporary realities.[165] Chinkin and

155 Case C–285/12 *Diakite v Commissaire General aux Refugies et aux Apatrides* [2014] 1 WLR 2477; subsidiary protection is defined in EU law where 'substantial grounds have been shown for believing that the person concerned [...], would face a real risk of suffering serious harm', which includes 'serious and individual threat to a civilian's life or person by reason of indiscriminate violence in situations of international or internal armed conflict' in Articles 2(f) and 15(c) Qualification Directive 2011.

156 *Diakite v Commissaire General aux Refugies et aux Apatrides* (n 155) para 20.

157 Ibid., paras 21–23.

158 See Article 31(3)(c) VCLT.

159 Article 3 of the Convention Relative to the Protection of Civilian Persons in Times of War (Fourth Geneva Convention) (adopted 12 August 1949, entered into force 21 October 1950) 75 UNTS 287; see for example Anthony Cullen, *The Concept of Non-International Armed Conflict in International Humanitarian Law* (CUP 2010).

160 Wouters, 'Conflict Refugees' (n 5) 823.

161 Chinkin and Kaldor, *International Law and New Wars* (n 115) in particular ch 6; Michael N. Schmitt, '21st Century Conflict: Can the Law Survive?' (2007) 8 *Melbourne Journal of International Law* 443.

162 See for example Helen Durham and Katie O'Byrne, 'The Dialogue of Difference: Gender Perspectives on International Humanitarian Law' (2010) 92 *International Review of the Red Cross* 31; Amy Barrow, 'UN Security Council Resolutions 1325 and 1820: Constructing Gender in Armed Conflict and International Humanitarian Law' (2010) 92 *International Review of the Red Cross* 221.

163 Theo Farrell and Olivier Schmitt, 'The Causes, Character and Conduct of Internal Armed Conflict and the Effects on Civilian Populations, 1990–2010' in Türk, Edwards and Wouters (eds), *In Flight from Conflict and Violence* 26.

164 Chinkin and Kaldor, *International Law and New Wars* (n 115) 230.

165 Chinkin and Kaldor, 'Gender and New Wars' (n 71) 169.

Kaldor have demonstrated that although the term 'armed conflict not of an international character' is often conflated with internal conflict, contemporary armed conflicts are generally characterised by violence across borders.[166] The conflicts in Syria and Iraq are a case in point.[167] Highlighting the difficulties experienced with classifying the conflict in Syria as an 'armed conflict not of an international character',[168] Chinkin and Kaldor therefore advocate that the classification of conflicts under international humanitarian law be abandoned altogether to ensure a more robust protective regime.[169] If international humanitarian law norms fail to reflect the realities of contemporary armed conflicts leading to calls for reform in this field, the extent to which these norms are pertinent as an aid to interpretation of international refugee law in the context of persons fleeing armed conflicts must be queried.

Furthermore, Chinkin and Kaldor argue that the international humanitarian law obligations of states generally offer a less protective framework than international human rights law.[170] For example, understanding 'gender' within the particular framework of international humanitarian law has been problematic because of the legal framework's foundations in state sovereignty.[171] More specifically, international humanitarian law provisions have been critiqued for focusing excessively on sex (biological factors) and ignoring more recent developments in international law regarding the notions of gender, including masculinities and femininities.[172] International humanitarian law has also been criticised for maintaining stereotypes of women as victims,[173] or for conceptualising violence against women as attacks on their honour rather than as human rights violations.[174] As a result, some scholars have claimed that the application of international humanitarian law norms discriminate against women.[175] Moreover, the Geneva Conventions fail to explicitly acknowledge men's experiences of sexual violence in conflict and thus lack the more inclusive conceptualisation of gender-based violence found in international human rights law.[176]

166 Chinkin and Kaldor, *International Law and New Wars* (n 115) 242.

167 See for example Fred H. Lawson, 'Syria's Mutating Civil War and Its Impact on Turkey, Iraq and Iran' (2014) 90 *International Affairs* 1351; Michael M. Gunter, 'Iraq, Syria, Isis and the Kurds: Geostrategic Concerns for the U.S. and Turkey' (2015) 22 *Middle East Policy* 102.

168 Chinkin and Kaldor, *International Law and New Wars* (n 115) 245–247.

169 Ibid., 245.

170 Ibid., 224–225, 248.

171 Christine M. Chinkin, 'A Gendered Perspective to the International Use of Force' (1992) 12 *Australian Yearbook of International Law* 279, 293; see also Judith Gardam, 'A Feminist Analysis of Certain Aspects of International Humanitarian Law' (1992) 12 *Australian Yearbook of International Law* 265.

172 For an overview of these norms, see Querton, 'Gender and the Boundaries of International Refugee Law' (n 74) 392–395.

173 See earlier international resolutions which were heavily framed in the language and approach of international humanitarian law such as the UN General Assembly (UNGA), Declaration on the Protection of Women and Children in Emergency and Armed Conflict Proclaimed by General Assembly Resolution 3318 (XXIX) of 14 December 1974, where women and children are grouped, described as particularly vulnerable and women's status as mothers is highlighted.

174 Article 27 Fourth Geneva Convention which covers 'international armed conflicts' states that 'Women shall be especially protected against any attack on their honour, in particular against rape, enforced prostitution, or any form of indecent assault.'

175 Judith Gardam and Hilary Charlesworth, 'Protection of Women in Armed Conflict' (2000) 22 *Human Rights Quarterly* 148, 152.

176 Barrow, 'UN Security Council Resolutions 1325 and 1820' (n 162) 224–225, describes the paradigm underpinning international humanitarian law as 'male as perpetrator, female as victim' at 233.

More recent developments in international criminal law have led scholars to engage with this branch of international law as a tool for interpretation of the Refugee Convention in situations of armed conflict.[177] The Statute of the International Criminal Court (ICC) first codified gender-based violence as an international crime.[178] The ICC Statute defines 'crime against humanity' as including the 'rape, sexual slavery, enforced prostitution, forced pregnancy, enforced sterilization, or any other form of sexual violence of comparable gravity' 'when committed as part of a widespread or systematic attack directed against any civilian population, with knowledge of the attack'.[179] In addition 'war crimes' may include 'committing rape, sexual slavery, enforced prostitution, forced pregnancy, [...] enforced sterilization, or any other form of sexual violence also constituting a grave breach of the Geneva Conventions' in situations of international armed conflicts,[180] or constituting 'a serious violation of article 3 common to the four Geneva Conventions' in situations of armed conflict not of an international character.[181] Thus, the development of international criminal law has led to the recognition of sexual violence and rape as crimes against humanity, war crimes and genocide.[182] More specifically the International Criminal Tribunal for Rwanda (ICTR) conceptualised sexual violence as 'other inhumane acts',[183] 'outrages upon personal dignity',[184] and 'serious bodily or mental harm'.[185] Further, the International Criminal Tribunal for the former Yugoslavia (ICTY) stated that whenever rape and other forms of sexual violence met the definition of torture such acts should be considered as such.[186]

Despite international criminal law arguably contributing to more gender-sensitive interpretation of international humanitarian law, support for drawing on international criminal law in the interpretation of the Refugee Convention definition is far from unanimous, with some commentators highlighting the important distinctions in how the term 'persecution' has been interpreted under each area of law and reminding that they serve very different purposes.[187] Further, although the jurisprudence of the international courts and tribunals have reconceptualised rape and sexual violence as a crime of harm rather than honour,

[177] Valerie Oosterveld, 'Gender at the Intersection of International Refugee Law and International Criminal Law' (2014) 12 *Journal of International Criminal Justice* 953; Magali Maystre, 'The Interaction between International Refugee Law and International Criminal Law with Respect to Child Soldiers' (2014) 12 *Journal of International Criminal Justice* 975; Idil Atak and James C. Simeon, 'Human Trafficking: Mapping the Legal Boundaries of International Refugee Law and Criminal Justice' (2014) 12 *Journal of International Criminal Justice* 1019; Holzer, *Refugees from Armed Conflict* (n 22) in particular 101–102; Oosterveld, 'Women and Girls Fleeing Conflict' (n 79) 193.

[178] Rome Statute of the International Criminal Court (adopted 17 July 1998, entered into force 1 July 2002) 2187 UNTS 3 (ICC Statute).

[179] Article 7(1)(g) ICC Statute. [180] Article 8(2)(b)(xxii) ICC Statute. [181] Article 8(2)I(vi) ICC Statute.

[182] *Prosecutor v Akayesu* (Judgment) ICTR-96-4-T, T Ch I (2 September 1998); Barrow, 'UN Security Council Resolutions 1325 and 1820' (n 162); Allison T. C. Milne, 'Prosecuting Cases of Gender Violence in the International Criminal Tribunal for Rwanda' (2005) 11 *Buffalo Human Rights Law Review* 107.

[183] Article 3(i) ICTR Statute. UN Security Council, *Statute of the International Criminal Tribunal for Rwanda* (as last amended on 13 October 2006), 8 November 1994.

[184] Articll(e) ICTR Statute. [185] Article 2(2)(b) ICTR Statute; *Prosecutor v Akayesu*, para 688.

[186] *Prosecutor v Delalic and Others* (Judgment) ICTY-IT-96-21-IT (16 November 1998) paras 494–496.

[187] UNHCR, *Expert Meeting on Complementarities between International Refugee Law, International Criminal Law and International Human Rights Law* (n 26) para 13.

scholars adopting a gender perspective have queried whether it may have created a high threshold against which sexual violence during armed conflict will be measured.[188] There are thus parallels with how international humanitarian law incorporates a higher standard of application than warranted under international refugee law.

Significantly, Chinkin and Kaldor argue that if 'new wars' are to be understood as a violation of human rights, international human rights law 'should be the predominant legal regime'.[189] Barrow argues that whereas more recent developments in international law have improved understandings of rape and sexual violence in situations of armed conflict, these developing norms may be insufficient to expand constructions of gender within the frames of international humanitarian law.[190] Thus, Barrow claims that without amendments to the international humanitarian law regime codified in the Geneva Conventions, alternative legal instruments approaching gender in a more sophisticated way are increasingly relevant.[191]

The discussion in this sub-section leads to the preliminary conclusion that international humanitarian law and international criminal law may not be adequate as aids to interpretation of the Refugee Convention definition in the cases of persons fleeing armed conflicts. The predominant reasons relate to the vastly differing purposes of these legal regimes, the high threshold requirements for their application and the state-centric perspective which fails to reflect the characteristics of contemporary armed conflicts and more nuanced understandings of gender dynamics. Comparatively, international human rights law shares the purpose of international refugee law, namely the protection of persons against human rights violations. Furthermore, there have been significant advances in the understanding of the relationship between gender and the exercise of violence made in the field of international human rights law.[192] It is suggested here that international human rights law provides a more flexible and dynamic body of international law to support the interpretation of international refugee law in the cases of persons fleeing contemporary armed conflicts from a gender perspective. This is explored in Section 2.2.2.

2.2.2 International Human Rights Law and Gender in the Context of Contemporary Armed Conflicts

Contrary to international humanitarian law, significant advances have been made within international human rights law,[193] and, as noted in Section 2.2.1, to some extent in international criminal law,[194] in recognising the particular context of armed conflicts for the protection of human rights from a gender perspective. The relation between armed conflicts and an increase in the risk of gender-based violence, including sexual violence, has been

188 Barrow, 'UN Security Council Resolutions 1325 and 1820' (n 162) 227–228; Oosterveld, 'Gender at the Intersection of International Refugee Law and International Criminal Law' (n 177).

189 Chinkin and Kaldor, *International Law and New Wars* (n 115) 230.

190 Barrow, 'UN Security Council Resolutions 1325 and 1820' (n 162).

191 Ibid., 234.

192 Querton, 'Gender and the Boundaries of International Refugee Law' (n 74).

193 Tanya Henderson, 'Protecting Women in Peace and Conflict: International Humanitarian and Human Rights Law at Work' (2011) 71 *Peace and Freedom* 17.

194 Although see in Section 2.2.1 concerns regarding the international criminal law regime serving a different purpose than international refugee law and requiring a high threshold for the commission of offences.

recognised within the international legal system.[195] More specifically, international law recognises that gender dynamics impact on the risk of exposure to serious harm, the type of harm and access to state protection.

For more than twenty-five years, the international community has expressed concerns at the fact that women may be particularly vulnerable to the risk of gender-based violence and the gendered tactics and strategies adopted by fighting parties in the context of armed conflicts. The Declaration on the Elimination of Violence against Women affirmed that violence against women constitutes a violation of the rights and fundamental freedoms of women and highlighted concerns that refugee women and women in situations of armed conflict are particularly vulnerable to violence.[196] The UNGA noted its deep concern for human rights violations occurring in the context of armed conflicts 'affecting the civilian population, especially women, children, the elderly and the disabled'.[197] In 2000, the UN Security Council (UNSC) adopted Resolution 1325 due to concerns regarding women civilians being increasingly affected by armed conflicts and targeted by combatants and armed forces.[198] The Istanbul Convention also acknowledges that women are particularly affected by ongoing human rights violations in times of armed conflicts and the potential for increased gender-based violence both during and after conflicts.[199] On the fifteenth anniversary of the Fourth World Conference on Women, the Commission on the Status of Women again endorsed the view that women and girls are differently impacted than men and boys by armed conflicts.[200]

What is more, the UN has long considered that the cause of the gender-differentiated impact of armed conflicts is the status of women in society and more recently the expected behaviour and norms assigned to men and women.[201] As early as 1995, during the Beijing Platform for Action, the fact that women and girls are particularly affected by armed conflicts was understood as being caused by their status in society and their sex.[202] The UN Secretary General's report on Women, Peace and Security, which had been called for by UNSC Resolution 1325, highlighted that the differential impact of armed conflicts on women was due to their status in society.[203]

In addition to recognising the gender-differentiated impact of armed conflicts due to a person's status in society, the UN agenda has raised the prospect of certain additional responsibilities on states. As a consequence of the risk of violence against women increasing during times of armed conflict, states have been asked to adopt special measures and

195 UNSC Resolution 1888 (30 September 2009) UN Doc S/RES/1888; UNSC Res 1820 (19 June 2008) UN Doc S/RES/1820.

196 UNGA /48/104, preamble.

197 Vienna Declaration and Programme of Action, adopted by the World Conference on Human Rights in Vienna on 25 June 1993, Part I, para 29; UNGA Res 48/121 (20 December 1993) UN Doc A/RES/48/121.

198 UNSC Res 1325 (31 October 2000) UN Doc S/RES/1325.

199 Convention on Preventing and Combatting Violence against Women and Domestic Violence (adopted 11 May 2011, entered into force 1 August 2014) CETS 210, preamble.

200 UN Commission on the Status of Women (54th Session) 'High-level round table on the implementation of the Beijing Declaration and Platform for Action and the outcomes of the twenty-third special session of the General Assembly and its contribution to shaping a gender perspective in the realization of the Millennium Development Goals' (10 March 2010) UN Doc E/CN.6/2010/CRP.5, para 16.

201 UN Fourth World Conference on Women, Platform for Action, September 1995 (n 52) para 135; UN Secretary-General, Women, Peace and Security: Study (n 50) para 6.

202 UN Fourth World Conference on Women (n 52) para 135.

203 UN Secretary-General, Women, Peace and Security: Study (n 50) para 6.

provide particular responses.[204] The Convention for the Elimination of All Forms of Discrimination against Women (CEDAW) Committee has noted how armed conflicts may 'often lead to increased prostitution, trafficking in women and sexual assault of women, which require specific protective and punitive measures'.[205] The Vienna Declaration placed specific emphasis on the treatment of women in situations of armed conflict which may require 'a particularly effective response' by states.[206]

UNSC Resolution 1325 also 'calls on all parties to armed conflict to take special measures to protect women and girls from gender-based violence, particularly rape and other forms of sexual abuse, and all other forms of violence in situations of armed conflict'.[207] However, scholars have criticised the focus on rape and sexual violence in international law as it neglects the numerous other type of violence which women experience in situations of armed conflict.[208] Further, the non-binding nature of UN Resolutions has led to varying success in the protection of women in times of armed conflicts.[209]

Nonetheless, the UN agenda on women in armed conflicts and soft law instruments reflect a more sophisticated approach to gender dynamics and understanding of the relationship between gendered relations and violence in situations of armed conflict than that provided in international humanitarian law. Moreover, the international community created some new roles designed to address what has been recognised as a pressing issue of concern to the international community as a whole.[210] The legal basis for these changes to the international legal regime stem from the UNSC's mandate for the maintenance of international peace and security. Hence international law in general and international human rights law in particular increasingly demonstrate a more nuanced understanding of the causes, characteristics and consequences of violence in situations of armed conflict from a gender perspective. As will be argued in Section 2.3.5, these constitute 'relevant rules of international law' that state parties to the Refugee Convention must take into account when interpreting the refugee definition.[211] These norms also provide the legal foundations for the conceptual model proposed in Chapter 3 as a framework to interpret the Refugee Convention definition when persons are fleeing armed conflicts. Section 2.3 thus sets out the claim that by virtue of the general rule of treaty interpretation, states must have regard to these norms and the conceptual framework when interpreting the Refugee Convention definition in order to ensure the effective protection of persons fleeing contemporary armed conflicts.

204 Vienna Declaration and Programme of Action (n 197) para 38.

205 CEDAW Committee, 'General Recommendation No 19' (n 50) para 16.

206 Vienna Declaration and Programme of Action (n 197) para 38.

207 UNSC Res 1325 (31 October 2000) UN Doc S/Res/1325, para 10.

208 Aisling Swaine, 'Beyond Strategic Rape and between the Public and Private: Violence against Women in Armed Conflict' (2015) 37 *Human Rights Quarterly* 755.

209 Alain-Guy Tachou-Sipowo, 'The Security Council on Women in War: Between Peacebuilding and Humanitarian Protection' (2010) 92 *International Review of the Red Cross* 197.

210 For example, the post of UN Special Representative to the Secretary-General on Sexual Violence in Conflict (SRSG-SVC) was created in 2009 by the Security Council, see UNSC Res 1888 (30 September 2009) UN Doc S/RES/1888, para 4. In 2010, the Office of the Special Adviser to the Secretary-General on Gender Issues and Advancement of Women (OSAGI) was set up and its responsibilities include monitoring the implementation of UNSC Res 1325 and promoting gender mainstreaming.

211 See Section 2.3.5.

2.3 International Refugee Law

This section will start by reviewing the historical context of refugee protection granted to groups of persons who were deemed to be in need of international protection as a result of events occurring in their countries of origin. This will show that legal instruments and international agreements for the protection of refugees originated in a concern for similarly situated groups of persons. It is an important context to explain why international protection, more recently codified at the international level through the Refugee Convention, is grounded in an attempt to address the needs arising from the forced displacement of large groups of persons sharing similar characteristics. Thus, although the adoption of the Refugee Convention marked a shift away from the international protection of refugees by categories, there is nothing in the terms of the Refugee Convention or in its drafting history that suggests a departure from the principle that groups of persons similarly situated may be entitled to international protection. The discussion will then turn to the obligation of states to interpret the terms of the Refugee Convention definition in their context and in light of the Refugee Convention's object and purpose under the VCLT.[212] It will be argued that states' duty to perform their obligations in good faith[213] requires a dynamic interpretation of the Refugee Convention definition to fulfil the treaty's purpose and ensure the effective protection of persons fleeing armed conflicts by having regard to present-day conditions, which include the nature and dynamics of violence in contemporary armed conflicts. In turn and more specifically, this contemporary reality can only be understood by incorporating existing knowledge in security and feminist studies.

2.3.1 Historical Approaches to the International Protection Needs of Refugees

From a historical perspective, the adoption of the Refugee Convention in 1951 followed a time when the protection of refugees was undertaken on a group basis rather than based on individual characteristics.[214] More specifically, between 1920 and 1935 international agreements were reached through the auspices of the League of Nations to recognise refugee status to groups of persons defined by their nationality.[215] In the case of Russian and Armenian refugees for example, the only conditions for protection were Russian or Armenian nationality and a lack of state protection in the Soviet Union or Turkey respectively. Thus, Jackson and Einarsen describe the refugee definitions under the League of Nations as definition by 'categories'.[216] Furthermore, group approaches to international protection were developed in response to the needs of persons fleeing armed conflict and widespread violence.[217] When the UNHCR suggested extending protection measures to other categories of refugees, the rapporteur noted they were in a condition akin to the similarly situated Russians and Armenians 'as a consequence of the war or events directly connected with the war'. Even those Council

212 Article 31(1) VCLT. 213 Article 26 VCLT.

214 James C. Hathaway, 'The Evolution of Refugee Status in International Law: 1920–1950' (1984) 33 *International and Comparative Law Quarterly* 348, 361.

215 Ibid., 350–357.

216 Ivor C. Jackson, *The Refugee Concept in Group Situations* (Martinus Nijhoff Publishers 1999) 25; Terje Einarsen, 'Drafting History of the 1951 Convention and the 1967 Protocol' in Andreas Zimmermann (ed), *The 1951 Convention Relating to the Status of Refugees and its 1967 Protocol: A Commentary* (OUP 2011) 44.

217 McAdam, *Complementary Protection in International Refugee Law* (n 8) 34.

of the League of Nations members who were anxious not to extend protection unreasonably noted that efforts should focus on 'those whose needs were greatest, those in fact whose needs had been caused by political circumstances, more specially the consequences of the war'.[218]

The period following the Second World War and just prior to the drafting of the Refugee Convention was also characterised by mass displacement.[219] During this time, the Constitution of the International Refugee Organisation (IRO), the predecessor to UNHCR, was adopted.[220] Annex 1 of the IRO Constitution defined persons of concern to the organisation within four categories. Most of the provisions defining categories of refugees of concern to the IRO referred to war as a historical context leading to events creating refugees.[221] More specifically, refugees were defined amongst other categories as victims of the Nazi, fascist or other regimes in the Second World War,[222] victims of Nazi persecution who were displaced from Austria and Germany as a result of 'enemy action' or 'war circumstances',[223] or 'war orphans',[224] and the definitions excluded war criminals.[225] Einarsen has concluded that under the IRO, refugees were defined as explicit or implicit victims of persecution, war circumstances and certain political regimes.[226] This very brief historical overview of the groups of persons defined as refugees and the reasons for their flight indicates that the concept of group-based refugee protection for reasons related to conflict and widespread violence was central to the legal framework of international protection in the period leading up to the adoption of the Refugee Convention.

2.3.2 *The Refugee Convention: A Shift in International Protection Approaches?*

Section 2.3.1 demonstrated that the adoption of the Refugee Convention in 1951 followed a tradition of establishing protection mechanisms for groups or categories of persons without the protection of their own states, including those fleeing wars. The Refugee Convention incorporates into its definition of a refugee those who had already been recognised as refugees under earlier agreements.[227] In addition, the Refugee Convention also defines a refugee as a person who has a 'well-founded fear of being persecuted for reasons of race, religion, nationality, membership of a particular social group or political opinion' to provide protection for the groups of persons displaced by the Second World War.[228] The additional definition was originally limited to persons displaced by events in Europe before 1 January 1951 but the geographical and temporal limitations were removed by the Refugee Protocol in 1967. As McAdam notes, the 'new legal refugee definition' did not eradicate the other categories of refugees,[229] and Melander claims that the Refugee Convention definition was heavily influenced by the practice of the IRO.[230]

218 Hathaway, 'The Evolution of Refugee Status in International Law' (n 214) 355, 356.
219 Charlotte Lülf, *Conflict Displacement and Legal Protection: Understanding Asylum, Human Rights and Refugee Law* (Routledge 2019) 20.
220 Constitution of the International Refugee Organization (adopted 15 December 1946, entered into force 20 August 1948) 18 UNTS 3.
221 Articles 1(a), 2, 3 and 4, Section A, Part 1, Annex 1. 222 Article 1(a). 223 Article 3. 224 Article 4.
225 Article 2. 226 Einarsen, 'Drafting History' (n 216) 46. 227 Article 1A(1) Refugee Convention.
228 Article 1A(2) Refugee Convention; Hathaway and Foster, *The Law of Refugee Status* (n 20) 175; Goodwin-Gill and McAdam, *The Refugee in International Law* (n 21) 35–36.
229 McAdam, *Complementary Protection in International Refugee Law* (n 8) 33.
230 Göran Melander, 'International Refugee Organization (IRO)' *Max Planck Encyclopaedia of Public International Law* (June 2007) <https://opil.ouplaw.com/view/10.1093/law:epil/9780199231690/law-9780199231690-e512#> accessed 12 July 2021, para 27.

After the adoption of the Refugee Convention, many countries applied the Refugee Convention in a prima facie manner to categories of persons deemed in need of international protection based primarily on the general situation in their countries of origin.[231] As Jackson has demonstrated, many groups of refugees in Africa were provided with UNHCR protection as Refugee Convention refugees, and where protection was enabled through UNHCR's good offices mandate, this was merely an instrumental choice reflecting prima facie group determination in light of the Refugee Convention definition.[232] However, after the removal of the geographical and temporal limitations to the refugee definition in 1967, Western states began undertaking assessments of the individual circumstances of persons fleeing Eastern Europe during the Cold War by means of individualised asylum procedures in order to determine whether the person in question had a well-founded fear of being persecuted for a Refugee Convention ground, generally for political reasons. Einarsen claims that a myth emerged in the 1970s/1980s to the effect that the Refugee Convention was a product of the Cold War, pursuing the aim of protecting individuals who were politically profiled, in order for states to adopt a more restrictive approach to interpretation.[233] As Chimni had already noted this was part of the myth of difference between refugees from Europe and the Global South, whereby the former but not the latter satisfied the individualist criteria of political persecution.[234]

This is reflected to some extent in EU MS's rejection of a prima facie approach to the grant of refugee status in the case of a mass influx of persons,[235] opting instead for temporary protection for those 'who have fled areas of armed conflict or endemic violence or persons at serious risk of, or who have been the victims of, systematic or generalised violations of their human rights' in the framework of the Temporary Protection Directive.[236] Thus, many scholars have pointed to the restrictive approach to the Refugee Convention by states[237] who interpret the refugee definition as 'individualistic' in nature.[238]

However, McAdam has argued that the incorporation of the earlier categories of group refugees into the Refugee Convention[239] broadens the Refugee Convention's conceptual basis of protection and thus challenges the view that the Refugee Convention does not provide legal status to persons fleeing armed conflicts or widespread violence.[240] Further, Einarsen claims that it was obvious to the drafters of the Convention that the definition included refugees fleeing situations affecting large numbers of persons and those fleeing for more specific individual reasons.[241] Hathaway and Foster note that despite the Refugee Convention's requirement to asses a well-founded fear of persecution on the basis of an applicant's individual circumstances, the history and context of the Refugee Convention demonstrate

[231] Jackson, *The Refugee Concept in Group Situations* (n 216) 236–237. [232] Ibid., 237.

[233] Einarsen, 'Drafting History' (n 216) 68.

[234] B. S. Chimni, 'The Geopolitics of Refugee Studies: A View from the South' (1998) 11(4) *Journal of Refugee Studies* 350, 356.

[235] European Commission, Proposal for a Council Directive on minimum standards for giving temporary protection in the event of a mass influx of displaced persons and on measures promoting a balance of efforts between Member States in receiving such persons and bearing the consequences thereof, COM(2000) 303 final, 24 May 2000, para 2.2.

[236] Article 2(c) Temporary Protection Directive.

[237] Goodwin-Gill and McAdam, *The Refugee in International Law* (n 21) 15.

[238] See for example Jackson, *The Refugee Concept in Group Situations* (n 216) 236.

[239] Article 1A(1) Refugee Convention.

[240] McAdam, *Complementary Protection in International Refugee Law* (n 8) 34–35.

[241] Einarsen, 'Drafting History' (n 216) 67.

that large groups of persons who fear widespread violence are within its protective scope.[242] Hathaway and Foster also claim that leading courts support the view that group-based risks fall within the well-founded fear criterion of the Refugee Convention definition.[243] As Jackson concludes, there is no inherent legal limitation to the Refugee Convention being applicable to group situations.[244]

Although there is one substantial difference between the Refugee Convention definition and the prior regime for the protection of refugees, namely the abandonment of the IRO practice to recognise as refugees persons who had experienced persecution in the past but who did not necessarily have a fear of persecution on return,[245] qualification as a refugee under the Refugee Convention does not require any evidence of past persecution.[246] Thus, the refugee definition in Article 1A(2) Refugee Convention merely removes the link to nationality but the definition is of general application and applies to everyone who has a well-founded fear of being persecuted for reasons of race, religion, nationality, membership of a particular social group or political opinion, which may include groups of persons fleeing widespread violence.[247]

However, some domestic administrative and appellate authorities are reading into the refugee definition a requirement that a person needs to be singled out for persecution, in the sense that they are personally targeted by actors of persecution.[248] As suggested earlier in this sub-section, this is the result of a restrictive approach to the Refugee Convention definition adopted by Western states during the Cold War, which ignores its historical context and past application. Although the adoption of the Refugee Convention marked a shift from refugees being defined by their nationality and being granted protection by categories to a refugee definition of general application detached from nationality, the adoption of the Refugee Convention never precluded the application of the definition on a prima facie basis where considered appropriate. Thus, recognising groups of persons as Refugee Convention refugees merely on the basis of the objective circumstances in their country of origin has been done extensively. Furthermore, the concern with protecting persons fleeing wars was very much an explicit concern of the international community in its various efforts to address the problem of forced displacement over time. Accordingly, it appears at odds with the history of refugee protection to claim that 'war refugees' are either excluded from the protection of the Refugee Convention per se or constitute a particular category of refugees whose entitlement to international protection under the Refugee Convention should be determined differently than persons fleeing circumstances unconnected with armed conflicts by, for example, requiring individuals to demonstrate that they have been singled out by actors of persecution.

2.3.3 *International Refugee Law and Regional Protection Frameworks*

The existence of regional protection frameworks that explicitly include persons fleeing generalised violence, internal conflicts and serious public disturbances amongst other reasons

[242] Hathaway and Foster, *The Law of Refugee Status* (n 20) 175. [243] Ibid., 180.

[244] Jackson, *The Refugee Concept in Group Situations* (n 216) 236.

[245] Hathaway and Foster, *The Law of Refugee Status* (n 20) 163. [246] Ibid., 165.

[247] The 'well-founded fear of being persecuted' element of the Refugee Convention definition is discussed in depth in Chapter 5.

[248] See Section 5.2 in Chapter 5.

has raised further doubts as to whether the Refugee Convention definition encompasses persons fleeing situations of armed conflict. The rationale for the adoption and scope of those regional mechanisms are briefly discussed here to set out from the outset that they were grounded in regional practical needs and therefore that no inferences can be drawn regarding an interpretation of the Refugee Convention definition which is limited to situations of relative peace outside of armed conflicts.

The notion that the Refugee Convention definition does not apply to persons fleeing armed conflicts is further compounded by reference to the expanded refugee definitions enshrined in regional instruments such as the Convention Governing the Specific Aspects of Refugee Problems in Africa[249] and the Cartagena Declaration on Refugees[250] in Latin America.[251] Some of the literature suggests that these regional refugee definitions were developed in response to the restrictive individualistic Refugee Convention definition.[252] Accordingly, the regional refugee definitions are sometimes described as expanding the Refugee Convention definition and filling a protection gap caused by the requirement under the Refugee Convention definition of individual targeting. However, as highlighted by UNHCR, the regional refugee definitions are explicitly complementary to the Refugee Convention definition.[253] This further emphasises that nothing in the Refugee Convention prevents its application to group-based risks.[254]

The OAU Convention defines a refugee by restating the Refugee Convention definition,[255] and adds that the term

> shall also apply to every person who, owing to external aggression, occupation, foreign domination or events seriously disturbing public order in either part or the whole of his country of origin or nationality, is compelled to leave his place of habitual residence in order to seek refuge in another place outside his country of origin or nationality.[256]

As Rutinwa noted, a number of scholars and policy-makers consider that the 'extended' definition of a refugee in the OAU Convention was adopted because the Refugee Convention definition was too stringent and did not ensure the protection of persons fleeing civil wars and other events seriously disturbing public order.[257] However, Rutinwa demonstrates through a historical perspective that African states did not view the OAU Convention as an alternative to the Refugee Convention but rather as a complement to it.[258]

[249] Organisation of African Unity Convention Governing the Specific Aspects of Refugee Problems in Africa, 10 September 1969 (OAU Convention).

[250] Cartagena Declaration on Refugees, 22 November 1984 (Cartagena Declaration).

[251] Türk, Edwards and Wouters, 'Introduction' (n 2) 13; Storey and Wallace, 'War and Peace' (n 147) 351.

[252] Andrew E. Shacknove, 'Who Is a Refugee?' (1985) 95 *Ethics* 274, 276; see also Arboleda describing the Refugee Convention definition as 'obsolete', Eduardo Arboleda, 'Refugee Definition in Africa and Latin America: The Lessons of Pragmatism' (1991) 3 *International Journal of Refugee Law* 185, 188; and more recently Simeon, who suggests amending the Refugee Convention definition to include 'war refugees' based on the practice in the African and Latin American regions, James C. Simeon, 'A New Protection Orientation and Framework for Refugees and Other Forced Migrants' (2017) 6 *Laws* 30, 3.

[253] UNHCR, *Guidelines on International Protection No. 12* (n 5) para 87.

[254] McAdam, *Complementary Protection in International Refugee Law* (n 8) 46.

[255] Article 1(1) OAU Convention. [256] Article 1(2) OAU Convention.

[257] Bonaventure Rutinwa, 'Relationship between the 1951 Refugee Convention and the 1969 OAU Convention on Refugees: A Historical Perspective' in Volker, Edwards and Wouters (eds), *In Flight from Conflict and Violence* 102–104.

[258] Ibid., 102.

His view is heavily influenced by Jackson's study of twelve refugee situations in Africa and the reasons for flight in the decade leading up to the adoption of the OAU Convention.[259] Rutinwa thus concludes that the distinction between 'political refugees' under the Refugee Convention and 'humanitarian refugees' protected under the 'extended' OAU Convention definition is erroneous and that the definitions overlap significantly.[260] He concludes that the real impetus for the 'extended' refugee definition in the OAU Convention was political, in avoiding a judgment regarding instances of persecution in African states, and practical, in avoiding the need to undertake costly individual refugee status determination.[261]

Sharpe supports this view based on an analysis of the historical record. She confirms that the objective of the OAU Convention was not to redress a perceived dissatisfaction with the scope of the Refugee Convention definition and that reliance on the 'extended' definition in practice is because it is more expedient and less resource intensive.[262] However, resort to a humanitarian approach to refugee protection under the OAU Convention definition has resulted in limited jurisprudence on the relationship between the concepts of 'external aggression, occupation, foreign domination or events seriously disturbing public order' and the concept of persecution in the Refugee Convention definition.[263] Accordingly, little support can be found in the practice of African states regarding the interpretation of the Refugee Convention definition, as reproduced in the OAU Convention, where persons are fleeing situations of armed conflict.[264] More significantly, it leaves an 'interpretation gap' which some scholars and decision makers take as an indication that the Refugee Convention definition does not apply to persons fleeing armed conflicts.[265]

As for the American region, the Cartagena Declaration calls on states to adopt the Refugee Convention definition,[266] and reiterates that

> the definition or concept of a refugee to be recommended for use in the region is one which, in addition to containing the elements of the 1951 Convention and the 1967 Protocol, includes among refugees persons who have fled their country because their lives, safety or freedom have been threatened by generalised violence, foreign aggression, internal conflicts, massive violation of human rights or other circumstances which have seriously disturbed public order.[267]

Cantor and Trimiño Mora highlight the particular nature of the Cartagena Declaration and emphasise how it requires a different approach to interpretation than the conventional rules of treaty law generally applied to the Refugee Convention.[268] Furthermore,

[259] Jackson, *The Refugee Concept in Group Situations* (n 216) 145–179.

[260] Rutinwa, 'Relationship between the 1951 Refugee Convention and the 1969 OAU Convention on Refugees' (n 257) 108, 115; see also Alice Edwards, 'Refugee Status Determination in Africa' (2006) 14 *African Journal of International and Comparative Law* 204, 233.

[261] Rutinwa, 'Relationship between the 1951 Refugee Convention and the 1969 OAU Convention on Refugees' (n 257) 114–115.

[262] Marina Sharpe, 'The 1969 OAU Convention in the Context of Individual Refugee Status Determination' in Volker, Edwards and Wouters (eds), *In Flight from Conflict and Violence* 121, 128.

[263] Rutinwa, 'Relationship between the 1951 Refugee Convention and the 1969 OAU Convention on Refugees' (n 257) 109.

[264] Ibid., 109. [265] Edwards, 'Refugee Status Determination in Africa' (n 260) 233.

[266] Conclusion III(1)–(2) Cartagena Declaration. [267] Conclusion III(3) Cartagena Declaration.

[268] David James Cantor and Diana Trimiño Mora, 'A Simple Solution to War Refugees? The Latin American Expanded Definition and Its Relationship to IHL' in Cantor and Durieux (eds), *Refuge from Inhumanity?* 213.

although Reed-Hurtado suggests that the Cartagena Declaration definition aimed to fill the protection gap left by the Refugee Convention due to its focus on the subjective and individual element of persecution, he also concludes that its aim was to ensure greater effectiveness in the process of granting protection, allowing group-based determination on grounds of objective factors leading to flight.[269] His finding that most cases from the seventeen countries surveyed resulted in the grant of refugee protection under the Refugee Convention indicates an overlap between the two definitions in Latin America as well and supports the claim that the Refugee Convention definition encompasses persons fleeing situations of armed conflict.[270]

In the EU, the codification of subsidiary protection into Article 15 Qualification Directive aimed at harmonising existing EU MS's domestic provisions for the grant of international protection to persons who did not qualify as refugees in light of EU MS's obligations arising from international human rights instruments.[271] Article 15(c) was designed to harmonise EU MS's practice of providing complementary protection to 'persons fleeing the indiscriminate effects of armed conflict or generalised violence without a specific link to Convention grounds'.[272] When the European Commission first proposed the Qualification Directive in 2001, it highlighted that 'persons in flight from civil war or internal or generalised armed conflict are not necessarily Convention refugees',[273] thereby strengthening the belief that persons fleeing armed conflicts are to be protected by distinct complementary protection regimes outside the confines of the Refugee Convention.

In 2001, the EU also set up an 'exceptional scheme'[274] for persons 'who have fled areas of armed conflict or endemic violence or persons at serious risk of, or who have been the victims of, systematic or generalised violations of their human rights' in the framework of the Temporary Protection Directive.[275] The Directive aimed to respond to any 'mass influx of displaced persons' and was designed to address any consequent pressure on the asylum systems of individual MS 'in a spirit of Community solidarity' and via the European Refugee Fund.[276] The mechanism requires a qualified majority Council decision following a proposal by the European Commission.[277] The Directive remained inactivated for twenty years before the European Commission proposed to repeal it.[278] However, following the invasion of Ukraine by Russia, the Directive was activated for the first time on 4 March 2022 by a unanimous decision of the European Council to respond

[269] Michael Reed-Hurtado, 'The Cartagena Declaration on Refugees and the Protection of People Fleeing Armed Conflict and Other Situations of Violence in Latin America' in Türk, Edwards and Wouters (eds), *In Flight from Conflict and Violence*' 151–152, 157.

[270] Ibid., 164–167. [271] McAdam, *Complementary Protection in International Refugee Law* (n 8) 55.

[272] Ibid., 70–71.

[273] European Commission, Proposal for a Council Directive on minimum standards for the qualification and status of third country nationals and stateless persons as refugees or as persons who otherwise need international protection (COM (2001) 510 final, 12 September 2001) Explanatory Memorandum, 21.

[274] Recital (2) Temporary Protection Directive; see also recital (13) and Article 2(a).

[275] Article 2(c) Temporary Protection Directive.

[276] Articles 1, 2(c), 24 and 25 Temporary Protection Directive.

[277] Article 5(1) Temporary Protection Directive.

[278] European Commission, Proposal for a Regulation of the European Parliament and of the Council addressing situations of crisis and force majeure in the field of migration and asylum, COM(2020) 613 final, recital (27).

to the influx of Ukrainians into the EU.[279] This further reinforces the perception that persons fleeing armed conflict should be covered by complementary forms of protection.[280]

The brief discussion in this sub-section demonstrates that the justifications for adopting regional protection frameworks were rooted in concerns regarding efficiency, recourse to group-based refugee status determination processes, diplomatic relations and regional harmonisation. The aims of regional protection regimes in Africa, Latin America and the EU were not to fill a real or perceived gap in the scope of the Refugee Convention definition. The main difference between the Refugee Convention definition and the regional definitions that have been briefly discussed is not the need to show any singling out in the former but rather the inclusion of persons fleeing situations of armed conflict for reasons unconnected to race, religion, nationality, membership of a particular social group or political opinion in the latter.[281]

As UNHCR noted in its Guidelines on Armed Conflict and Violence, the statement at paragraph 164 of the UNHCR Handbook that 'persons compelled to leave their country of origin as a result of international or national armed conflicts are not normally considered refugees under the 1951 Convention or 1967 Protocol' is addressed to persons fleeing armed conflicts in the absence of causal link between the well-founded fear of being persecuted and the Refugee Convention grounds.[282] Thus, the question of how the Refugee Convention reasons for persecution are applied and interpreted in the asylum claims of persons fleeing situations of armed conflict is essential as it constitutes the key difference between the recognition of Refugee Convention status and complementary forms of protection under regional protection mechanisms.[283] However, as will be seen, the practice of appellate authorities in the EU reveals their perception that the principal difference between refugee status and subsidiary protection status is the requirement of a concrete risk of persecution evidenced by being singled out or individually targeted in the Refugee Convention definition.[284] Consequently, persons fleeing armed conflicts are refused refugee status on this basis even before appellate authorities consider the application of the Refugee Convention reasons for persecution.

2.3.4 *A Purposive Interpretation of the Refugee Definition*

As an international treaty, the Refugee Convention must be interpreted in light of the general rule of treaty interpretation as set out in the VCLT.[285] Although the VCLT was adopted after the Refugee Convention came into force, its terms reflect customary international law and thus its rules apply to the interpretation of any international treaty, whether or not state parties to the treaty have ratified the VCLT.[286] The general rule of interpretation provides

[279] Council Implementing Decision (EU) 2022/382 of 4 March 2022 establishing the existence of a mass influx of displaced persons from Ukraine within the meaning of Article 5 of Directive 2001/55/EC, and having the effect of introducing temporary protection [2022] OJ L 71/1.

[280] Although the Directive stipulates that temporary protection does not prejudge the recognition of refugee status, MS may provide that the statuses cannot be enjoyed concurrently; Articles 3(1) and 19 Temporary Protection Directive.

[281] UNHCR, *Guidelines on International Protection No. 12* (n 5) para 7. [282] Ibid., para 10.

[283] See Chapter 6. [284] See Chapter 5. [285] Articles 31–32 VCLT.

[286] *Reservations to the Convention on Genocide* (Advisory Opinion) [1951] ICJ Reports 15, pp 21–23.

that 'a treaty shall be interpreted in good faith in accordance with the ordinary meaning to be given to the terms of the treaty in their context and in the light of its object and purpose'.[287] The wording of this provision has sparked debates regarding the proper approach to interpretation, namely whether the primary focus should be on the terms of a treaty, also known as the 'literal' approach, or whether any interpretation should give precedence to the object and purpose of the treaty, known as the 'purposive' approach. Article 31 of the VCLT, however, is expressed as a singular rule of interpretation, suggesting a holistic approach to interpretation. Such an approach reconciles some commentators' views that although the ordinary meaning of the terms in their context is the starting point in interpreting a treaty, this is nonetheless determined in light of the object and purpose of the relevant treaty.[288] This perspective is endorsed by Hathaway and Foster who argue that the interpretation of the Refugee Convention, in accordance with this legal framework, requires a holistic assessment combining an analysis of the text in its context and in light of the Refugee Convention's object and purpose.[289] There appears to be a general agreement within refugee law scholarship that resort to the 'ordinary meaning' of the terms of the Refugee Convention definition in their context is unsatisfactory to interpret the definition in any event because its terms are 'inherently vague and broadly framed', leaving the definition itself 'ambiguous'.[290]

Furthermore, Hathaway and Foster assert the predominant requirement of interpreting the treaty in 'good faith' as a central principle of international law, meaning that states have to interpret the Refugee Convention in a manner that ensures its object and purpose.[291] This obligation is enshrined in Article 26 VCLT, which states that 'every treaty in force is binding upon the parties to it and must be performed by them in good faith'. This basic principle explicitly requires state parties to comply with the obligations set out in the Refugee Convention in good faith. Finally, in interpreting the terms of the Refugee Convention, consideration may also be given to supplementary means of interpretation,[292] but only to the extent that these supplementary means add to, rather than replace, the ordinary meaning to be given to the terms in their context and in the light of the treaty's object and purpose.[293] The VCLT provides that supplementary means include the preparatory work of the treaty and the circumstances of its conclusion, including the historical context.[294]

[287] Article 31(1) VCLT.

[288] I. M. Sinclair, *The Vienna Convention on the Law of Treaties* (2nd edn, Manchester University Press 1984) 130; Rebecca M. M. Wallace and Olga Martin-Ortega, *International Law* (7th edn, Sweet & Maxwell/ Thomson Reuters 2013) 280.

[289] Hathaway and Foster, *The Law of Refugee Status* (n 20) 7.

[290] Einarsen, 'Drafting History' (n 216) 49; Jane McAdam, 'Interpretation of the 1951 Convention' in Zimmermann (ed), *The 1951 Convention Relating to the Status of Refugees and Its 1967 Protocol* 86; Storey highlights the 'minimalist provisions' of the definition, in Hugo Storey, 'Persecution: towards a Working Definition' in Vincent Chetail and Céline Bauloz (eds), *Research Handbook on International Law and Migration* (Edward Elgar 2014) 459.

[291] Hathaway and Foster, *The Law of Refugee Status* (n 20) 5; Eirik Bjørge, *The Evolutionary Interpretation of Treaties* (OUP 2014) 70; Mark W. Janis, *International Law* (6th edn, Wolters Kluwer 2012) 28.

[292] Article 32 VCLT.

[293] Oliver Dörr and Kirsten Schmalenbach, *Vienna Convention on the Law of Treaties: A Commentary* (Springer 2012) 571–572.

[294] Wallace and Martin-Ortega, *International Law* (n 288) 281.

Looking firstly at the terms of the Refugee Convention, it is notable that the Refugee Convention does not make any explicit references to persons fleeing armed conflicts and widespread violence. As the 'ordinary meaning' of the terms of the Refugee Convention is merely the starting point in the process of interpreting the refugee definition, the absence of reference to the context of armed conflict cannot be taken to mean that persons fleeing armed conflicts are excluded from its protective ambit. In support of the argument that the drafters of the Refugee Convention considered the definition to be broad and applicable to almost all known groups of refugees, Einarsen points to the explicit Refugee Convention exclusion provisions.[295] Applying this rationale, the absence of explicit exclusion of persons fleeing armed conflicts from the Refugee Convention definition entails their inclusion within its scope. Hathaway and Foster claim, in the light of the plain language of the Refugee Convention definition, that it should be interpreted in the same manner irrespective of the context and thus that no additional requirement should be expected merely due to the fact that the person is fleeing a situation of armed conflict.[296]

Although the terms constituting the definition of a refugee may be vague and general, their context remains relevant.[297] The VCLT provides that a treaty's context includes its preamble and annexes.[298] There is general agreement that the Refugee Convention's preamble demonstrates its human rights focus.[299] More specifically, it highlights the 'principle that human beings shall enjoy fundamental rights and freedoms without discrimination'[300] and cites the UN Charter[301] and the Universal Declaration of Human Rights (UDHR).[302] The UN Charter sets out as one of its principal objectives, and the UDHR enshrines, the protection of human rights of all human beings without distinction of any kind, including on the basis of sex.[303] The preamble also emphasises that the UN has expressed serious concerns for refugees and worked towards assuring 'refugees the widest possible exercise of these fundamental rights and freedoms'.[304] It is thus clear that the process of interpretation of the constituent terms of the Refugee Convention definition requires the incorporation of human rights norms.[305]

The human rights focus of the preamble also assists in identifying the object and purpose of the Refugee Convention.[306] Hence, one of the principal aims of the Refugee Convention is to extend the protection of the international community to refugees,[307] and 'to ensure the protection of the specific rights of refugees'.[308] Overall, the Refugee Convention is an instrument whose purpose is to strengthen the protection of refugees[309] by shifting the obligation of protection from the country of origin to the international community.[310] A purposive approach thus entails interpreting the Refugee Convention definition in a broad and inclusive manner.[311] Section 2.3.5 argues that effective protection for persons

[295] Einarsen, 'Drafting History' (n 216) 67. See Articles 32 and 33(2) Refugee Convention.

[296] Hathaway and Foster, *The Law of Refugee Status* (n 20) 181, cite the Australian judgment of *Minister for Immigration and Multicultural Affairs v Abdi* [1999] 87 FCR 280, para 290, in support.

[297] Article 31(1) VCLT. [298] Article 31(2) VCLT.

[299] Hathaway and Foster, *The Law of Refugee Status* (n 20) 9. [300] Preamble Refugee Convention.

[301] UN Charter. [302] UDHR (adopted 10 December 1948) UNGA Res 217 A(III).

[303] Articles 1–2 UDHR; Article 1(3) UN Charter. [304] Preamble Refugee Convention.

[305] UNHCR, Interpreting Article 1 of the 1951 Convention Relating to the Status of Refugees, April 2001, para 4.

[306] McAdam, 'Interpretation of the 1951 Convention' (n 290) 91.

[307] Goodwin-Gill and McAdam, *The Refugee in International Law* (n 21) 8.

[308] UNHCR, Interpreting Article 1 (n 305) para 3.

[309] Goodwin-Gill, 'The Dynamic of International Refugee Law' (n 109) 655.

[310] McAdam, 'Interpretation of the 1951 Convention' (n 290) 90.

[311] Hathaway and Foster, *The Law of Refugee Status* (n 20) 10.

fleeing armed conflicts requires states to adopt a dynamic approach to interpretation of the Refugee Convention, treating it as a living instrument by taking into account the realities of contemporary armed conflicts. This, in turn, necessitates states to have regard to the gendered dynamics of violence arising from the changing nature of contemporary armed conflicts.

2.3.5 A Dynamic Approach to Interpretation: Ensuring the Effective Protection of Refugees in Light of Contemporary Realities

As set out, interpreting the Refugee Convention definition in light of the general rule of interpretation does not limit the definition to the meaning given to its terms at the time of the treaty's adoption. On the contrary, interpretation of the refugee definition should be guided by the principle of good faith and a holistic approach having regard to its terms in their context and in the light of the Refugee Convention's object and purpose. Furthermore, together with the context of the relevant terms, the VCLT also requires states to take into account 'any relevant rules of international law applicable in the relations between the parties'.[312] It is suggested here that international human rights law constitutes 'relevant rules' applicable between the parties to the Refugee Convention for the purpose of treaty interpretation. International human rights law is relevant because its objective coincides with the Refugee Convention's aim to protect the fundamental human rights of individuals. As set out in Section 2.3.4, the preamble of the Refugee Convention reiterates the importance of the universal protection of human rights. The Refugee Convention itself is often described as a human rights instrument,[313] and although this is debated,[314] the near universal acceptance of the human rights paradigm for the interpretation of the refugee definition supports the proposition that international human rights norms are 'relevant rules' of international law for the purpose of interpreting the terms of the refugee definition together with the context.[315] Accordingly, international human rights law norms of relevance to gender and armed conflicts discussed earlier must therefore be taken into account by states when interpreting the Refugee Convention definition.[316] These norms have acknowledged and sought to respond to the increase in gender-based violence in situations of armed conflict and the impact of gender dynamics on the nature of violence.

An obligation of states to have regard to later developments in international law leads to an evolutive approach to interpretation that treats an international treaty as a living instrument to be interpreted in the light of present-day conditions.[317] Cassese acknowledges that it may result in an expansion of the normative scope of treaties,[318] and Goodwin-Gill equates a dynamic approach[319] to interpretation with the progressive development of

[312] Article 31(3)(c) VCLT.

[313] Erika Feller, 'Foreword' in Zimmermann (ed), *The 1951 Convention Relating to the Status of Refugees and Its 1967 Protocol* vii; McAdam, *Complementary Protection in International Refugee Law* (n 8) 14.

[314] Vincent Chetail, 'Are Refugee Rights Human Rights? An Unorthodox Questioning of the Relations between Refugee Law and Human Rights Law' in Ruth Rubio-Marín (ed), *Human Rights and Immigration* (OUP 2014).

[315] As first set out in James C. Hathaway, *The Law of Refugee Status* (1st edn, Butterworths 1991).

[316] See Section 2.2.2. [317] Malcolm N. Shaw, *International Law* (8th edn, CUP 2017) 710.

[318] Antonio Cassese, *International Law* (2nd edn, OUP 2005) 179.

[319] McAdam defines this as the 'evolutionary approach' in McAdam, 'Interpretation of the 1951 Convention' (n 290) 103; Sinclair describes this as the 'emergent purpose' doctrine in Sinclair, *The Vienna Convention on the Law of Treaties* (n 288) 131.

international refugee law.[320] Subsequent state practice in the application of the Refugee Convention supports a dynamic approach to interpretation.[321] Thus, the Australian High Court noted that 'it would be an error to construe the definition so as to ignore the changing circumstances of the world in which the Convention now operates',[322] and the UK House of Lords has also endorsed treating the Refugee Convention as a 'living instrument'.[323] Accordingly, the Refugee Convention should be approached as a living instrument to be interpreted in the light of current circumstances such as contemporary armed conflicts.

As demonstrated in Chapter 1, the role of domestic authorities is often to determine whether persons fleeing situations of contemporary armed conflict across national borders meet the Refugee Convention definition. This requires a process of interpretation of the terms of the refugee definition to assess the meaning of 'a well-founded fear of being persecuted' for 'reasons of race, religion, nationality, membership of a particular social group or political opinion'. The discussion in Section 2.3.4 highlighted that the task of interpreting the Refugee Convention definition is challenging because the definition is vague, ambiguous and minimalist. In practice however, if domestic authorities considered that two different interpretations of the Refugee Convention definition were possible, only the interpretation which ensured the appropriate effect should be utilised.[324] This approach reasserts the Refugee Convention's relevance by ensuring it continues to function within its 'present social reality and contemporary legal context'.[325]

Accordingly, the general rule of treaty interpretation mandates a dynamic approach to interpreting the Refugee Convention definition in the cases of persons fleeing armed conflicts, by taking into account relevant norms of international law and international human rights law that better reflect the contemporary realities of armed conflicts. Compliance with states' good faith obligations towards the effective protection of refugees can only be achieved by consideration of and engagement with interdisciplinary knowledge of the nature of violence in situations of contemporary armed conflict, which will be discussed in Chapter 3. This approach does not lead to an interpretation that stretches the Refugee Convention definition beyond the ordinary meaning of its terms to recognise as refugees persons whom the drafters did not intend to include in the definition. As shown, the historical development of refugee protection by the international community was in response to the needs of groups of persons, often in the context of wars and armed conflicts. The drafting history of the Refugee Convention also demonstrates that persons fleeing group-based risks in the context of wars and armed conflicts were in the drafters' mind at the time of the Conference of Plenipotentiaries. Furthermore, even if the characteristics of armed conflicts have inherently changed since the international framework for the protection of refugees was first developed and since the drafting of the Refugee Convention, a purposive and dynamic approach to interpretation as mandated by the

[320] Goodwin-Gill, 'The Dynamic of International Refugee Law' (n 109) 661.

[321] Article 31(3)(b) VCLT also mandates taking into account 'any subsequent practice in the application of the treaty which establishes the agreement of the parties regarding its interpretation'.

[322] Per Kirby J in *A and Another v Minister for Immigration and Ethnic Affairs and Another* [1997] AHC 190 CLR 225, para 227.

[323] See for example Lord Hope in *Asfaw, R v* [2008] AC 1061, para 55; *Sepet & Anor, R (on the application of) v Secretary of State for the Home Department* [2003] UKHL 15, para 6.

[324] International Law Commission, 'Draft Articles on the Law of Treaties with Commentaries' (1966) II *Yearbook of the International Law Commission* 219.

[325] Hathaway and Foster, *The Law of Refugee Status* (n 20) 6; see also Guy Goodwin-Gill, 'The Search for the One, True Meaning' in Goodwin-Gill and Lambert (eds), *The Limits of Transnational Law* 207, 220.

VCLT supports the view that the concept of a refugee is not static nor fixed to historical intention. Therefore, interpretation of the Refugee Convention definition in the cases of persons fleeing armed conflicts without attention to evolving relevant norms of international human rights law and the dynamics of violence in contemporary armed conflicts does not fulfil the obligations of states to ensure the effective protection of refugees.

2.4 The Interpretation of International Refugee Law in the EU

This section examines how the claim that interpretation of the Refugee Convention definition to ensure the effective protection of refugees fleeing armed conflicts can only be guaranteed by consideration of relevant norms of international human rights law and feminist and security studies scholarship is affected when the process of interpretation takes place within the EU. This question concerns the relationship between international law and EU law, which is highly debated.[326] The issue is particularly relevant in the context of international protection in the EU because the legal obligations of EU MS arise from both international refugee law and the EU asylum *acquis*, as set out in Chapter 1.[327] Accordingly, when determining asylum claims, domestic authorities in EU MS are required to comply with both the Refugee Convention, an international treaty, and the Qualification Directive, an instrument of EU law.[328] In EU law, the refugee definition is found in Article 2(d) Qualification Directive, which reproduces the Refugee Convention definition but for the exclusion of EU nationals and those covered by Article 12 of the Directive.

There are express references in EU law to the need to respect international law. Thus, Article 3(5) Treaty on European Union sets out that the Union shall contribute 'to the strict observance and the development of international law'.[329] Moreover, the CJEU has also regularly reiterated the principle that EU competences must be exercised in accordance with international law.[330] As EU MS transferred powers to the Union in the aim of developing a common policy on asylum, they must apply the provisions of the Common European Asylum System (CEAS), including the Qualification Directive, in accordance with international law. More specifically, Article 78 Treaty on the Functioning of the European Union (TFEU) sets out that 'this policy must be in accordance with the Geneva Convention of 28 July 1951 and the Protocol of 31 January 1967 relating to the status of refugees, and other relevant treaties'. The provisions of the Qualification Directive and their interpretation must thus comply with the Refugee Convention and other relevant international human rights treaties.[331]

[326] See for example Martti Koskenniemi, *International Law Aspects of the European Union* (Kluwer Law International 1998); Jan Wouters, André Nollkaemper and Erika De Wet, *The Europeanisation of International Law: The Status of International Law in the EU and Its Member States* (CUP 2008).

[327] See Section 1.1.1 in Chapter 1.

[328] On the effect of EU law on domestic law generally, see Case 6/64 *Costa v Enel* [1964] ECR-585.

[329] Consolidated versions of the Treaty on European Union and the Treaty on the Functioning of the European Union 2012/C 326/01, Official Journal C 326, 26/10/2012 P. 0001–0390.

[330] In a series of cases raising the question whether a UNSC Resolution (as a provision of international law) should take primacy over EU law: Case C–402/05 P and C–415/05 P. *Kadi and Al Barakaat International Foundation v Council and Commission* [2008] ECR I–6351; Case T–85/09 *Kadi v Commission* [2010] ECR II-05177; Joined Cases C–584/10 P, C–593/10 P and C–595/10 P *Commission, Council and United Kingdom v Kadi* (Kadi II), Judgment of 18 July 2013.

[331] María-Teresa Gil-Bazo, 'Refugee Status, Subsidiary Protection, and the Right to be Granted Asylum under EC Law', 20 November 2006 (UNHCR Research Paper No 136) 4.

Overall, EU Treaty provisions and CJEU case law establish that there is a close relationship between international law and EU law generally, and thus between the Refugee Convention and the Qualification Directive specifically.

However, the duty to comply with international law in the exercise of EU law does not call into question the autonomy of the EU legal order.[332] In this respect, the EU system has been defined as a 'new legal order' developing independently of other branches of international law.[333] Moreno-Lax has demonstrated the complex relationship between international law and EU law, highlighting how the application of specific rules of interpretation has varied according to internal or external matters, types of EU instruments or their purpose in particular circumstances.[334] Accordingly, it is necessary to delineate the relationship between the definition of a refugee found in the Refugee Convention and that adopted in the Qualification Direction, and between the definition of a refugee and a beneficiary of subsidiary protection, both in the Qualification Directive.

Bearing in mind the requirement in the Treaties to comply with international law whilst simultaneously interpreting EU provisions autonomously, the CJEU held, in the case of *CILFIT*, that 'every provision of [EU] law must be placed in its context and interpreted in the light of the provisions of [EU] law as a whole, regard being had to the objectives thereof and to its state of evolution at the date on which the provision in question is to be applied'.[335] Where a provision of EU secondary legislation is ambiguous or incomplete, a teleological interpretation is applied which requires the provision to be interpreted in light of the objectives it pursues.[336] The refugee definition in Article 2(d) Qualification Directive must thus be interpreted in light of the objectives it pursues. Numerous provisions of the Qualification Directive's preamble emphasise that the CEAS is based on the full and inclusive application of the Refugee Convention.[337] The Qualification Directive thus states that the Refugee Convention is the 'cornerstone of the international legal regime for the protection of refugees',[338] and that the purpose of the Qualification Directive is to 'introduce common criteria for recognising applicants for asylum as refugees within the meaning of [the Refugee Convention definition]'.[339] In terms of interpreting the Qualification Directive, the CJEU has reiterated that the Refugee Convention 'constitutes the cornerstone of the international legal regime for the protection of refugees' and that the Qualification Directive was 'adopted to guide the competent authorities of the Member States in the application of that convention on the basis of common concepts and criteria'.[340] The CJEU has concluded that the Directive has to be interpreted in the light of its general scheme and purpose and in a manner consistent with the Refugee Convention.[341] The Qualification Directive is part of the broader scheme of the CEAS whose objective is to

332 Koen Lenaerts and Jose A. Gutiérrez-Fons, 'To Say What the Law of the EU Is: Methods of Interpretation and the European Court of Justice' (2014) 20 *Columbia Journal of European Law* 3, 6.

333 Violeta Moreno-Lax, 'Of Autonomy, Autarky, Purposiveness and Fragmentation' in Cantor and Durieux (eds), *Refuge from Inhumanity?* 297.

334 Ibid., 312–314.

335 Case 283/81 *Srl CILFIT and Lanificio di Gavardo SpA v Ministry of Health* [1982] ECR I-03415, para 20.

336 See discussion in Lenaerts and Gutiérrez-Fons, 'To Say What the Law of the EU Is' (n 332) 32.

337 Recital (3) Qualification Directive 2011; see also recitals (4), (23), (24), (29), (33) and Articles 5(3) and 9 for example.

338 Recital (4) Qualification Directive 2011.

339 Recital (24) Qualification Directive 2011.

340 Joined Cases C-443/14 and C-444/14 *Kreis Warendorf v Alo and Osso v Region Hannover* [2016] 3 CMLR 11 para 28; see also recital (23) Qualification Directive 2011.

341 *Kreis Warendorf v Alo and Osso v Region Hannover* para 29.

offer 'appropriate status to any third-country national requiring international protection and ensuring compliance with the principle of *non-refoulement*'.[342] The object and purpose of the Qualification Directive are thus aligned to the objectives of the Refugee Convention to extend and strengthen the protection of the international community to refugees.[343] Accordingly, the definition of a refugee in Article 2(d) of the Qualification Directive is identical to the Refugee Convention definition but for the exclusion of EU nationals from its scope.[344]

With respect to the interpretation of Article 15(c) Qualification Directive, Lenaerts and Gutiérrez-Fons suggest that the 'principle of systematic interpretation' in EU law requires that the subsidiary protection provisions of Article 15 Qualification Directive be interpreted in a manner that has regard to the general scheme of international protection in the EU.[345] Equally, each provision needs to be given its own scope of application to ensure its *effet utile*.[346] As the CJEU established that Article 15(c) contains an autonomous concept of EU law,[347] the meaning of its terms may differ from the way in which they are defined in the domestic law of EU MS. Accordingly, any interpretation of the provision must take into account the normative context of the provisions of the Qualification Directive as a whole and the objectives it seeks to achieve.[348] As just discussed, those objectives reflect the purposes of the Refugee Convention.

UNHCR's Executive Committee has emphasised the primacy of the Refugee Convention over other forms of complementary protection, arising for example from obligations under international human rights law or the EU Qualification Directive.[349] The primacy of the Refugee Convention over subsidiary protection in EU law is reflected in the definition of subsidiary protection itself in Article 2(f), which explicitly states that a person can only be a beneficiary of subsidiary protection when they are not already a refugee. This is reiterated in the recital to the Qualification Directive.[350] At procedural level, the Asylum Procedure Directive reflects this relationship.[351] Tsourdi has emphasised that the primacy of the refugee protection regime over subsidiary protection in EU law is unambiguous.[352]

342 Article 78 TFEU. 343 See Section 2.3.4.

344 Lambert argues the exclusion is in contravention of international law, Helene Lambert, 'The EU Asylum Qualification Directive, Its Impact on the Jurisprudence of the United Kingdom and International Law' (2006) 55 *International and Comparative Law Quarterly* 161, 178; although Gil-Bazo has argued that EU MS remain free to fulfil their international obligations towards EU nationals, Gil-Bazo, 'Refugee Status' (n 331) 10.

345 Lenaerts and Gutiérrez-Fons, 'To Say What the Law of the EU Is' (n 332) 20. 346 Ibid. 17.

347 *Diakite v Commissaire General aux Refugies et aux Apatrides* (n 155).

348 Lenaerts and Gutiérrez-Fons, 'To Say What the Law of the EU Is' (n 332) 7; see also *Srl CILFIT and Lanificio di Gavardo SpA v Ministry of Health* para 20; Joined Cases C–402 and 415/05 *Kadi v Council & Commission (Common Foreign & Security Policy)* [2008] ECR I-6351.

349 UNHCR Executive Committee, 'Conclusion on the Provisions of International Protection Including through Complementary Forms of Protection' No 103 (LVI) 2005, <www.unhcr.org/uk/excom/exconc/43576e292/conclusion-provision-international-protection-including-complementary-forms.html> accessed 12 July 2021.

350 Recital 4 Qualification Directive.

351 Article 10(2) Directive 2013/32/EU of the European Parliament and of the Council of 26 June 2013 on common procedures for granting and withdrawing international protection OJ L 180, 29.6.2013 states that 'when examining applications for international protection, the determining authority shall first determine whether the applicants qualify as refugees and, if not, determine whether the applicants are eligible for subsidiary protection'.

352 Evangelia Tsourdi, 'What Protection for Persons Fleeing Indiscriminate Violence? The Impact of the European Courts on the EU Subsidiary Protection Regime' in Cantor and Durieux (eds), *Refuge from Inhumanity?* 287.

Applying these principles to the interpretation of the refugee and subsidiary protection definitions in the Qualification Directive indicates that the Refugee Convention retains its primacy in the framework of international protection in the EU. Furthermore, there is significant overlap in the object and purpose of the Qualification Directive and the Refugee Convention in ensuring the protection of refugees. For example, the protection of refugees on a group basis in international refugee law, discussed earlier,[353] has also been recognised in the EU context, where the EU Joint Position acknowledged that entire groups of people may be at risk of persecution.[354] The provisions of the Qualification Directive are termed such that the two international protection statuses must be interpreted in succession according to the same principles of interpretation as they both share the same objectives. Accordingly, a teleological approach to interpretation of the refugee and subsidiary protection definitions in EU law that conforms to international law entails taking into account relevant norms of international human rights law and the dynamics of violence in contemporary armed conflicts by incorporating existing feminist and security studies knowledge.[355] In other words, failure to have regard to the dynamics of violence in contemporary armed conflicts when interpreting the EU international protection provisions does not ensure the effective protection of refugees in the EU legal order. Section 2.4.1 considers the outcome of asylum decisions in the EU in order to place this interpretative duty in its relevant context.

2.4.1 Outcome of Asylum Decisions in the EU

Statistics suggest that on average first-instance decisions for all nationalities between 2013 and 2016 in the EU resulted in a higher proportion of refugee status than subsidiary protection status.[356] However, there was a substantial increase in the grant of subsidiary protection status from 9 per cent in 2015 to 23 per cent in 2016 and a lowering of refugee status outcomes from 38 per cent in 2015 to 33 per cent in 2016. As first-instance decisions are not necessarily taken in the same year as asylum applications are made and recorded, it may be suggested that the significant increase in the number of applications in 2015 may explain the subsequent change in first-instance decisions outcomes in 2016. By 2020, however, refugee protection rates had reduced to 20 per cent, equivalent to the combined subsidiary protection and humanitarian protection rates.[357] The rates of protection statuses between men and women did not differ significantly and the group with the highest proportion of grants alternated between 2013 and 2016.[358]

[353] See Sections 2.3.1 and 2.3.2.

[354] Joint Position of 4 March 1996 defined by the Council on the basis of Article K.3 of the Treaty on European Union on the harmonised application of the definition of the term 'refugee' in Article 1 of the Geneva Convention of 28 July 1951 relating to the status of refugees (96/196/JHA) [1996] OJ L63/2, para 2.

[355] See Sections 2.3.4 and 2.3.5.

[356] It is important to note that the subsidiary protection rates indicated in Eurostat statistics is protection awarded under Article 15(a)–(c) Qualification Directive. Some countries make use of non-harmonised humanitarian protection statuses in significant numbers such as Germany for example.

[357] Statistics compiled from Eurostat, 'First Instance Decisions on Applications by Citizenship, Age and Sex – Annual Aggregated Data (Rounded)', <https://ec.europa.eu/eurostat/databrowser/view/migr_asydcfsta/default/table?lang=en> last updated 18 November 2021, accessed 21 November 2021. Figures from 2020 exclude the UK.

[358] See Table B.1 in Appendix B.

The outcome of final decisions in the EU for the same period (2013–2016) displays a similar trend as appellate authorities are more likely to recognise appellants as refugees rather than as beneficiaries of subsidiary protection. The year 2016, however, did not see an increase in the rate of subsidiary protection status as observed in first-instance decisions.[359] The outcome of final decisions in the EU for Afghan, Iraqi and Syrian nationals also show that refugee status was granted in higher proportion than subsidiary protection.[360] The only exception was that, in 2013, appellate authorities recognised almost twice as many Syrians as beneficiaries of subsidiary protection than as refugees.[361] Reflecting the first-instance decisions outcome, the rates of protection statuses between men and women did not differ significantly and the group with the highest proportion of grants alternated between 2013 and 2016.

The trends described represent an EU-wide average however, and comparing the proportion of Afghan appeals allowed on Refugee Convention grounds or subsidiary protection grounds in Belgium, Denmark, Spain, France, the Netherlands and the UK shows that there are significant disparities in final decision outcomes in these EU MS, both in respect of refugee status and subsidiary protection status.[362] The percentage of final decisions in Afghan appeals resulting in the grant of refugee status in 2016 for example ranged from 1.3 per cent in Belgium to 57.21 per cent in the UK. The percentage of final decisions in Afghan appeals resulting in the grant of subsidiary protection status in 2014 for example ranged from 0 per cent in Belgium and Spain to 59.32 per cent in France. Whereas appellate authorities in Belgium and the UK barely recognised any Afghans as beneficiaries of subsidiary protection over the relevant period, the French Court allowed such appeals on average in almost 50 per cent of cases. On average over the relevant period, the Dutch Courts recognised Afghans as beneficiaries of subsidiary protection in 27 per cent of cases and the Danish Refugee Appeal Board in 18 per cent of cases. As noted in the methodology, there were significantly fewer appeals determined in Spain.[363] The Spanish National High Court (Audiencia Nacional, AN) made merely five decisions in appeals brought by Afghan nationals in the relevant period and all were dismissed.[364]

The outcome of final decisions for Iraqi nationals in Belgium, Denmark, Spain, France, the Netherlands and the UK also varied significantly.[365] The Eurostat statistics for Spain suggest that the Spanish Court made no or less than five decisions in Iraqi appeals in

[359] See Table B.2 in Appendix B. [360] See Tables B.3–B.5 in Appendix B.

[361] See Table B.5 in Appendix B. [362] See Tables B.6–B.7 in Appendix B. [363] See Section 1.2.3 in Chapter 1.

[364] In 2013 there were two Afghan appeals, in 2014 there were two Afghan appeals and in 2015 there was one Afghan appeal. Eurostat data are rounded to the nearest five, hence the number of final decisions is given as zero every year between 2013 and 2016, see Eurostat Metadata, 'Decisions on Applications and Resettlement (migr_asydec)' <https://ec.europa.eu/eurostat/cache/metadata/fr/migr_asydec_esms.htm> accessed 12 July 2021, para 3.1. For statistics regarding Spain, the more specific figures provided by the Spanish Office for Asylum and Refuge (Oficina de Asilo y Refugio, OAR) were used; OAR, 'Asilo en Cifras 2016' October 2017 <www.interior.gob.es/opencms/pdf/servicios-al-ciudadano/oficina-de-asilo-y-refugio/datos-e-informacion-estadistica/Asilo_en_cifras_2016_126150899.pdf> accessed 12 July 2021; OAR, 'Asilo en Cifras 2015' undated <www.interior.gob.es/opencms/pdf/servicios-al-ciudadano/oficina-de-asilo-y-refugio/datos-e-informacion-estadistica/Asilo_en_cifras_2015_126150899.pdf> accessed 12 July 2021, p 50; OAR, 'Asilo en Cifras 2014' September 2015 <www.interior.gob.es/opencms/pdf/servicios-al-ciudadano/oficina-de-asilo-y-refugio/datos-e-informacion-estadistica/Asilo_en_cifras_2014_126150899.pdf> accessed 12 July 2021, p 63; OAR, 'Asilo en Cifras 2013' September 2014 <www.interior.gob.es/opencms/pdf/servicios-al-ciudadano/oficina-de-asilo-y-refugio/datos-e-informacion-estadistica/Asilo_en_cifras_2013_126140719.pdf> accessed 12 July 2021, p 66.

[365] See Tables B.8–B.9 in Appendix B.

the relevant period. The figures from OAR indicate there was merely one Iraqi appeal in 2013, which was dismissed.[366] Both Belgium and Denmark had a consistently minimal rate of successful Iraqi appeals under the Refugee Convention. Although France and the Netherlands had a proportion of successful Iraqi refugee appeals between approximately 15 per cent and 30 per cent from 2013 to 2015, the grant of refugee status by appellate authorities from both countries then significantly reduced in 2016. The UK retained a consistent proportion of successful Iraqi appeals resulting in the grant of refugee status over the relevant period.

The statistics show that only appellate authorities in France and the Netherlands allowed Iraqi appeals under the subsidiary protection provisions to a meaningful extent. Although appellate authorities in Belgium, Denmark and the UK did allow appeals under the subsidiary protection provisions, the proportion was minimal. This stood in stark contrast to the grant of subsidiary protection status in over 47 per cent of Iraqi appeals by the Dutch Courts in 2016. The proportion of allowed Iraqi appeals by the Belgian Court was consistently low at less than 7 per cent with respect to both types of statuses. Overall, there were significant disparities, in particular between France and the Netherlands on the one hand and Belgium, Denmark and the UK on the other.

In respect of final decisions in Syrian appeals, the statistics again demonstrate significant differences in outcomes between select EU MS.[367] The proportion of final decisions in Syrian appeals show again that the Belgian Courts allow appeals under the Refugee Convention in a low number of cases. The Dutch Courts allowed no appeals under the Refugee Convention in 2013 and 2014 although by 2016 this had risen to approximately one quarter of decisions. Demonstrating a similar trend to the Dutch Courts, the Spanish Courts allowed no appeals under the Refugee Convention from 2013 to 2014 and made no decisions in Syrian appeals in 2015. The success rate then increased significantly to 60 per cent in 2016. In 2016, Denmark, France and the UK allowed Syrian appeals under the Refugee Convention in approximately 45 to 50 per cent of cases.

The statistics showing the proportion of successful Syrian appeals resulting in the grant of subsidiary protection status reveal a stark contrast between the Netherlands and the other EU MS sampled for this study. The Dutch Courts were the only appellate authorities out of the six jurisdictions consistently to recognise subsidiary protection for Syrian nationals in the range of 50 to 70 per cent. On the contrary, the other appellate authorities granted this status in a minimal number of cases from 2015 onwards. Thus, the application of Article 15(c) by appellate authorities in the EU since 2015 has been generally consistent in rejecting recognition of Syrian appellants as beneficiaries of subsidiary protection. Simultaneously, recognition of Syrians as refugees was inconsistent across the EU in the period examined, culminating in recognition rates varying between 10 per cent in Belgium to 60 per cent in Spain.

Overall, these figures demonstrate that despite an obligation to comply with the same international and European legal standards and definitions, including methods of interpretation, there are substantial disparities in the outcome of appellate decision-making in the EU. Identifying the precise reasons for divergence in asylum decision-making is complex because identical outcomes can only be expected in identical cases. As the determination of asylum claims requires consideration of both the personal characteristics of each applicant and the general conditions in the country of origin, the outcome of asylum claims

[366] OAR, 'Asilo en Cifras 2013' September 2014 (n 364) p 66. [367] See Tables B.10–B.11 in Appendix B.

is partly determined by the unique individual circumstances of each applicant, which are inevitably different in each EU MS. However, in cases where individuals are fleeing countries experiencing protracted armed conflicts characterised by a material level or spread of violence affecting the civilian population, more consistent outcomes would be expected as the objective conditions in the country of origin become increasingly determinative of the outcome, rather than the personal circumstances of each claimant. Thus, although some level of divergence in asylum decision outcomes across EU MS may be justified by the differences in individual asylum cases, where persons flee situations of armed conflict, inconsistencies are less likely to be warranted as factors independent of individual applicants increasingly take precedence.[368]

An EU-level decision to grant protection to persons fleeing armed conflicts such as that required under the Temporary Protection Directive, illustrated by the case of Ukrainians fleeing the Russian military invasion in February 2022, naturally results in consistent outcomes across the EU. In July 2022, the EU Agency for Asylum reported that 3.8 million persons fleeing Ukraine had been registered for temporary protection.[369] This stands in stark contrast to the 112,660 persons granted refugee status and 61,385 granted subsidiary protection across the EU for the whole of 2021.[370]

With respect to the interpretation of the Refugee Convention definition, Chapter 5 will demonstrate how all the appellate authorities surveyed require asylum appellants to be singled out by actors of persecution. Consequently, this suggests that the most important variable in determining the recognition of refugee status is whether individual claimants have been singled out for persecution and whether their account is considered credible. The proportion of appellate decisions leading to refugee status in each EU MS is thus dependent on the individual facts of each case and the assessment of credibility rather than the objective conditions in Afghanistan, Iraq and Syria. As will be discussed in Chapter 6, if attention was paid to the dynamics of violence in situations of armed conflict, including the gendered strategies and tactics adopted by fighting parties, as a lens to interpret the Refugee Convention definition rather than focus on past events demonstrating having been singled out,[371] appellate decision outcomes would likely be more consistent across EU MS.

2.5 Conclusion

This chapter started by engaging with the relationship between international refugee law and other fields of international law in the context of contemporary armed conflicts. It discussed the deficiencies of international humanitarian law and to a lesser extent international criminal law as an aid to interpretation of the Refugee Convention definition. Instead, it was argued that international human rights law had more potential in framing the risk of human rights violations in the context of armed conflicts from a gender perspective. Consideration was then given to historical approaches to international protection and the conclusion was drawn that historically group-based risks in the context of situations of

368 These factors are discussed in Chapter 3.

369 EU Agency for Asylum, 'Analysis on Asylum and Temporary Protection in the EU+ in the Context of the Ukraine Crisis Week 28 (11–17 July) 2022', 20 July 2022 <https://euaa.europa.eu/publications/analysis-asylum-and-temporary-protection-eu-context-ukraine-crisis-14> accessed 26 July 2022, 1.

370 Eurostat, 'First Instance Decisions on Applications by Citizenship, Age and Sex' (n 35).

371 As argued in Section 2.3.

war and widespread violence formed the basis for refugee protection arrangements. This was followed by a discussion of the shift in international approaches to the protection of refugees with the adoption of the Refugee Convention in 1951. The claim was made that this shift was limited to a departure from a refugee definition based on nationality and lack of state protection but that the Refugee Convention definition is nonetheless of general application. This view was supported by the brief overview of the rationales for adopting regional protection frameworks in Africa, the Americas and Europe that contain provisions explicitly addressing persons fleeing generalised violence, internal conflicts and serious public disturbances. Thus, the principle of group-based risk where a high number of similarly situated persons are equally at risk due to widespread violence did not cease to apply when the Refugee Convention was adopted.

This context led to the main argument of this chapter that relevant norms of international human rights law and the nature of violence in contemporary armed conflicts are essential considerations in the interpretation of the Refugee Convention definition in accordance with the general rule of interpretation. More specifically, the chapter argued for an approach to interpretation of the Refugee Convention definition in light of the treaty's object and purpose and in accordance with the principles of good faith and effectiveness. Ensuring the effective protection of persons fleeing armed conflicts can only be achieved by incorporating the wealth of knowledge and empirical evidence that the characteristics of armed conflicts and the nature of violence in situations of widespread human rights violations have changed. Finally, it was claimed that the relationship between international refugee law and EU law is such that the process of interpretation of the refugee definition under the Qualification Directive in the context of the EU legal order is to be guided by the same approach.

UNHCR claims that the protection gap arising out of asylum claims in situations of armed conflict is the result of inadequate interpretation of the Refugee Convention that is contrary to an inclusive application of the treaty.[372] As set out in this chapter, the Refugee Convention requires dynamic interpretation due to its status as a living instrument to be interpreted in light of modern-day situations and applied to reflect changing realities and developments in international law.[373] The substantive content of those contemporary circumstances are set out in a conceptual framework as a means to interpret the Refugee Convention definition in accordance with state parties' legal obligations in Chapter 3.

[372] Türk, Edwards and Wouters, 'Introduction' (n 2) 2, 21.

[373] McAdam, 'The Enduring Relevance of the 1951 Refugee Convention' (n 8); Goodwin-Gill, 'The Search for the One, True Meaning' (n 325) 207; Türk, Edwards and Wouters, 'Introduction' (n 2) 7; Madeline Garlick, 'Protection in the European Union for People Fleeing Indiscriminate Violence in Armed Conflict' in Türk, Edwards and Wouters (eds), *In Flight from Conflict and Violence* 247.

3

Contemporary Armed Conflicts, Violence and Gender in International Refugee Law

3.1 Introduction

The previous chapter claimed that interpreting the Refugee Convention definition in a way that ensures the effective protection of persons fleeing armed conflicts requires taking into account the nature of violence in the context of contemporary armed conflicts. An interdisciplinary approach to legal interpretation enables these features to be adequately recognised in the process of refugee status determination. Accordingly, the present chapter proposes a conceptual framework drawing on security studies and gender perspectives as a subset of international relations scholarship to reframe the interpretation of the Refugee Convention in the context of persons fleeing armed conflicts. In light of the changing nature of violence in contemporary armed conflicts, including the increasing complexity of actors, parties' objectives and fighting strategies, and the dynamics and impact of violence, this framework reasserts the Refugee Convention as the cornerstone of international protection.

In the field of international refugee law, only Lambert, Farrell and Schmitt have considered the relevance of security studies literature for the international protection of persons fleeing armed conflicts.[374] However, the theoretical models they draw on are concerned with investigating the onset of armed conflicts. As a result, the value of this interdisciplinary research as an explanatory framework for the general conditions in countries of origin is limited to understanding the broad causes of armed conflict onset rather than the ongoing dynamics of violence in situations of armed conflict. More specifically, Lambert and Farrell have adopted a modified perspective of the greed or grievance theory first propounded by Collier and Hoeffler to explain reasons for conflicts.[375] Although Lambert and Farrell aim to shed light on the changing character of armed conflicts for the purpose of international protection, their analysis is limited to the statement that 'new wars are not waged for reasons of state but rather for a mix of motives involving greed and grievance: wars are fought to secure resources, and to avenge for perceived past wrongs'.[376] Later, in the context of United Nations High Commissioner for Refugees' (UNHCR's) Consultations on the international protection of persons fleeing armed conflicts and violence, Farrell and Schmitt investigated the causes, character, conduct and effect on civilians of armed conflict from the perspective

[374] Lambert and Farrell, 'The Changing Character of Armed Conflict' (n 6); Lambert, 'The Next Frontier' (n 6); Farrell and Schmitt, 'The Causes, Character and Conduct of Armed Conflict' (n 163).

[375] Paul Collier and Anke Hoeffler, 'Greed and Grievance in Civil War' (2004) 56 *Oxford Economic Papers* 563.

[376] Lambert and Farrell, 'The Changing Character of Armed Conflict' (n 6) 257; 'reasons of state' is a term found in the field of international relations meaning the interests of states; see Jonathan Haslam, *No Virtue Like Necessity: Realist Thought in International Relations since Machiavelli* (Yale University Press 2002) 17.

of political science.[377] However, Farrell and Schmitt deal only briefly with the causes of armed conflict,[378] do not seek to explore those causes from a gender perspective,[379] and do not propose a solution to the problems they identify.[380] Significantly, Farrell and Schmitt endorse the approach first suggested by Lambert and Farrell when stating that conflicts are generally spurred by a mix of drivers, including ethnic differences (the grievance motive) and economic conditions (the greed motive).[381] Consequently, existing contributions focus mostly on the causes of conflicts and the political economy of conflicts rather than enabling an understanding of violence as a process and not merely as an outcome.[382] Moreover, the conventional dichotomy between the notion of criminal and political violence is inherent in the greed and/or grievance theory.

The approach therefore imports preconceptions about the nature of violence in armed conflicts with significant consequences for international protection. The absence of greater consideration of the nature of violence in armed conflicts and instead on armed conflicts more broadly, is illustrated by the focus in the literature on qualification by persons fleeing armed conflicts as beneficiaries of subsidiary protection rather than refugee protection.[383] This has led to a focus on technical questions surrounding subsidiary protection such as how to measure levels of 'indiscriminate violence'.[384] Instead, this chapter proposes a framework to adequately explain and understand the nature and dynamics of violence in contemporary armed conflicts of relevance to the Refugee Convention, the cornerstone of international protection.

This chapter claims that the ongoing dynamics of violence in situations of armed conflict provides a more valuable lens to interpret the Refugee Convention definition where persons flee armed conflicts as it focuses on the nature of violence, including its continuum, features, application, direction, motivation and impact. A micro-level analysis of this type also enables the identification of gender dynamics that are essential in understanding violence in armed conflicts. Conversely, macro-level explanations for the causes of armed conflicts result in treating armed conflicts and violence as synonymous instead of conceptually different notions. Accordingly, the present chapter proposes an original conceptual framework built on gender and security studies and supported by existing international legal standards and norms. This framework outlines the knowledge that should be incorporated into the

[377] Farrell and Schmitt, 'The Causes, Character and Conduct of Armed Conflict' (n 163).

[378] Barely two and a half pages are devoted to the issue in the UNHCR Research Series Paper, see Theo Farrell and Olivier Schmitt, *The Causes, Character and Conduct of Armed Conflict, and the Effects on Civilian Populations, 1990–2010* (UNHCR 2012); whilst the topic is reduced to barely half a page in the subsequent publication, Farrell and Schmitt, 'The Causes, Character and Conduct of Armed Conflict' (n 163).

[379] In relation to issues of gender, the research is limited to highlighting that gender-based violence is prevalent during times of conflict without specifically investigating its causes and consequences.

[380] At most Farrell and Schmitt note that it is ironic that the Refugee Convention does not explicitly provide international protection to persons fleeing armed conflicts in light of the historical context of its drafting; see Farrell and Schmitt, 'The Causes, Character and Conduct of Armed Conflict' (n 163) 35.

[381] Farrell and Schmitt, 'The Causes, Character and Conduct of Armed Conflict' (n 163); as endorsed by Wouters in 'Conflict Refugees' (n 5) 816–820; it was also endorsed by Clark and Simeon in Tom Clark and James C. Simeon, 'War, Armed Conflict, and Refugees: The United Nations' Endless Battle for Peace' (2016) 35 *Refugee Studies Quarterly* 35, 43, 68, although in the context of addressing root causes of refugees.

[382] Kalyvas, *The Logic of Violence in Civil War* (n 41) 21, 35.

[383] See for example Lambert and Farrell, 'The Changing Character of Armed Conflict' (n 6); Lambert, 'The Next Frontier' (n 6); Hélène Lambert, 'Causation in International Protection from Armed Conflict' in Cantor and Durieux (eds), *Refuge from Inhumanity?*.

[384] Under Article 15(c) Qualification Directive and the national legislation transposing it.

process of interpreting the refugee definition to ensure effective protection of refugees fleeing armed conflicts. Overall, the framework contributes to a consistent and inclusive interpretation of the refugee definition in the asylum claims of persons fleeing contemporary armed conflicts.

Chinkin and Kaldor define 'old wars' as intra-state wars, on the one hand, as conducted between two or more regular armed forces using conventional weaponry and strategies to achieve territorial occupation.[385] 'New wars', on the other hand, are distinct from 'old wars' or traditional forms of warfare in terms of their goals and constructed identities, actors, tactics and sources of financing, issues which are not easily separated.[386] It is generally agreed within the literature on conflict that the main characteristics of contemporary conflicts are the increase in internal conflicts,[387] rather than conventional forms of warfare between organised armies,[388] and the majority of civilian casualties rather than male soldiers.[389] Almost 90 per cent of casualties during armed conflicts are now civilians.[390] Civilians have not only become victims of conflict, as casualties, but effectively become incorporated into conflicts on a widespread scale,[391] as they are being deliberately targeted by parties to conflicts,[392] thereby blurring the distinction between combatants and civilians.[393] This is a distinction which underpins international humanitarian law and further justifies consideration of a conceptual framework that better reflects twenty-first-century practice. The changing nature of armed conflicts shapes the origins and consequences of forced displacement and requires further examination to ensure that the Refugee Convention retains its contemporary application.[394]

Thompson has pointed out that new theories of conflict must be addressed by the literature on gender and conflict by better engaging with the nature of contemporary conflicts and challenging traditional understandings of conflict that war is largely fought by men, acting in formal roles as soldiers, defined and contained within the framework of the state, seeking to acquire or retain state power and that violence against civilians is an unfortunate consequence of war.[395] The representations of men and women in war have often been

385 Chinkin and Kaldor, *International Law and New Wars* (n 115) 3.

386 Ibid., 8; Laura Sjoberg and Sandra Via, 'Introduction' in Laura Sjoberg and Sandra Via (eds), *Gender, War, and Militarism: Feminist Perspectives* (Praeger 2010) 5.

387 UN Secretary-General, Women, Peace and Security: Study (n 50) para 3.

388 Ruth Jacobson, Susie Jacobs and Jen Marchbank, 'Introduction: States of Conflict' in Susie Jacobs, Ruth Jacobson and Jen Marchbank (eds), *States of Conflict: Gender, Violence and Resistance* (Zed Books 2000) 3.

389 Wenona Giles and Jennifer Hyndman, 'Introduction' in Wenona Giles and Jennifer Hyndman (eds), *Sites of Violence: Gender and Conflict Zones* (University of California Press 2004) 3; UN Security Council (UNSC) Resolution 1674 (28 April 2006) UN Doc S/RES/1674, preamble; UNSC Res 1820 (19 June 2008) UN Doc S/RES/1820, preamble.

390 Giles and Hyndman, 'Introduction' (n 389) 5; UN Secretary-General, Women, Peace and Security: Study (n 50) para 3.

391 Cynthia Cockburn, 'The Continuum of Violence: A Gender Perspective on War and Peace' in Giles and Hyndman (eds), *Sites of Violence* 35.

392 Jacobson, Jacobs and Marchbank, 'Introduction' (n 388) 4; UN Secretary-General, Women, Peace and Security: Study (n 50) para 4.

393 Lambert, 'The Next Frontier' (n 6); Cockburn, 'The Continuum of Violence' (n 391) 35; Türk, Edwards and Wouters, 'Introduction' (n 2) 4.

394 Alexander Betts, Gil Loescher and James Milner, *The United Nations High Commissioner for Refugees (UNHCR): The Politics and Practice of Refugee Protection* (2nd edn, Routledge 2012) 133.

395 Martha Thompson, 'Women, Gender, and Conflict: Making the Connections' (2006) 16 *Development in Practice* 342, 343.

determined by essentialist perspectives of men as fighters and women as pacifists.[396] Kaldor, in her more recent work with Chinkin, has now highlighted the critical role of gender in developing an alternative approach to the conceptualisation of war,[397] although arguably more could be done to intrinsically engender this 'new war' theory.[398] The literature on feminist conflict theory has traditionally focused on the experiences of women although this is increasingly being challenged.[399] Whilst it is gradually recognised that men and boys are subjected to sexual violence in situations of armed conflict too, the claim that women are disproportionally affected by war endures.[400] The literature in this field highlights that gender subordination continues in situations of armed conflict as a driver for violence and that participation in violence is intrinsically linked to traditional masculinity.[401] Scholars have made statistically relevant findings that societies are more likely to experience armed conflict and resort to violence where gender inequality is highest.[402] Therefore, a gender analysis of armed conflict should take into account constructions of masculinity as this matters in militarisation and consequently in how conflicts are carried out.[403] Furthermore, adopting wider parameters for analysis, to include both women and men, allows for 'context-specific analysis of the various gender identities to which both men and women are expected to conform, and of the relationship of both violence and militarisation'.[404]

Although there have been calls for a broader enquiry into the complex character of violence and the lived experiences of persons fleeing armed conflict,[405] there is still a gap in international refugee law literature in this respect. Moreover, notwithstanding the wide recognition within the literature on conflict and gender that most conflicts have a gender dimension,[406] this is almost entirely overlooked within international refugee law scholarship.[407]

[396] Miriam Cooke and Angela Woollacott, 'Introduction' in Miriam Cooke and Angela Woollacott (eds), *Gendering War Talk* (Princeton University Press 1993) ix.

[397] Chinkin and Kaldor, *International Law and New Wars* (n 115) 4.

[398] The notion of 'engendering' is used here as the action of applying a gender lens to all aspect of the theory.

[399] Heleen Touquet and Ellen Gorris, 'Out of the Shadows? The Inclusion of Men and Boys in Conceptualisations of Wartime Sexual Violence' (2016) 24 *Reproductive Health Matters* 36; Ellen Anna Philo Gorris, 'Invisible Victims? Where Are Male Victims of Conflict-Related Sexual Violence in International Law and Policy?' (2015) 22 *European Journal of Women's Studies* 412; Ayşe Gül Altınay and Andrea Pető, 'Europe and the Century of Genocides: New Directions in the Feminist Theorizing of Genocide' (2015) 22 *European Journal of Women's Studies* 379.

[400] Sjoberg and Via, 'Introduction' (n 386) 6.

[401] Michael Flood and David Duriesmith, 'Gender, War, and Male Disadvantage' (21 July 2017) <www.xyonline.net/content/gender-war-and-male-disadvantage> accessed 12 July 2021.

[402] Mary Caprioli, 'Primed for Violence: The Role of Gender Inequality in Predicting Internal Conflict' (2005) 49 *International Studies Quarterly* 161; Erik Melander, 'Gender Equality and Intrastate Armed Conflict' (2005) 49 *International Studies Quarterly* 695; although the importance of nuance in this statistical relationship was later highlighted and political representation of women in Parliament was found not to be an indicator of gender equality in East Asia, see Erik Melander and Elin Bjarnegård, 'Revisiting Representation: Communism, Women in Politics, and the Decline of Armed Conflict in East Asia' (2013) 39 *International Interactions* 558.

[403] Thompson, 'Women, Gender, and Conflict' (n 395) 351; Jacobson, Jacobs and Marchbank, 'Introduction' (n 388) 3; Cockburn, 'The Continuum of Violence' (n 391) 24, 26.

[404] Judy El-Bushra, 'Fused in Combat: Gender Relations and Armed Conflict' (2003) 13 *Development in Practice* 252, 264.

[405] Lambert, 'Causation in International Protection from Armed Conflict' (n 383) 15.

[406] Jacobson, Jacobs and Marchbank, 'Introduction' (n 388) 1.

[407] This dichotomy is reflected in law in general, as Conaghan notes the enhanced visibility of sex and gender stands in stark contrast to the continued adherence of mainstream legal discourse to a conceptual and normative framework in which gender has no place, Conaghan, *Law and Gender* (n 69) 7.

More specifically, there is a general consensus in the conflict and gender literature and within the international community that men and women experience conflict differently, both in terms of the likelihood of being exposed to violence and the nature and characteristics of violence as a result both of their sex and gender dynamics.[408] Lived experiences are influenced by a set of expected standards for behaviour based on gender,[409] and as 'wars are lived and felt as gendered', gender should be an essential element in how conflicts are thought of and defined.[410] Despite this knowledge, there has never been a detailed analysis of how theories of conflict applied through a gender lens may provide a new perspective on the interpretation and application of the Refugee Convention in the asylum claims of persons fleeing armed conflicts. As the majority of asylum claims lodged in Europe in the last decade originate from persons fleeing situations of armed conflict and widespread violence, the potential contribution of this model is significant.

In light of this, the changed nature of contemporary armed conflicts is further examined in this chapter through Kaldor's conceptualisation of 'new wars' to better understand contemporary armed conflicts in the twenty-first century, and its relevance for asylum decision-making is explored.[411] Situated at the intersection of gender and new theories of conflict, a novel framework is proposed to revisit the interpretation of international refugee law which better responds to not only personal experiences of conflict but also the characteristics, underlying causes and consequences of violence. Applying this lens also contributes to uncovering the impact of traditional normative understandings of international refugee law on the international protection of persons fleeing situations of armed conflict. As the number of persons fleeing armed conflict increases, this original framework to better understand the contemporary nature of armed conflicts will contribute to international refugee law scholarship.

Drawing on feminist security studies scholarship, as a subset of international relations, which posits that one cannot understand the role of violence without reference to gender,[412] this framework is premised upon the theory that understanding gendered dynamics within a particular society is required in impartially interpreting and applying the refugee definition and helps reframe the debate around gender inequality as a politicised issue.[413] Such consideration is necessary for example in understanding the nature of political violence, the motivation behind that violence and structural and societal responses to it. Particular inspiration is drawn from the works of Sjoberg who has argued that there is insufficient attention being paid to the gendering of conflict in the fields of international relations and security studies and that a 'feminist theory of war' is therefore indispensable to an adequate understanding of the politics of war.[414] By analogy, a claim for asylum based on a fear of persecution in the context of armed conflict cannot be adequately determined without an understanding of the

[408] Chinkin and Kaldor, 'Gender and New Wars' (n 71) 169.

[409] Sjoberg and Via, 'Introduction' (n 386) 4.

[410] Christina Weber, 'Review – Gendering Global Conflict: Toward a Feminist Theory of War' (2015) 29 *Gender & Society* 448, 450; Sara Meger, 'Gender and Politics: A Discussion of Laura Sjoberg's Gendering Global Conflict: Toward a Feminist Theory of War' (2014) 12 *Perspectives on Politics* 168, 169; Miriam Cooke, 'Wo-man, Retelling the War Myth' in Cooke and Woollacott (eds), *Gendering War Talk* 177.

[411] Kaldor, *New and Old Wars* (n 3); Cooke and Woollacott adopt the terms 'postmodern wars' or 'contemporary wars' in Cooke and Woollacott, 'Introduction' (n 396) xi.

[412] Sjoberg, 'Gender/Violence in a Gendered/Violent World' (n 4) 539.

[413] Jeffrey C. Isaac, 'Gender and Politics' (2014) 12 *Perspectives on Politics* 1, 2.

[414] See for example the symposium reviewing Laura Sjoberg's book entitled *Gendering Global Conflict: Towards a Feminist Theory of War* (Columbia University Press 2013) and commenting on the theme of the gendering of global conflicts in the special issue of *Perspectives on Politics* (2014) 12(1).

gendered dynamics of violence in armed conflicts. States therefore need to identify the gendered nature, causes and consequences of violence in conflict if they are to deliver on their international legal obligations towards refugees under the Refugee Convention.

3.2 The Temporality of Armed Conflicts

Feminist literature on the gendered impact of conflict in both the social and political sciences has consistently pointed to the fact that violence in the context of conflict generally does not end with official ceasefire declarations.[415] As a consequence, the traditional frames for explaining gender-based violence during armed conflicts artificially conceptualise times of armed conflicts as exceptional situations outside the norm of 'peacetime'. This has a significant impact on understanding the reasons for and the risks and impact of violence in situations of armed conflicts and this matters for the determination of asylum claims from persons fleeing armed conflicts.

Empirical research has demonstrated that gender-based violence does not materialise in the course of events described as armed conflicts without continuum to pre- and post-conflict situations. Rather, there is often a build-up of gendered violence in the lead-up to situations of armed conflict, and the impact of that violence continue in 'post-conflict' situations, often creating new risks and challenges.[416] Cultures of violence and discrimination against women existing prior to the onset of hostilities tend to be exacerbated during conflict.[417] Thus, socially constructed relations such as notions of shame, stigma and exclusion are carried over in later times,[418] which may lead to new forms of violence as social support networks and opportunities are no longer available.[419] Many women who were raped during conflict in communities where honour is an important notion later had to resort to prostitution for survival because they had been excluded from their communities.[420] Brownmiller has explored rape in wartime and claims that the cultural context shaped by expressions of power and dominance in female/male relations detrimentally affects responses to rape victims.[421]

415 Sjoberg and Via, 'Introduction' (n 386) 7; Caroline O. N. Moser and Fiona Clark, 'The Gendered Continuum of Violence and Conflict' in Caroline O. N. Moser and Fiona Clark (eds), *Victims, Perpetrators or Actors? Gender, Armed Conflict and Political Violence* (Zed Books 2001) 36; Liz Kelly, 'Wars against Women: Sexual Violence, Sexual Politics and the Militarised State' in Jacobson, Jacobs and Marchbank (eds), *States of Conflict* 61; Giles and Hyndman, 'Introduction' (n 389) 3; Cockburn, 'The Continuum of Violence' (n 391) 43.

416 CEDAW Committee, Concept Note (n 50) 24.

417 UN Secretary-General, Women, Peace and Security: Study (n 50) para 6.

418 Kelly, 'Wars against Women' (n 415) 53.

419 In Iraq for example, the practice of 'encouraging' through monetary compensation or forcing young girls into a form of temporary marriage (*muta'ah*) traditionally practised by Shi'ites is used as a cover for prostitution. There are no consequences for the male partner as the marriage contract can be ended at any time whereas the girls are left in an increasingly vulnerable situation due to the stigma and the potential pregnancy and sexually transmitted diseases. The violence experienced and risk of future ill-treatment thus continues beyond the termination of the marriage contract, see Henia Dakkak, 'Tackling Sexual Violence, Abuse and Exploitation' (2007) Special Issue: 'Iraq's Displacement Crisis: The Search for Solutions', *Forced Migration Review* 39 40.

420 Kelly, 'Wars against Women' (n 415) 54; see also Nira Yuval-Davis, *Gender and Nation* (Thousand Oaks 1997) 110.

421 Susan Brownmiller, *Against Our Will: Men, Women and Rape* (Penguin 1975); Carol Riddell, 'Review: Susan Brownmiller – Against Our Will: Men, Women and Rape' (1977) 11 *Sociology* 389.

Men who have been raped also suffer significantly from a particular stigma after the 'end' of conflicts,[422] and may experience shame associated with their sexuality.[423] The Convention for the Elimination of All Forms of Discrimination against Women (CEDAW) Committee has noted that sexual violence generally persists after the cessation of hostilities.[424] The Committee overseeing the International Convention on the Elimination of All Forms of Racial Discrimination (CERD) has highlighted how consequences of racial discrimination may affect women predominantly, including suffering from post-rape pregnancies and ostracism.[425] What is more, there is an extensive body of scholarship and international resolutions which conclude that post-conflict reconstruction presents itself differently for women and men.[426] Extensive evidence regarding how violence as a result of armed conflicts is experienced over time has been acknowledged by the international community and international human rights bodies. The UNSC and the CEDAW Committee have highlighted the difficulties of bringing hostilities to an end and the continuation of violence against women in post-conflict situations.[427]

The failure to consider this continuum of violence, including sexual violence, not only during armed conflict but also in the build-up to conflict and beyond situations of conflict does not accurately reflect the experiences of those who have suffered from violence during conflict.[428] Militarism, understood as the 'underlying system of institutions, practices, values, and cultures', occurs outside specifically defined times of conflict and is instrumental to the preparation and justification of armed fighting.[429] The extension of military practices into everyday life blurs the war/peace and military/civilian dichotomy and refutes the assumption that situations of conflict are remote from normal life.[430] Such a perspective

[422] Sandesh Sivakumaran, 'Male/Male Rape and the "Taint" of Homosexuality' (2005) 27 *Human Rights Quarterly* 1274, 1293–1294.

[423] Hebah H. Farrag, 'Engendering Forced Migration: Victimization, Masculinity and the Forgotten Voice' (2009) 2 *Surfacing: Gender and Conflict* 1, 9.

[424] CEDAW Committee, Concept Note (n 50) 8.

[425] International Convention on the Elimination of All Forms of Racial Discrimination (CERD) (adopted 21 December 1965, entered into force 4 January 1969) 660 UNTS 195; CERD, 'General Recommendation No 25: Gender Related Dimensions of Racial Discrimination' (20 March 2000) UN Doc A/55/18, para 2.

[426] Cockburn, 'The Continuum of Violence' (n 391) 40; Paul Chaney, 'Civil Society and Gender Mainstreaming: Empirical Evidence and Theory-Building from Twelve Post-Conflict Countries 2005–15' (2016) 83 *World Development* 280; see for example in the case of the Western Balkans, Ioana-Bianca Berna, 'Gender Politics and Post-Conflict Reconstruction in the Western Balkans' (2013) 3 *Journal of Research in Gender Studies* 128; in the case of Sierra Leone, Hazel McFerson, 'Women and Post-Conflict Society in Sierra Leone' (2011) 12 *Journal of International Women's Studies* 127; UNSC Res 1674 (28 April 2006) UN Doc S/RES/1674, para 11; UN Secretary-General, Women, Peace and Security: Study (n 50) para 14.

[427] UNSC Res 1820 (19 June 2008) UN Doc S/RES/1820, preamble; CEDAW Committee, Concept Note (n 50) 24.

[428] Kelly, 'Wars against Women' (n 415) 61. [429] Sjoberg and Via, 'Introduction' (n 386) 7.

[430] Ibid., 7. In Syria for example, continued and intensified militarism played a crucial role in the ruling party's (the Baath Party) hold on power and treatment of political dissidents. Syria has experienced a 'continual state of war' since 1948 through ongoing armed conflicts with Israel, Iraq, Turkey and Lebanon, which led to military commanders installing a single-party state and the state of emergency declared in 1963. In this context, political opposition was viewed as a threat to national unity and justified authoritarian forms of governance on the basis of nationality security. 'Perpetual warfare' modified state structures as military spending increased and material and political resources were vested in the military establishment. This had a severe impact on the state's response to civil society and dissident forces, see Fred H. Lawson, 'Syria' in Michele Penner Angrist (ed), *Politics and Society in the Contemporary Middle East* (Lynne Rienner Publishers 2010) 424–429.

stands in stark contrast to the manner in which situations of armed conflict have historically been approached in asylum jurisprudence. Oosterveld found that there was inconsistent practice regarding attention being paid to gender-based violence in post-conflict situations in asylum appeals.[431] More specifically, the actual impact of ceasefires or peace agreements on the nature and extent of gender-based violence was rarely examined by judicial decision makers.[432]

As it is difficult to precisely determine when conflicts start and end,[433] the war/peace dichotomy, an essential concept underpinning international law, is an inadequate lens to understand the lived experiences of persons in sites of conflict or to acknowledge the exercise of violence across a continuum. A significant failing in the Common European Asylum System (CEAS) is the existence of a distinct subsidiary protection status for persons fleeing 'indiscriminate violence in situations of international or internal armed conflict' attracting a lesser set of rights than refugee status because it is built on this dichotomy. By considering that situations of armed conflict have a special character, domestic courts have applied restrictive interpretations of the Refugee Convention, requiring asylum applicants to demonstrate a higher level of risk over and above the rest of the general population.[434] In light of this, it becomes apparent that the legal concepts which pervade the CEAS legislative framework, national provisions and the manner in which they are interpreted do not adequately respond to international protection needs. The European Union (EU) legal framework has resulted in the judiciary battling to determine the definition of an 'internal armed conflict' and how to measure levels of 'indiscriminate violence'.[435] International refugee law scholarship has consequently spent considerable resources examining this issue.[436] Accordingly, it is suggested that asylum decision-making should be informed by considering the context of armed conflicts by reference to violence as a continuum rather than a simple war/peace dichotomy.[437]

3.3 The Rise of Non-State Actors in Contemporary Armed Conflicts

One of the main characteristics of violence in contemporary armed conflicts is that it is exercised by a broader range of non-state actors such as armed groups.[438] Chinkin and Kaldor describe participants in 'new wars' as malleable networks of state and non-state actors that

[431] Oosterveld, 'Women and Girls Fleeing Conflict' (n 79) 213. [432] Ibid., 207.

[433] Kelly, 'Wars against Women' (n 415) 61; Cockburn, 'The Continuum of Violence' (n 391) 39.

[434] An approach described as a 'differential risk analysis' see Holzer, *Refugees from Armed Conflict* (n 22) 110–112; Christel Querton, 'Women Fleeing Armed Conflict: Seeking International Protection in the United Kingdom' in Efrat Arbel, Catherine Dauvergne and Jenni Millbank (eds), *Gender in Refugee Law: From the Margins to the Centre* (Routledge 2014).

[435] Case C–465/07 *Elgafaji v Staatssecretaris van Justitie* [2009] ECR I-921; Case C–542/13 *M'Bodj v Belgium* [2015] 1 WLR 3059; *Diakite v Commissaire General aux Refugies et aux Apatrides* (n 155).

[436] See for example Garlick, 'Protection in the European Union' (n 373); Lambert and Farrell, 'The Changing Character of Armed Conflict' (n 6); Lambert, 'The Next Frontier' (n 6); Roger Errera, 'The CJEU and Subsidiary Protection: Reflections on *Elgafaji* – and After' (2011) 23 *International Journal of Refugee Law* 93; Céline Bauloz, 'The Definition of Internal Armed Conflict in Asylum Law: The 2014 Diakité Judgment of the EU Court of Justice' (2014) 12 *Journal of International Criminal Justice* 835.

[437] Giles and Hyndman, 'Introduction' (n 389) 3.

[438] David E. Cunningham, Kristian Skrede Gleditsch and Idean Salehyan, 'Non-State Actors in Civil Wars: A New Dataset' (2013) 30 *Conflict Management and Peace Science* 516.

cross borders made up of factions from 'the regular armed forces, paramilitary groups, warlords, jihadists, terrorists, mercenaries, private security contractors and criminal groups'.[439] This would suggest that commonly used terms in international law, such as 'non-state actors', may not adequately reflect contemporary realities. For this reason, this book generally adopts the term 'armed groups' rather than non-state actors when discussing parties to armed conflicts. Furthermore, armed groups play an increasing role in the conduct of armed conflicts and, as a result, an increasing number of civilian casualties are attributed to these groups.[440] The traditionally state-centric nature of international refugee law is contested by the resulting diminishing character of state sovereignty and its close association to the authority to use force.[441]

Prior to the development of the CEAS, the practice of EU Member States (MS) regarding the interpretation of non-state actors as agents of persecution differed widely.[442] Although the EU Council in 1996 recognised non-state actors as agents of persecution it also appeared to require the encouragement, permission or a *deliberate* failure to act by the authorities.[443] As a result, persons originating from failed states in the midst of armed conflicts such as Afghanistan and Somalia were refused asylum by those EU MS which considered that non-state actors could not be defined as agents of persecution under international law. More specifically, asylum decision makers considered that in the absence of a functioning infrastructure, authority and control over the country, the country of origin could not be considered to have instigated or tolerated the violence feared.[444] Equally, persons fearing gender-based violence within the family or the community were refused refugee status due

[439] Chinkin and Kaldor, *International Law and New Wars* (n 115) 11. In Iraq, fighting parties include Islamic State of Iraq and Syria (ISIS), Kurdish *peshmergas*, different Shi'ite militias including the Madhi Army and the Badr Corps, see Chinkin and Kaldor, *International Law and New Wars* (n 115) 12; Patrick Cockburn, 'War against ISIS: US Strategy in Tatters as Militants March On' *Independent on Sunday* (London, 12 October 2014) <www.independent.co.uk/voices/comment/war-against-isis-us-strategy-in-tatters-as-militants-march-on-9789230.html> accessed 12 July 2021. In Syria, the government relies on armed groups and militias such as the National Defence Forces often recruited from the national army and trained by the Iranian Revolutionary Guard, Hezbollah and Shabbiya/Shabiha (an Alawite militia) to fight ISIS and anti-government forces including the Syrian Democratic Forces, an alliance of anti-government forces composed of Kurdish brigades, moderate rebels and Islamist militias (such as the Al-Qaeda affiliate Jabhat al-Nusra), see Chinkin and Kaldor, *International Law and New Wars* (n 115) 12; Chinkin and Kaldor, 'Gender and New Wars' (n 71) 170.

[440] Aaron Karp, 'The Changing Ownership of War: States, Insurgencies and Technology' in Keith Krause (ed), *Armed Groups and Contemporary Conflicts: Challenging the Weberian State* (Routledge 2010) 181, 187; Minwoo Yun, 'Insurgency Warfare as an Emerging New Mode of Warfare and the New Enemy' (2010) 22 *Korean Journal of Defense Analysis* 111.

[441] Chinkin and Kaldor, *International Law and New Wars* (n 115) 79.

[442] Wilsher, 'Non-State Actors and the Definition of a Refugee' (n 62). See for example the UK House of Lords decision not to return asylum seekers to Germany and France because Mr Adan feared clan violence and there was no functioning state in Somalia and Mr Aitseguer feared an Islamic group in Algeria which the state did not support or condone, *Secretary of State for the Home Department, Ex Parte Adan R v Secretary of State for the Home Department Ex Parte Aitseguer, R v* [2001] 1 All ER 593 (19 December 2000).

[443] Joint Position of 4 March 1996 (n 354) para 5.2.

[444] Magner, 'Does a Failed State Country of Origin Result in a Failure of International Protection?' (n 64) 715; Of the EU MS considered by Magner, she highlights Austria, France, Germany and the Netherlands as countries that failed to recognise non-state actors as agents of persecution. Belgium and the UK on the other hand had adopted the concept in their practice.

to the absence of state involvement.[445] The concept of non-state actors as agents of persecution was one of the most controversial during the negotiations of the first iteration of the Qualification Directive due to inconsistent state practice,[446] but was strongly supported by UNHCR.[447] The eventual adoption of the concept within the Directive[448] was hailed as an achievement by civil society and academics.[449]

In addition to the explicit recognition of non-state actors as agents of persecution in the original Qualification Directive, the Court of Justice of the European Union (CJEU) has recognised the increasing role played by armed groups in contemporary armed conflicts in the context of subsidiary protection. The CJEU noted that whether an 'internal armed conflict' exists must

> be determined by considering its usual meaning in everyday language, while also taking into account the context in which it occurs and the purposes of the rules of which it is part. The usual meaning in everyday language of "internal armed conflict" is a situation in which a State's armed forces confront one or more armed groups or in which two or more armed groups confront each other.[450]

By adopting this definition of 'internal armed conflict' the CJEU envisages situations of armed conflict which do not even engage the state.

However, the changes in the exercise of violence in situations of contemporary armed conflict, which tend to arise in the wake of weak states and the breakdown of states' traditional monopoly over organised violence,[451] has led to the blurring of traditional distinctions between state and non-state actors.[452] Contemporary armed conflicts are thus particularly complex and characterised by political vacuums due to the diversity of fighting parties and the weakened political authority of social and economic institutions.[453] The increasing number of armed groups in armed conflicts, their relative power over the exercise of violence, their size, strategies and resources are some of the biggest challenges to refugee protection because international refugee law has traditionally been interpreted through a state-centric lens.

445 Catherine Phuong, 'Persecution by Non-State Agents: Comparative Judicial Interpretations of the 1951 Refugee Convention' (2002) 4 *European Journal of Migration and Law* 521, 530, discusses the practice in Germany.

446 Ibid., 531.

447 UNHCR, 'UNHCR Annotated Comments on the EC Council Directive 2004/83/EC on Minimum Standards for the Qualification and Status of Third Country Nationals or Stateless Persons as Refugees or as Persons Who Otherwise Need International Protection and the Content of the Protection Granted (OJ L 304/12 of 30.9.2004)', (January 2005) <www.unhcr.org/protect/PROTECTION/43661eee2.pdf> accessed 12 July 2021.

448 Article 6 Qualification Directive 2004; Article 6 Qualification Directive 2011.

449 Storey, 'Persecution' (n 290) 484; Mullally, 'Domestic Violence Asylum Claims' (n 63) 460.

450 *Diakite v Commissaire General aux Refugies et aux Apatrides* (n 155) paras 27–28.

451 Kaldor, *New and Old Wars* (n 3); Graeme Cheeseman, 'Review: The European Rupture: The Defence Sector in Transition/Restructuring the Global Military Sector Volume I: New Wars/Restructuring the Global Military Sector Volume II: The End' (1999) 53 *Australian Journal of International Affairs* 212.

452 Cheeseman, 'Review' (n 451) 213.

453 In the context of Syria, see Khuloud Alsaba and Anuj Kapilashrami, 'Understanding Women's Experience of Violence and the Political Economy of Gender in Conflict: The Case of Syria' (2016) 24 *Reproductive Health Matters* 5, 6.

3.4 Weak States in Situations of Armed Conflict

Not only are contemporary armed conflicts characterised by a rise in armed groups, but many states involved as parties to protracted conflicts are increasingly weak. Thus, a relevant matter in understanding violence in armed conflicts is the process of economic globalisation which both weakens the governance structures of the nation-state and has been identified as a potential cause for the onset of fighting.[454] Barkawi claims that neoliberal economic policies led to political violence and war around the world after the Cold War.[455] Cockburn suggests that several armed conflicts in the 1990s arose in places that experienced an intensification of structural violence in the 1980s through a combination of economic adjustment policies resulting in economic distress and high unemployment rates amongst young men who became attracted to crime or militarism and a rise in nationalist movements.[456] Farrell and Schmitt consider that it is unnecessarily limiting to consider armed conflicts to be driven primarily by economic conditions.[457] Rather, the role of globalisation in the diffusion of technology, the movement of people, terrorism, organised crime and the proliferation of weapons outside traditional military structures[458] has seen a parallel trend in the weakening of states and the resulting decline in structural responses to violence in the context of armed conflicts.[459]

Failed and fragile states are further undermined as fighting parties, which are often based on ethnic, religious or tribal identity, battle for control over the state and its resources.[460] Failed and fragile states are described in this manner as they lack the capacity for governance. As a result, states are unable to administer justice or enforce rights domestically.[461] The Peace Fund Fragile States Index 2021 lists Syria, Afghanistan and Iraq in its top twenty fragile states list, with Syria at Very High Alert, Afghanistan at High Alert and Iraq at Alert.[462] In turn, state fragility is a contributing factor to further violence,[463] thereby creating a cyclical trend of cause and effect between the governance of state structures and violence.

In times of conflict issues such as domestic violence may be less of a concern for states, with the resulting lack of protection from state agencies. Protracted armed conflicts are often associated with increase in unemployment and a parallel increase in domestic violence as men feel frustrated and powerless due to losing their masculine roles as income earners.[464] Moreover, evidence[465] suggests that during armed conflict domestic violence increases and

[454] Giles and Hyndman, 'Introduction' (n 389) 304; Tarak Barkawi, *Globalization and War* (Rowman & Littlefield 2006) xi.

[455] Barkawi, *Globalization and War* (n 454) xii.

[456] Cockburn, 'The Continuum of Violence' (n 391) 31.

[457] Farrell and Schmitt, 'The Causes, Character and Conduct of Armed Conflict' (n 163) 27.

[458] Barkawi, *Globalization and War* (n 454) xi.

[459] Jacobson, Jacobs and Marchbank, 'Introduction' (n 388) 6.

[460] Betts, Loescher and Milner, *The United Nations High Commissioner for Refugees* (n 394) 143.

[461] Ibid., 143.

[462] The Fund for Peace, 'Fragile States Index 2021' <https://fragilestatesindex.org/wp-content/uploads/2021/05/fsi2021-report.pdf> accessed 12 July 2021.

[463] Türk, Edwards and Wouters, 'Introduction' (n 2) 4–5.

[464] In the case of Afghanistan, see for example Asha Hans, 'Escaping Conflict: Afghan Women in Transit' in Giles and Hyndman (eds), *Sites of Violence* 242; in the case of Northern Uganda see Jeannie Annan and Moriah Brier, 'The Risk of Return: Intimate Partner Violence in Northern Uganda's Armed Conflict' (2010) 70 *Social Science & Medicine* 152.

[465] In the case of Iraq, see for example Dakkak, 'Tackling Sexual Violence' (n 419) 40.

is more lethal due to incidents with weapons,[466] and daily security is affected by the expansion of small arms and light weapons.[467] Ultimately, where there is a lack of structures and resources for state authority, law reform to address sex discrimination is unlikely.[468]

The characteristics of state institutions and the political economy are thus relevant factors both to the onset and protraction of violence, including gender-based violence.[469] As conflict is associated with state collapse it thereby impacts on states' ability and willingness to provide protection and ensure fundamental human rights. This process is in itself gendered. The changing nature and weakened role of the nation-state, particularly during and around times of armed conflict, challenge one of the core principles of international refugee law, namely the notion of international protection as surrogate protection due to the breakdown of the relationship between a person and their country of origin.[470] An approach which better reflects the realities of countries experiencing situations of armed conflict must reflect the ability of state institutions in responding to violence and selective choice regarding available protection in situations of armed conflicts.

3.5 The Definition of Objectives by Parties to Contemporary Armed Conflicts

As noted, there has been little research looking specifically at the determination of asylum claims made by persons fleeing armed conflicts under the Refugee Convention. Goodwin-Gill and McAdam, however, highlight that a closer examination of the background to conflicts and the ways in which they are fought may often establish a link to the Refugee Convention.[471] Holzer found that the causes and characteristics of armed conflicts, including the methods of warfare, are not taken into account systematically by domestic courts and there is inconsistent practice in this respect.[472] In her research regarding women and girls fleeing armed conflict, Oosterveld also found examples of judicial decisions which did not examine the political and ethnic dimensions of conflicts.[473] Although the existing literature provides some insight into judicial practice and recommended approaches to determining asylum claims in the context of armed conflicts, the analyses are based on a conceptualisation of conflicts as time-bounded events with well-defined causes and objectives.

466 Kelly, 'Wars against Women' (n 415) 59.

467 Cockburn, 'The Continuum of Violence' (n 391) 32; ICRC, *Addressing the Needs of Women Affected by Armed Conflict* (International Committee of the Red Cross 2004) 27; Suneel Kumar, 'Small Arms and Light Weapons: A Global Threat to Human Security and Development' (2008) 69 *The Indian Journal of Political Science* 787; C. J. Chivers, 'Small Arms, Big Problems: The Fallout of the Global Gun Trade' (2011) 90 *Foreign Affairs* 110; Josef Danczuk, 'The Global Spread of Arms: The Link between State Collapse, Small Arms Proliferation, and Global Conflict' (2016) 96 *Military Review* 42.

468 Kelly, 'Wars against Women' (n 415) 60.

469 Alsaba and Kapilashrami, 'Understanding Women's Experience of Violence' (n 453); Sara Meger, *Rape Loot Pillage: The Political Economy of Sexual Violence in Armed Conflict* (OUP 2016).

470 Atle Grahl-Madsen, *The Status of Refugees in International Law*, vol 1 (A. W. Sijthoff 1966) 79; Shacknove, 'Who Is a Refugee?' (n 252) 283; Maria O'Sullivan, 'Acting the Part: Can Non-State Entities Provide Protection under International Refugee Law?' (2012) 24 *International Journal of Refugee Law* 85, 89; Hathaway and Foster, *The Law of Refugee Status* (n 20) 288–289; Holzer, *Refugees from Armed Conflict* (n 22) 165.

471 Goodwin-Gill and McAdam, *The Refugee in International Law* (n 21) 126.

472 Holzer, *Refugees from Armed Conflict* (n 22) 189–190.

473 Oosterveld, 'Women and Girls Fleeing Conflict' (n 79) 196, 198.

As explained in Section 3.1, framing the relevant considerations for refugee status determination as the causes of armed conflict is of limited assistance to the question of interpretation because it amalgamates the concepts of armed conflicts and violence. What is more, the literature on conflict onset is characterised by quantitative macro-level analysis. This body of literature claims for example that there is no correlation between cultural factors such as ethnic and religious diversity or polarisation and the onset of armed conflict,[474] although there are disagreements as to whether homogeneity or diversity of cultural factors contribute to higher conflict risks.[475] However, in light of the fluid temporality of armed conflicts explored, it is suggested that for the purpose of refugee protection, the relevant consideration is the dynamics of violence identified through the characteristics of violence, including the strategic objectives of the violence as defined by fighting parties and their justifications for violence in situations of armed conflict to better understand how to interpret the Refugee Convention in such claims, rather than merely potential correlations between factors such as ethnicity and religion and the *onset* of fighting, broadly defined as the objectives of conflicts.[476] More specifically, it is claimed that irrespective of whether these factors contribute to the *start* of armed conflicts, it is necessary to examine how that violence is exercised, motivated and sustained in the assessment of asylum claims. This approach is made possible by drawing on gender and conflict studies scholarship to understand and explain the circumstances of and the reasons why people flee violence in situations of armed conflict.

Therefore, this section explores the drivers of violence in armed conflicts by examining how 'identities', including political, religious, national and gendered identities, are created, shaped and transformed in situations of armed conflict in order to justify and sustain that violence. It examines the manner in which identities are socially constructed by the myriad of actors involved in contemporary armed conflicts through a gender lens and how this perspective supports the interpretation of the Refugee Convention definition to better respond to present-day realities. Moreover, it explains how those identities intersect and how this impacts on the risk of violence in situations of armed conflict, the characteristics of such violence and its consequences. It is claimed here that an understanding of constructed identities is essential in adequately applying the Refugee Convention to the asylum claims of persons fleeing armed conflicts.

Kaldor states that the reason why civilians are being increasingly targeted is due to contemporary conflicts being fought on the basis of 'identity politics',[477] which generally have an important gender dimension.[478] Chinkin and Kaldor claim that contemporary armed

[474] James D. Fearon and David D. Laitin, 'Ethnicity, Insurgency, and Civil War' (2003) 97 *American Political Science Review* 75; Collier and Hoeffler, 'Greed and Grievance in Civil War' (n 375); Bethany Lacina, 'Explaining the Severity of Civil Wars' (2006) 50 *Journal of Conflict Resolution* 276.

[475] Collier and Hoeffler adjusted their previous model which examined solely motivations of conflicts (greed versus grievance) to an examination of both motivations and structural factors making armed conflict feasible, Paul Collier, Anke Hoeffler and Dominic Rohner, 'Beyond Greed and Grievance: Feasibility and Civil War' (2009) 61 *Oxford Economic Papers* 1.

[476] Collier, Hoeffler and Rohner recognise the limitations of their positivist approach as follows: 'Quantitative analysis based on global data sets has its own severe limitations imposed by data constraints and so should be seen as complementing qualitative in-country research rather than supplanting' (ibid., 2).

[477] Kaldor, *New and Old Wars* (n 3); see in particular ch 4.

[478] Chinkin and Kaldor, *International Law and New Wars* (n 115) 9; Chinkin and Kaldor, 'Gender and New Wars' (n 71) 167.

conflicts are increasingly being fought in the name of identity, including ethnic, religious or tribal identities rather than the political ideas and ideology which characterised wars and armed conflicts during the Cold War.[479] The objective of such violence is said to be exclusive access to the state for those identified with a particular label at the expense of those with other ascribed identities.[480] Religious wars may be about ideas such as the imposition of fundamental interpretation of Islamic law or about the right to political power for specific religious identities.[481] Chinkin and Kaldor highlight the multiplicity of identities which are constructed in situations of armed conflict and that those identities are closely linked to gender.[482]

Despite persons generally having multiple identities, identities are constructed and 'fixed' by fighting parties deploying a narrative of 'us' against 'them' in situations of armed conflict.[483] Opponents to the same conflict thus propound different war narratives by assigning different meanings to events in order to justify the onset and the protraction of violence.[484] Barkawi claims that during armed conflict, people interconnect with the opposing party through an 'intensified awareness' of one another and a reconstruction of self and other.[485] In other words, conflicts 'are opportunities for voices within communities to redefine and refashion dominant identities'.[486] Such identities may be transformed not only by forces within communities but also by external influences.[487] Fighting parties in contemporary armed conflicts thus construct and assign unitary identities to themselves and to their opponents. Once identities are attributed, changing 'sides' is no longer possible, a characteristic which further contributes to the protraction and severity of violence. In building those identities and differentiating others through labels, identity politics tend to the extremes, justifying ever more severe and public forms of violence. As armed conflicts are transformative of politics, sectarian identity is an outcome of armed conflict rather than a cause of its onset.[488] This perspective does not diminish its relevance as a frame for the interpretation of the refugee definition, however. On the contrary, the relevant issue here is not one of conflict causality but rather the reasons for the violence, human rights violations and ultimately persecution, which may be imputed.

Peterson highlights that, if all experience is gendered, the study of political identities requires an analysis of gender identities as informed by masculinities and femininities.[489] Scholars have for some time recognised that the gender-based expectations of human

[479] Chinkin and Kaldor, *International Law and New Wars* (n 115) 8.

[480] Ibid., 8. [481] Ibid., 8.

[482] Chinkin and Kaldor, 'Gender and New Wars' (n 71) 171; Chinkin and Kaldor, *International Law and New Wars* (n 115) 9.

[483] Chinkin and Kaldor, *International Law and New Wars* (n 115) 8.

[484] As an example, Osama Bin Laden dates the beginning of what is commonly referred to as the 'War on Terror' by Western states back to the breakup of the Ottoman Empire, see Barkawi, *Globalization and War* (n 454) 130.

[485] Ibid., xiii. [486] Ibid., 166.

[487] Lawson notes in the context of Syria that influences such as the French Imperial administration, its armed resistance, the Syrian armed forces, the Baath Party and Iraqi refugees all contributed to heightened tensions between ethnic and sectarian minorities in Lawson, 'Syria' (n 430) 430–432.

[488] Mary Kaldor, 'Identity and War' (2013) 4 *Global Policy* 336, 336; Barkawi, *Globalization and War* (n 454) 167.

[489] V. Spike Peterson, 'Political Identities/Nationalism as Heterosexism' (1999) 1 *International Feminist Journal of Politics* 34, 37.

behaviour have been essential in narratives explaining or justifying war.[490] Yuval-Davis claims that national identities are closely linked to the concept of nations which cannot properly be understood without reference to gender and vice versa.[491] She analysed nationalist ideologies by highlighting that the concept of the nation-state is premised upon the complete correspondence between ethnic composition and territorial borders. Such a perception allows the construction of ethnic minorities as outside the norm and justifies their exclusion from important power resources.[492] There is an inherent connection between ethnicity and nationalism, and nationalist demands make claims for political representation of the collective.[493]

Yuval-Davis proposes three main types of nationalist projects, all of which are of relevance in thinking about the causes of violence in situations of armed conflict and the Refugee Convention grounds. The first type is that built on the specific origin of people (or their race) which tends to be the most exclusionary project.[494] As Linke examines the relation between military patterns of rape and racial stratification,[495] Pittaway and Bartolomei identify the root causes of displacement in situations of armed conflict as racial and ethnic tensions.[496] The second nationalist project identified by Yuval-Davis is the nationalist project based on culture 'in which the symbolic heritage provided by language and/or religion and/or other customs and tradition is constructed as the "essence" of "the nation"' and finally the nationalist projects based on citizenship as determining the boundaries of the nations.[497] Those dimensions are highly gendered, for example questions regarding whether women have children or not, how many and when, are identified by certain nationalist projects as issues which need to be controlled. If membership in the collective could only be achieved by birth, 'control of marriage, procreation and therefore sexuality would thus tend to be high on the nationalist agenda'.[498] Conflicts fought along nationalistic lines are often heavily influenced, motivated and conducted on the basis of gender identities where women are seen as bearers of 'tradition' and national culture and men as protectors of the faith or nation and its property.[499] Nationalist projects built on culture and tradition often have strong gender symbols. Women are perceived as reproducers of those traditions, as embodiments of the collective and its cultural reproducers.[500]

490 Sjoberg and Via, 'Introduction' (n 386) 4. The USA, for example, relied heavily on the stereotype of the feminised victim and a narrative of women's liberation in justifying military intervention in Afghanistan; see Carol Stabile and Deepa Kumar, 'Unveiling Imperialism: Media, Gender and the War on Afghanistan' (2005) 27 *Media Culture and Society* 765; and Krista Hunt, 'The Strategic Co-optation of Women's Rights' (2002) 4 *International Feminist Journal of Politics* 116.

491 Yuval-Davis, *Gender and Nation* (n 420) 21.

492 Ibid., 11. 493 Ibid., 16. 494 Ibid., 21.

495 Uli Linke, 'Gendered Difference, Violent Imagination Blood, Race, Nation' (1997) 99 *American Anthropologist* 559.

496 Eileen Pittaway and Linda Bartolomei, 'Refugees, Race, and Gender: The Multiple Discrimination against Refugee Women' (2001) 19 *Refuge* 21, 22.

497 Yuval-Davis, *Gender and Nation* (n 420) 21. 498 Ibid., 22.

499 Giles and Hyndman, 'Introduction' (n 389) 8; Pittaway and Bartolomei, 'Refugees, Race, and Gender' (n 496) 23.

500 Yuval-Davis, *Gender and Nation* (n 420) 23. For example, Algerian men wrote about the Algerian revolution from the perspective of protectors of wives and daughters and consequently as those who had much to lose by being deprived of control, see Cooke, 'Wo-man, Retelling the War Myth' (n 410) 184.

The loss of personal security as a result of armed conflict is thus highly gendered.[501] Contemporary nationalist and ethnic-nationalist movements represent a renewal of traditional gender norms as applied to both women and men.[502] This ethnic nationalism, as a social phenomenon, generates structural violence and gender-specific crimes,[503] including widespread sexual violence against women as political acts of aggression.[504] In light of those observations, Enloe has posited that 'the militarisation of any nationalist movement occurs through the gendered workings of power'.[505] In such a context men must prove their masculinity and women must become sufficiently acquiescent to meet the needs of the militaries.[506] Sjoberg notes that militarisation is gendered in its aims (competitive power and strength), its means and its impact, which disproportionately and negatively affect women.[507] Struggles by the oppressed, who are called upon to 'reclaim their manhood' through violence,[508] aim to gain power rather than transform power relations within society. These 'national liberation' movements often bring further oppression of women and other disadvantaged groups within the new social order.[509]

Viewed in this light, what has traditionally been considered as a matter falling outside the realm of the Refugee Convention becomes an essential element of a political project, particularly in the context of armed conflict where control over state power and resources is violently contested. The impact on and consequences for women of violence in situations of armed conflict due to the particular identities created by the intersection of race, ethnicity, religion, disability, age, class, caste or other factors and gender has been recognised by the United Nations (UN) and the CEDAW Committee.[510] Such an intersectional approach to the dynamics of violence and discrimination against women allows for a more comprehensive understanding and explanation of the issue.[511] The relevance of this perspective to the Refugee Convention reasons for persecution is further discussed in Chapter 6.

501 Giles and Hyndman, 'Introduction' (n 389) 4; Jacobson, Jacobs and Marchbank, 'Introduction' (n 388) 5–6.

502 Giles and Hyndman, 'Introduction' (n 389) 9; Cockburn, 'The Continuum of Violence' (n 391) 32.

503 Cockburn relies on Galtung and describes structural violence as situations where the political development of a group is held back by the conditions of a relationship such as the unequal distribution of power and resources; Cockburn, 'The Continuum of Violence' (n 391) 30.

504 Giles and Hyndman, 'Introduction' (n 389) 13; Pittaway and Bartolomei, 'Refugees, Race, and Gender' (n 496) 23; UN Division for the Advancement of Women, 'Gender and Racial Discrimination: Report of the Expert Group Meeting' (21–24 November 2000) Section D.

505 Cynthia Enloe, *The Morning After: Sexual Politics at the End of the Cold War* (University of California Press 1993) 246.

506 V. Spike Peterson and Anne Sisson Runyan, *Global Gender Issues* (Westview Press 1993) 83–84.

507 Sjoberg and Via, 'Introduction' (n 386) 8.

508 Yuval-Davis, *Gender and Nation* (n 420) 113.

509 Ibid., 113.

510 UN Fourth World Conference on Women, Beijing Platform for Action, September 1995 (n 52) para 32; UN Committee on the Elimination of All Forms of Discrimination against Women, 'General Recommendation No 25, on article 4, paragraph 1, of the Convention on the Elimination of All Forms of Discrimination against Women, on Temporary Special Measures' in 'Compilation of General Comments and General Recommendations Adopted by Human Rights Treaty Bodies' (2004) UN Doc HRI/GEN/1//Rev.7, para 12.

511 UN Division for the Advancement of Women, 'Gender and Racial Discrimination—' Section I; Aisha Davis, 'Intersectionality and International Law: Recognizing Complex Identities on the Global Stage' (2015) 28 *Harvard Human Rights Journal* 205.

3.6 Gendered Strategies and Tactics of Fighting Parties

In contemporary armed conflicts, fighting is no longer conducted through traditional military battles between interstate armies; rather, the myriad of actors involved in conflicts operate strategies that reflect their objectives and means. Kalyvas and Balcells demonstrate how armed groups are increasingly unable to match conventional state armed forces because they do not have the means to equal the military capacity of the state. This explains the change in the majority of contemporary armed conflicts from conventional warfare to asymmetric fighting.[512] Thus territory is captured through political control of the population rather than military advances.[513] The notion of political control of territory by the state military or militia groups seeking to dominate and coerce the population is an important concept in explaining the characteristics of strategies deployed in contemporary armed conflicts.[514] Thompson describes how globalisation has displaced the centrality of the role of the nation-state in light of the rise of non-state actors who depend on terror, exercised through violence, to control populations and territory in the absence of sophisticated weaponry.[515] Armed groups engage in highly visible forms of violence and human rights violations to create fear and force the population to flee. The consequences of contemporary armed conflicts are fewer battle deaths and increased forced displacement.[516] As a result of those tactics of control, violence during conflicts is mainly directed at civilians who have or are perceived by the fighting parties to have a different identity.[517] Consequently, civilians are deliberately attacked, including through sexual and gender-based violence, as a way of targeting identity.[518] In recognition of the increasing deliberate targeting of civilians in armed conflict and its impact, the protection of civilians in armed conflict has remained a central part of UNSC's mandate since 1999 because of its threat to international peace and security.[519]

Moreover, as strategies involve terrorising the population in order to exercise control, parties seek to mediatise their actions. Cooke identifies this as a phenomenon of

512 Kalyvas and Balcells, 'International System and Technologies of Rebellion' (n 44).
513 Kaldor, *New and Old Wars* (n 3) 9.
514 See for example Farrell and Schmitt, 'The Causes, Character and Conduct of Armed Conflict' (n 163) 29; Alsaba and Kapilashrami, 'Understanding Women's Experience of Violence' (n 453) 6; Immigration and Refugee Board of Canada, 'Afghanistan: Whether the Taliban Has the Capacity to Pursue Individuals after They Relocate to Another Region; Their Capacity to Track Individuals over the Long Term; Taliban Capacity to Carry Out Targeted Killings (2012–January 2016)' (Immigration and Refugee Board of Canada, 2016).
515 Thompson, 'Women, Gender, and Conflict' (n 395) 344.
516 Chinkin and Kaldor, *International Law and New Wars* (n 115) 14.
517 Ibid., 13–14; Kaldor, *New and Old Wars* (n 3) 9.
518 Kaldor, *New and Old Wars* (n 3) 9; Chinkin and Kaldor, *International Law and New Wars* (n 115) 15; Alsaba and Kapilashrami, 'Understanding Women's Experience of Violence' (n 453) 10; the concept of 'identity politics' and objectives in contemporary armed conflicts was explored in Section 3.2.4.
519 UN Secretary-General, Report to the Security Council on the Protection of Civilians in Armed Conflict, UN Doc S/1999/957, 8 September 1999, para 1; UNSC Res 1265 (17 September 1999) UN Doc S/RES/1265; UNSC Res 1296 (12 April 2000) UN Doc S/RES/1296; UNSC Res 1325 (31 October 2000) UN Doc S/RES/1325; UNSC Res 1674 (28 April 2006) UN Doc S/RES/1674; UNSC Res 1738 (23 December 2006) UN Doc S/RES/1738; UNSC Res 1820 (19 June 2008) UN Doc S/RES/1820; UNSC Res 1894 (11 November 2009) UN Doc S/RES/1894, paras 3–4; UN Office for the Coordination of Humanitarian Affairs (OCHA), Security Council Norms and Practice on the Protection of Civilians in Armed Conflict: Analysis of Normative Developments in Security Council Res 2009–2013 (OCHA Policy and Studies Series 008, May 2014) 4.

'hyperrepresentation' which occurs in contemporary conflicts, in other words the increased accessibility of and to media which allows all sides of a conflict to strive to represent themselves and their cause to the local population and the wider world. Chinkin and Kaldor point to ISIS's highly skilled reliance on communications techniques for propaganda and mobilisation.[520] In such a context, kidnappings and hijackings are perceived as more successful because of the potential wider impact of such strategic choices of violence.[521]

The violence adopted by fighting parties in contemporary armed conflicts thus serves very specific objectives. Evidence from conflicts across the globe has demonstrated that sexual and gender-based violence against civilians is systematic and being purposefully used by fighting parties to exercise control and to assert dominance over the population and other armed groups or to punish the population associated with the opposition in the absence of traditional resources for military occupation.[522] Rape is used by fighting parties as strategies of war to shame and demoralise entire communities.[523] As Wouters notes this makes it an effective tool to terrorise civilian populations.[524] This pervasive strategic violence is a major contributor to and often a deliberate instrument for forced displacement. The International Committee of the Red Cross (ICRC) has noted that threats of killing, torture and rape create an 'atmosphere of terror' which often causes populations to flee.[525] Acts of sexual violence were found by the International Criminal Tribunal for Rwanda (ICTR) to 'form an integral part of the process of destruction, specifically, targeting Tutsi women and contributing to their destruction and the destruction of the Tutsi as a group'.[526] Indictments before the ICTR explicitly raised the causal relation between sexual violence and 'political, ethnic or racial grounds'.[527] Sexual violence is also increasingly seen as a tactic or strategy of war which specifically targets civilians.[528] Witnesses of the Rwandan genocide before the ICTR recounted that sexual violence was perpetrated as a tactic of war.[529] A 2015 report from the UN Special Representative to the Secretary-General on Sexual Violence in Conflict (SRSG-SVC) led the UN Secretary-General to raise grave concerns regarding the prevalence of sexual violence perpetrated by states and non-state actors 'including those pursuing extremist ideologies' in conflict situations, such as Iraq and Syria amongst others.[530]

520 Chinkin and Kaldor, *International Law and New Wars* (n 115) 14.

521 Cooke, 'Wo-man, Retelling the War Myth' (n 410) 181.

522 See for example in the case of Iraq – Dakkak, 'Tackling Sexual Violence' (n 419) 39; in the case of Syria – UN General Assembly, Human Rights Council Report of the Independent International Commission of Inquiry on the Syrian Arab Republic A/HRC/23/58, 18 July 2013, paras 91–95; in the case of the DRC – Sara Meger, 'Toward a Feminist Political Economy of Wartime Sexual Violence: The Case of the Democratic Republic of the Congo' (2015) 17 *International Feminist Journal of Politics* 416, 423; in the case of Bosnia, Eritrea, Guatemala, Mozambique and Rwanda – Martin, *Refugee Women* (n 54) 31–32.

523 Pittaway and Bartolomei, 'Refugees, Race, and Gender' (n 496) 21.

524 Wouters, 'Conflict Refugees' (n 5) 817.

525 ICRC, *Addressing the Needs of Women Affected by Armed Conflict* (n 467) 37.

526 *Prosecutor v Kayishema and Ruzindana* (Judgment) ICTR-95-1-T (May 1999) para 95.

527 *Prosecutor v Kajelijeli* (Judgment) ICTR-98-44A-I (25 January 2001) count 7 of the indictment.

528 UNSC Res 1888 (30 September 2009) UN Doc S/RES/1888, para 1.

529 Milne, 'Prosecuting Cases of Gender Violence' (n 182) 113.

530 UNSC, 'Conflict-Related Sexual Violence: Report of the Secretary-General' (23 March 2015) UN Doc S/2015/203, para 8.

Violence experienced during contemporary armed conflicts therefore has clear and significant gendered dimensions.[531] Literature on gender and conflict shows that gender relations have been relied on in situations of widespread violence to motivate and increase violence.[532] There appears to be a general agreement within this body of literature that women may be particularly targeted,[533] and subjected to sexual violence in particular.[534] However, there is increasing evidence pointing to men and boys also being exposed to sexual and gender-based violence in situations of armed conflict.[535] This highlights the importance of avoiding equating gender with women and girls and of categorising 'gender-related asylum claims' as a small subset of asylum claims mostly populated by women.[536] Sexual violence has been shown not to be related to the perpetrators' or survivors' sexuality but is rather explained as an expression of power.[537] In this situation, it is possible to identify the intersection between gender and systems of dominance/oppression and inequality based on race, ethnicity, religion, class, sexuality and ability.[538] Henry considers that this approach allows for a much deeper understanding of the causes, consequences and impact of rape in times of conflict.[539]

The discussion here highlights the difficulties with the concept of 'indiscriminate violence' as it fails to adequately characterise the manner in which violence in contemporary armed conflicts is exercised. In this light, violence against civilians is not understood as indiscriminate violence but as a deliberate strategy of control which has significant gendered dimensions. Viewing contemporary armed conflicts in this frame challenges the rationale of subsidiary protection in the Qualification Directive which explicitly comprises terms such as 'indiscriminate violence', the interpretation of those provisions and debates regarding the manner in which levels of 'indiscriminate violence' should be measured. An understanding of violence as indiscriminate presents a challenge not only for subsidiary protection but also for refugee protection. Oosterveld's research identified a significant number of judicial decisions which discounted gender-based violence occurring in situations of armed conflict on the basis that this amounted to 'the general indiscriminate consequences of conflict'.[540]

531 See for example in the case of Syria – Alsaba and Kapilashrami, 'Understanding Women's Experience of Violence' (n 453) 12; in the case of Iraq – Mallory Wankel, 'Obscuring the Realities of Gender-Based Violence: European Policies on Iraqi Asylum Claims' (2009) 2 *Surfacing: Gender and Conflict* 18, 19; in the case of Sierra Leone – Thompson, 'Women, Gender, and Conflict' (n 395) 350; Human Rights Watch, '"We'll Kill You If You Cry": Sexual Violence in the Sierra Leone Conflict' (January 2003) Vol 15(1A) <www.hrw.org/reports/2003/sierraleone/sierleon0103.pdf> accessed 12 July 2021, 54.

532 Giles and Hyndman, 'Introduction' (n 389) 4.

533 Heaven Crawley and Trine Lester, Comparative Analysis of Gender-Related Persecution in National Asylum Legislation and Practice in Europe (EPAU/2004/05, May 2004) para 244.

534 Sjoberg and Via, 'Introduction' (n 386) 10.

535 Grey and Shepherd, '"Stop Rape Now?" (n 73) 16–17; Farrag, 'Engendering Forced Migration' (n 423) 8; House of Lords Select Committee on Sexual Violence in Conflict, *Sexual Violence in Conflict: A War Crime* (12 April 2016, HL123) <https://publications.parliament.uk/pa/ld201516/ldselect/ldsvc/123/123.pdf> accessed 12 July 2021, para 228; Cecile Allegra, 'Revealed: Male Rape Used Systematically in Libya as Instrument of War' *The Guardian* (London, 3 November 2017) <www.theguardian.com/world/2017/nov/03/revealed-male-used-systematically-in-libya-as-instrument-of-war> accessed 12 July 2021.

536 Querton, 'Gender and the Boundaries of International Refugee Law' (n 74).

537 Farrag, 'Engendering Forced Migration' (n 423) 9.

538 For an outline of intersectionality more generally, see Kimberle Crenshaw, 'Mapping the Margins: Intersectionality, Identity Politics, and Violence against Women of Color' (1991) 43 *Stanford Law Review* 1241; Davis, 'Intersectionality and International Law' (n 496).

539 Nicola Henry, 'Theorizing Wartime Rape' (2016) 30 *Gender & Society* 44.

540 Oosterveld, 'Women and Girls Fleeing Conflict' (n 79) 196–198.

The theoretical, empirical and legal approaches put forward in this section contradict such a conceptualisation of violence being indiscriminate, in the sense of fighting parties exercising violence without particular strategies, targets and objectives. Overall, the strategies and tactics of fighting parties in contemporary armed conflicts matter for the application and interpretation of the Refugee Convention because they impact on civilians in gendered ways. Taking these into consideration in refugee status determination exposes incidents or attacks in situations of armed conflict that are traditionally considered in asylum jurisprudence to be indiscriminate or criminal as strategic and political.

3.7 Conclusion

Although Oosterveld has pointed to obstacles for persons fleeing armed conflict in obtaining refugee protection, the express terms of the subsidiary protection provision which establishes that a person qualifies for subsidiary protection only if they are not a refugee, reinforce the claim that the Refugee Convention is the principal international protection mechanism also for persons fleeing contemporary armed conflicts. The Refugee Convention's status as the cornerstone of international protection and its role as a living instrument ground the novel conceptual framework proposed in this chapter for revisiting its interpretation and application.

The gender and security studies literature supports the proposition that it is more accurate to look at violence during armed conflicts as a continuum rather than a simple war/peace dichotomy and this perspective should inform interpretation of international refugee law accordingly. The rise in the number and relative power of armed groups in armed conflicts means that the nature of violence is increasingly determined by their means and choices. This challenges the state/non-state actors dichotomy, and the focus on state sovereignty and state monopoly over the use of force in international law. Contemporary armed conflicts are characterised by weak states, increasing the likelihood that states are unable or unwilling to ensure protection against violence. Further, existing protection is gendered and limited to a select few. Violence in armed conflicts is targeted at civilians and is justified and maintained on the basis of identity politics. In this context, fixed identities justify ever more serious human rights violations and as changing sides is increasingly impossible, armed conflicts become protracted. The social construction of these political identities is highly gendered, in the sense that these identities are based on gender norms. Strategies and tactics of armed groups are determined by their means so that when armed groups do not have military capacity to control territory, they use terror, including violence and threats of violence, to control populations and by extension territory. Other strategic means to terrorise populations include highly visible forms of human rights violations such as kidnappings, rape, sexual violence and gender-based violence.

On that basis, a more detailed examination of armed groups' strategies and tactics in conflicts and their means provides a better understanding of their reliance on violence against civilians to control populations and territories and support the financial costs of fighting. The objective of the various strategies adopted by fighting parties during armed conflicts is to terrorise populations as a whole as defined by their race, ethnicity, religion or national identity to control geographical areas and/or force displacement. Viewed in this manner, the nature of violence experienced by persons in situations of armed conflict presents itself as motivated, tactical and most importantly, political. This indicates that violence in armed conflicts is far from being indiscriminate; rather, it is strategically deployed and highly gendered. This illustrates the limited protective scope of subsidiary protection provisions designed for persons fleeing 'indiscriminate violence', such as Article 15(c) Qualification Directive, and instead amplifies the relevance of the Refugee Convention. This understanding is essential in applying and interpreting the Refugee Convention definition as it translates into the forms of ill-treatment, its targeted nature and the reasons for the exercise of violence, as will be discussed in Chapters 4 to 6.

4

Judicial Constructions of Risk on Return to Situations of Contemporary Armed Conflict

4.1 Introduction

The present chapter enquires into judicial constructions of risk on return to situations of contemporary armed conflict. It demonstrates how appellate authorities approach situations of armed conflict predominantly through the perspective of conventional warfare, as defined by Kalyvas and Balcells in their typology of internal armed conflicts,[541] and a notion of territoriality in a manner which ignores the wealth of theoretical and empirical knowledge of contemporary conflicts. A conventional warfare perspective driven by an emphasis on territoriality means that the judicial assessment of conflicts in appellants' country of origin is centred on traditional battlefronts, armed confrontations and occupation of territory.

However, as demonstrated in Chapter 3, contemporary armed conflicts are no longer characterised by these aspects. Instead, states' use of force and means of combat have been displaced as the decisive factors determining the conduct of hostilities and the characteristics of armed conflicts. A conventional warfare perspective infers that violence arising out of fighting methods traditionally adopted by conventional state armed forces, such as ground engagements between parties to the conflict, is more severe than violence occurring in areas where territory is not physically disputed. Such judicial interpretation does not give credence to relevant matters for the purpose of interpreting international protection legislation, such as the nature and impact of violence exercised by armed groups which reflects their gendered strategies, non-conventional fighting methods and their relative power over the conduct of hostilities. More specifically, it fails to acknowledge that one of the main strategies of fighting parties is to establish political control over territory by forcibly displacing and terrorising populations through the exercise of highly visible forms of human rights violations. Consequently, appellate authorities' adoption of a conventional warfare perspective and their focus on the geographical location of combats, the intensity of armed confrontations between fighting parties, and the military and administrative control of territory in the determination of asylum appeals where the risk of persecution and serious harm arises in situations of armed conflict have important implications for international protection.

The Qualification Directive requires asylum decision makers to firstly examine whether individuals qualify for refugee protection and only afterwards, if the refugee claim has been refused, to examine whether they may nonetheless be eligible for subsidiary protection,[542] whether persons flee situations of armed conflict or not. All European Union (EU) Member

541 Kalyvas and Balcells, 'International System and Technologies of Rebellion' (n 44).

542 Article 2(f) Qualification Directive 2011 defines a 'person eligible for subsidiary protection' as 'a third-country national or a stateless person who does not qualify as a refugee'; see also UK: *AA (Article 15(c)) Iraq CG* [2015] UKUT 544, para 88 and UK: *AK (Article 15(c)) Afghanistan CG* [2012] UKUT 00163, para 154.

States (MS) have now instated a single procedure to determine qualification for both statuses sequentially.[543] However, the research findings show that the existence of these two distinct international protection statuses in EU law has had a significant impact on how appellate authorities in EU MS approach the determination of asylum appeals in the cases of persons fleeing armed conflicts. In particular, the existence of a subsidiary protection regime under Article 15(c) Qualification Directive, whose specific aim is the international protection of persons fleeing armed conflicts, provides appellate authorities with an alternative form of protection instead of examining the circumstances of widespread violence under the Refugee Convention.

The analysis of Afghan, Iraqi and Syrian asylum appeals demonstrates that appellate authorities give prominence to subsidiary protection in the cases of persons fleeing armed conflicts even if entitlement to refugee protection is examined first, as required by the Qualification Directive. The findings confirm McAdam's concerns, raised shortly after the Qualification Directive was first adopted, that in a regime that differentiates between protection needs based on the reasons for flight, recognising an individual as a beneficiary of subsidiary protection without considering the application of the Refugee Convention may result in the latter's development being impeded.[544] The codification of subsidiary protection in EU law and appellate authorities' obligation to consider refugee status and subsidiary protection sequentially brings to the fore judicial misconceptions that persons fleeing situations of armed conflict do not meet the criteria of the Refugee Convention definition because of the generalised nature of the risk. Durieux explained this misconception as the mistaking of 'generalised' or 'widespread' violence for 'indiscriminate' violence.[545] As a result, appellate authorities in the EU rarely, if ever, examine how the general conditions of violence in the country of origin that characterise contemporary armed conflicts impact on appellants' entitlement to refugee protection.

To illustrate the point, prior to legislative changes in Denmark introducing Temporary Protection Status in 2015, the Danish Refugee Appeals Board (Flygtningenævnet, DRAB) asserted that the general conditions in the country of origin could not lead to asylum under section 7 of the Aliens Act. DRAB explained that claims based on generalised violence fell outside its jurisdiction because they were not covered by section 7. More specifically, it stated that 'the competence of the Board is [...] limited to assessing questions relevant to asylum, that is, individual risk of persecution or harm, and it is therefore outside the competence of the Board to assess whether, a residency permit for other and more humanitarian reasons, for instances, because of temporary, generalised violence where the applicant does not fulfil the criteria of Section 7' and the 'general security situation in a country cannot by itself constitute grounds for asylum according to Section 7 of the Aliens' Act'.[546]

The misconstruction has led the UK Upper Tribunal (UT) to clarify that 'to skip over refugee eligibility would be to lend support to the misconception that persons fleeing

543 Directive 2013/32/EU of the European Parliament and of the Council of 26 June 2013 on common procedures for granting and withdrawing international protection, Recital (11) and Article 10(2).

544 McAdam, *Complementary Protection in International Refugee Law* (n 8) 61. This is further discussed in Chapters 5 and 6.

545 Durieux, 'Of War, Flows, Laws and Flaws' (n 42) 165.

546 Liv Feijen, 'Filling the Gaps? Subsidiary Protection and Non-EU Harmonized Protection Status(es) in the Nordic Countries' (2014) 26 *International Journal of Refugee Law* 173 179–180.

armed conflict cannot fall within the Article 1A(2) Refugee Convention definition. That has never been so, even if there has been recurrent hesitation about the criteria that should apply to [asylum-related claims based wholly or significantly on risks arising from situations of armed conflict and indiscriminate violence].'[547] Further, the Spanish Supreme Court (Tribunal Supremo, TS) has also had to confirm that, contrary to the government's policy of refusing refugee status and granting instead subsidiary protection to Syrians, the widespread nature of the conflict does not exclude the application of the Refugee Convention when the legal requirements of the definition are met.[548] Overall, despite some higher courts reiterating that the Refugee Convention may apply to persons fleeing armed conflicts, Chapters 5 and 6 demonstrate that judicial practice consistently rejects refugee status in cases of widespread violence, thus displacing the Refugee Convention as the cornerstone of international protection. This chapter will first explore judicial constructions of risk on return arising from widespread violence in situations of contemporary armed conflict, which, as explained, occurs predominantly in the context of subsidiary protection. The chapter starts by providing a typology of armed conflicts to explain the different types of conflicts defined by conventional or asymmetric warfare in order to better explain how appellate authorities in the EU perceive contemporary armed conflicts. The remainder of the chapter then sets out in more detail the factors characterising conventional warfare which constitute the focal point of analysis by appellate authorities, namely armed confrontations between parties to the conflict, territory as a strategic military objective and effective control over territory.[549]

4.2 Typology of Armed Conflicts

Kalyvas and Balcells set out that situations of conventional warfare arise in internal armed conflicts, where the military capacity of both sides to the conflict are matched at a high level and armed groups are able to confront states using heavy weaponry, including field artillery and armour. Fighting in such types of conflicts is characterised, on the one hand, by direct confrontations 'across well-defined front lines or between armed columns; clashes often take the form of set battles, trench warfare, and town sieges'.[550] On the other hand, where armed groups are unable to match conventional military tactics employed by state forces, asymmetrical or irregular conflicts are said to exist.[551] In a third situation, the military capacity of both the state forces and the insurgents are low. Such an armed conflict may be characterised as symmetrical non-conventional.[552]

The principal objectives, strategies and means of non-state armed groups explored in Chapter 3 illustrate how asymmetrical conflicts are the most widespread type of conflicts today. There is a general agreement within security studies scholarship that asymmetric

[547] UK: *AK (Article 15(c)) Afghanistan* CG [2012] UKUT 00163, para 154.

[548] Spain (ES): TS STS 1182/2016 16.03.2016 (Syria) 10–11.

[549] Illustrated predominantly by the asylum appeals of Afghan and Iraqi nationals as there is limited discussion of the general conditions of widespread violence in Syria in judicial determinations. Limited judicial enquiry is due to most Syrian appellants having already been granted subsidiary protection by administrative authorities, their Syrian nationality being disbelieved, or the appeals concerning return to safe third countries.

[550] Kalyvas and Balcells, 'International System and Technologies of Rebellion' (n 44) 418–419.

[551] Ibid. [552] Ibid.

warfare, also described as insurgency, has become the main type of warfare.[553] Whereas the coalition forces in Afghanistan and Iraq employed conventional military tactics from the outset of the conflicts, armed groups were unable to match these tactics and methods, using instead tactics aimed at exercising control over local communities through fear and intimidation.[554] Non-state armed groups in Syria have been described as possessing both conventional and non-conventional fighting capacities,[555] although they display significant similarities with the characteristics of non-state actors in non-conventional conflicts in other parts of the world.[556] The conflicts in Iraq, Afghanistan and Syria are thus better understood as asymmetrical or at the very least contain some significant characteristics of non-conventional conflicts, as in the case of Syria.[557]

Contrary to this wealth of knowledge however, appellate authorities in EU MS view situations of contemporary armed conflict predominantly from the perspective of conventional warfare. This approach perceives armed conflicts as events with defined spatial boundaries wherein fighting parties engage in combat along identifiable front lines in order to establish physical and administrative control over territory. A traditional warfare lens undermines judicial understandings of armed conflicts and an adequate interpretation of the Refugee Convention definition as it focuses solely or excessively on conventional fighting. Consequently, it attributes more weight to violence exercised through fighting methods and capacities traditionally adopted by state military forces, such as ground engagements and heavy artillery used on the battlefronts, and the impact of this type of violence. This obscures the nature, extent and impact of violence arising as a result of the objectives of other parties to the conflict, their diverse strategies and methods, and means available.

Significantly, a conventional warfare perspective also ignores the relative power of non-state armed groups over the conduct of hostilities. As non-state armed groups have increasing influence over the conduct of fighting,[558] and an increasing number of civilian casualties are attributed to these groups, the impact on refugee protection of failing to properly enquire into their objectives, tactics, methods and means is significant. For example, most civilian casualties in Afghanistan are attributed to 'Anti-Government Elements' and they have been

[553] See for example William Banks, 'Toward an Adaptive International Humanitarian Law: New Norms for New Battlefields' in William Banks (ed), *New Battlefields/Old Laws, Critical Debates on Asymmetric Warfare* (Columbia University Press 2011) 3; Eugene Miakinkov, 'The Agency of Force in Asymmetrical Warfare and Counterinsurgency: The Case of Chechnya' (2011) 34 *Journal of Strategic Studies* 647, 653; Karp, 'The Changing Ownership of War' (n 440) 181; Yun, 'Insurgency Warfare as an Emerging New Mode' (n 440).

[554] Kaldor, *New and Old Wars* (n 3) 166–172.

[555] Özlem Kayhan Pusane, 'How to Profile PYD/YPG as an Actor in the Syrian Civil War: Policy Implications for the Region and Beyond' in Özden Zeynep Oktav, Emel Parlar Dal and Ali Murat Kurşun (eds), *Violent Non-State Actors and the Syrian Civil War: The ISIS and YPG Cases* (Springer 2018) 75.

[556] Ivan Briscoe, 'Non-Conventional Armed Violence and Non-State Actors: Challenges for Mediation and Humanitarian Action' (Norwegian Peacebuilding Resource Centre, 2013) <www.clingendael.org/sites/default/files/pdfs/Non-conventional%20armed%20violence%20and%20non-state%20actors,%20challenges%20for%20mediation%20and%20humanitarian%20action.pdf> accessed 12 July 2020, 2.

[557] Özden Zeynep Oktav, Emel Parlar Dal and Ali Murat Kurşun, 'Reframing and Reassessing the VNSAs in Syrian Conflict: An Introduction' in Oktav, Dal and Kurşun (eds), *Violent Non-State Actors and the Syrian Civil War* 2; John F. Murphy, 'International Law in Crisis: Challenges Posed by the New Terrorism and the Changing Nature of War' (2011) 44 *Case Western Reserve Journal of International Law* 59, 74.

[558] Karp, 'The Changing Ownership of War' (n 440) 181, 187.

responsible for between 61 and 74 per cent of civilian casualties since 2013.[559] Further, a traditional warfare lens also fails to account for how the nature of violence in situations of armed conflict may evolve over time. Warfare never remains static as fighting parties adapt and modify their tactics.[560] It is precisely this ability to adapt which led to the emergence of asymmetrical warfare as the main type of conflict today.

4.3 Armed Confrontations between Parties to the Conflicts

Appellate authorities disproportionately focus on direct confrontations between parties to the conflict, and more specifically on establishing the location, number and intensity of those battles. Notably, the Belgian Court (Belgian Council for Alien Law Litigation, CCE/RvV) places excessive weight on the extent of what it terms 'open combat' situations. Although the term 'open combat' situations is not defined in Belgian legislation or jurisprudence, the Belgian Court uses the term in English to refer to battles or direct confrontations between national armies and insurgents. In relation to the situation in Central Iraq, the Court thus stated that the analysis of the security situation in Kirkuk indicated the occurrence of sporadic severe attacks but this was not a situation of 'open combat'.[561] Similarly, the Court stated that the analysis of the security situation in Baghdad indicated that there were serious attacks but that this was not a situation of 'open combat'.[562] In the assessment of a risk on return to the city of Jalalabad in Afghanistan, the Court noted that no mention could be made of a situation of 'open combat' or of violent and continuous or uninterrupted fighting notwithstanding the fact there were regular terror attacks,[563] complex attacks,[564] or high-profile attacks.[565] With respect to the situation in Afghanistan's capital Kabul, although the Court noted there were regular complex attacks, there could be no mention of a situation of 'open combat' or of violent and continuous or uninterrupted fighting.[566] The Court also found in respect of returns to Kabul that there was no situation of 'open combat', nor reports of violent and continuous or uninterrupted fighting between insurgents and government forces despite the occurrence of various attacks causing civilian casualties,[567] complex high-profile attacks,[568] or asymmetrical attacks.[569]

Likewise, the UK First-Tier Tribunal (FTT) describes regions in Iraq characterised by 'ongoing fighting' as 'contested areas'.[570] The FTT's approach reflects its application of the UT Country Guidance on Iraq that only violence generated by all-out fighting is considered

559 All of the United Nations Assistance Mission in Afghanistan's (UNAMA's) annual reports on the 'Protection of Civilians in Armed Conflict' are available <https://unama.unmissions.org/protection-of-civilians-reports> accessed 12 July 2021.

560 Williamson Murray, *Military Adaptation in War* (Institute for Defence Analyses 2009) <www.ida.org/-/media/feature/publications/m/mi/military-adaptation-in-war/ida-paper-p-4452.ashx> accessed 12 July 2021, 8–6.

561 Belgium (BE): RvV 97 614 21.02.2013 (Iraq).

562 BE: RvV 94 655 09.01.2013 (Iraq).

563 BE: RvV 165 409 08.04.2016 (Afghanistan).

564 BE: RvV 160 102 15.01.2016 (Afghanistan).

565 BE: RvV 108 480 22.08.2013 (Afghanistan).

566 BE: RvV 147 398 08.06.2015 (Afghanistan).

567 BE: RvV 122 391 11.04.2014 (Afghanistan).

568 BE: RvV 116 849 14.01.2014 (Afghanistan); see also BE: RvV 154 649 15.10.2015 (Afghanistan).

569 BE: RvV 111 940 14.10.2013 (Afghanistan); see also BE: RvV 114 377 25.11.2013 (Afghanistan); BE: RvV 105 426 20.06.2013 (Afghanistan).

570 UK: UT(IAC) 05.10.2015 (Iraq): based on findings of facts made in earlier decision by UK: FTT(IAC) 25.02.2015 (Iraq).

a 'contested area' whereas 'violence in Baghdad is largely generated by asymmetrical warfare (i.e. sporadic terrorist attacks) rather than by "all out fighting", such as is to be seen in the contested areas'.[571] On this basis, the Iraqi Governorates of Anbar,[572] Diyala, Kirkuk, Ninewah and Salah Al-din are defined as 'contested areas'.[573] This is contrasted by the UT with the area in the north of the Babil Governorate, characterised by the lack of evidence of 'very recent conflict between ISIL and state authorities'.[574] The UK UT's Iraq Country Guidance was explicitly endorsed by the Dutch District Court (Rechtbank, Rb), which cited passages from the reported UK judgment.[575] The Rb concluded in several instances that violence in Baghdad city was mainly caused by sporadic terrorist attacks and not by 'all-out fighting', a term which the Court used in English.[576] Although Denmark is not bound by the Qualification Directive, the explanatory statement to the Bill which brought in the Temporary Protection Status in 2015 suggests a similar approach.[577] It sets out the specific factors decision makers would consider when assessing eligibility for this status including whether 'the battles are geographically limited or widespread and the number of civilian deaths, injured or displaced as a result of the battles'.[578] The explanatory statement thus specifically lists the geographical spread of ground engagements and the impact of violence arising from those battles, characteristics of conventional warfare, as the central criteria of relevance in the assessment of asylum claims.

On the whole, judicial approaches reveal a dichotomy between risk on return arising from all-out fighting characterised by ground engagements between parties to the conflict and risk on return resulting from attacks conducted by armed groups outside these areas. The assessment of the characteristics of the armed conflicts in Afghanistan and Iraq demonstrates a disproportionate emphasis on conventional military battles and ground engagements. Moreover, this is often contrasted with asymmetrical warfare. The judicial reasoning clearly discloses an expectation of conflicts involving battlefronts and direct confrontations between national armed forces and insurgents, exposing the implicit belief that violence in armed conflicts is mainly exercised in the context of two or more fighting parties engaging each other through conventional military operations. In this manner, appellate authorities disclose an assumption of the extent, severity and impact of violence according to this classification. Hence, although attacks and 'security incidents' occurring outside sites of ground engagements instigated by armed groups were described as serious or severe, the violence was not of such intensity to create a risk on return because the attacks were sporadic. Regular attacks by armed groups were insufficient to create a risk on return; instead, appellate authorities in Belgium, the Netherlands and the UK consider that

571 UK: *AA (Article 15(c)) Iraq* CG [2015] UKUT 544, para 130.

572 Iraq is divided into eighteen Governorates, the non-government organisation (NGO) Coordination Committee for Iraq hosts a website with in-depth profiles for each Governorate including their history, population, geography, economy and humanitarian overview, 'Iraqi Governorate Profiles' undated <www.ncciraq.org/en/about/about-iraq/iraqi-governorate-profiles> accessed 12 July 2021.

573 UK: *AA (Article 15(c)) Iraq* CG [2015] UKUT 544 (IAC), paras 101–106.

574 Ibid., para 111.

575 Ibid., paras 118–126.

576 The Netherlands (NL): Rb AWB 15/22446 31.03.2016 (Iraq); see also NL: Rb AWB 16/13425 11.07.2016 (Iraq); NL: Rb AWB 16/2368 03.03.2016 (Iraq): making similar findings by relying on the judgment of the UK UT (Immigration and Asylum Chamber, IAC).

577 S. 7(3) Aliens Act.

578 Forslag til Lov om ændring af udlændingeloven, Folketingstidende A, Lovforslag nr. L 72, 14 November 2014, para 2.1.2, p 7.

the violence is sufficiently intense only if the attacks are continuous or persistent in a manner akin to conventional fighting along battlefronts.[579]

Undertaking an assessment of situations of armed conflict in Afghanistan and Iraq primarily by an examination of ground engagements between fighting parties is at odds with the wealth of knowledge in the field of security studies and publicly available information regarding the nature of violence in conflict that 'open combat between armed fighters is probably now the exception rather than the rule'.[580] The approach adopted by appellate authorities instigates a search for evidence of conventional warfare which ignores the generally accepted proposition that insurgency has become the main type of warfare as a result of armed groups' increasing number and relative power and influence over the conduct of hostilities.[581] A conventional warfare perspective imports into the assessment of risk on return the assumption that the extent and severity of the violence and its impact is highest when it results from armed clashes between fighting parties. Significantly, it means that appellate authorities consider that a risk of serious harm due to widespread violence in situations of armed conflict only arises when a person's area of return coincides with the site of armed confrontations between parties to the conflict.

4.4 Territory as a Strategic Military Objective

A corresponding trend to the one identified in Section 4.3 emerges from the analysis, namely that appellate authorities consider territory to be the principal issue at stake between the parties to the conflict. Thus, appellate authorities are guided by a notion of territoriality when determining asylum appeals from persons fleeing armed conflicts. Although the principle of territoriality has featured prominently in the field of international relations and security studies, it has generally been used as an explanatory framework and variable for evaluating the likelihood of interstate war onset based on quantitative research.[582] However in internal conflicts 'identity, discrimination, and territory coexist in ways that generate armed conflict'.[583] Hence, the role of territory in the inception of internal armed conflicts is less significant than in situations of international armed conflicts as other factors such as identity and discrimination are equally important.[584] Furthermore, whereas the notion may be useful in understanding and predicting conflict onset, it is less useful as a concept for understanding the nature of violence in situations of armed conflict.

579 As noted in the methodology, the features of the asylum systems in Denmark and Spain mean the characteristics of armed conflicts and the violence exercised in this context are not scrutinised at appeal.

580 Editorial, '*The Guardian* View on Afghanistan: War Quickens as Politicians Falter' *The Guardian* (London, 30 January 2015) <www.theguardian.com/commentisfree/2015/jan/30/guardian-view-afghanistan-war-quickens-politicians-falter> accessed 12 July 2021.

581 Karp, 'The Changing Ownership of War' (n 440) 181, 187; Yun, 'Insurgency Warfare as an Emerging New Mode' (n 440).

582 Monica Toft, 'Territory and War' (2014) 51 *Journal of Peace Research* 185. In the context of international armed conflicts see for example Bryan A. Frederick, Paul R. Hensel and Christopher Macaulay, 'The Issue Correlates of War Territorial Claims Data, 1816–20011' (2017) 54 *Journal of Peace Research* 99; Hemda Ben-Yehuda, 'Territoriality and War in International Crises: Theory and Findings 1918–2001' (2004) 6 *International Studies Review* 85, 87.

583 Patrick M. Regan, 'Civil War and Territory? Drawing Linkages between Interstate and Intrastate War' (2009) 35 *International Interactions* 321, 324.

584 See Chapter 3 generally.

This trend is illustrated by the French National Asylum Court's (Cour Nationale du Droit d'Asile, CNDA's) assumption that the occupation of territory is one of the central objectives of fighting parties. Although the CNDA does not give the same prominence to conventional battles and direct armed confrontations between parties to conflicts as the Belgian, Danish,[585] Dutch and UK appellate authorities, it nonetheless appears to focus mostly on identifying territory, such as particular regions or cities, as strategic military targets in its assessment of the armed conflicts in Afghanistan and Iraq.[586] The CNDA is thus to a certain extent also guided by a notion of territoriality when determining the extent of violence in the assessment of risk of return to situations of armed conflict.

Following this approach, the CNDA highlighted that Logar Province in Afghanistan was a strategic zone for the Taliban as a major gateway to the capital due to its geographical position south of Kabul Province.[587] Furthermore, Kabul Province remained a privileged target of the insurgents due to its symbolic and strategical importance.[588] Regarding the conflict in Iraq, the Court noted that the city of Kirkuk was very coveted by all belligerents and that Sulaymaniyah, an important oil city, was also one of Daesh's objectives.[589] Similarly, the Court placed emphasis on the announcement by the Islamic State of Iraq and Syria (ISIS) spokesperson of the insurgents' intentions to attack Baghdad.[590] Overall, the CNDA's approach suggests it considers the physical occupation of territory to be one of the main objectives of armed groups' strategies. To a certain extent, the UK UT also places emphasis on the strategic importance of particular cities or towns for parties to armed conflicts. With respect to Iraq, the UT identified the town of Ramadi, in the Anbar Governorate,[591] or the north of Babil Governorate because of its proximity to Baghdad and its border with Anbar.[592] In an Afghanistan Country Guidance case, the UT noted that Kabul remained 'a persistent strategic target for high-profile attacks and assassination attempts'.[593] It also noted that Ghazni city and the southern and eastern districts of Ghazni Province were the targets of 'much of the insurgent activity'.[594] Thus, overall, there is a significant emphasis by appellate authorities on armed confrontations between parties to the conflicts and/or on territory as a strategic military objective in their examination of the situations of armed conflict.[595]

Appellate authorities' perspective of conventional warfare fails to reflect that the gendered strategies of armed groups are of central relevance in understanding the nature of violence in situations of armed conflict, as argued in Chapter 3. More specifically, it stands in stark contrast to the growing consensus within security studies scholarship that strategies and tactics adopted by armed groups in contemporary armed conflicts aim to achieve control of territory not through ground engagements and military occupation but by the control of population through highly visible forms of human rights violations

[585] See n 579.

[586] France (FR): CNDA 16024864 26.10.2016 (Afghanistan); FR: CNDA 150018199 18.02.2016 (Iraq); FR: CNDA 13034393/13034396 25.11.2014 (Iraq); FR: CNDA 12026005 05.07.2013 (Afghanistan); FR: CNDA 12001368 22.05.2013 (Afghanistan).

[587] FR: CNDA 16024864 26.10.2016 (Afghanistan).

[588] FR: CNDA 12026005 05.07.2013 (Afghanistan); see also FR: CNDA 12001368 22.05.2013 (Afghanistan).

[589] FR: CNDA 15018199 18.02.2016 (Iraq). [590] FR: CNDA 13034393/13034396 25.11.2014 (Iraq).

[591] UK: *AA (Article 15(c)) Iraq* CG [2015] UKUT 544, para 102. [592] Ibid., para 111.

[593] UK: *AK (Article 15(c)) Afghanistan* CG [2012] UKUT 00163, para 77. [594] Ibid., para 81.

[595] As noted, the asylum systems of Denmark and Spain mean that these issues were not canvassed by their respective appellate bodies.

directed at civilians. Appellate authorities thus generally fail to acknowledge that territory, in the geographical sense of the term, plays a lesser role in contemporary armed conflicts than previously.

4.5 Effective Control over Territory

The claim that appellate authorities adopt a territorial lens in the determination of risk on return to situations of armed conflict is further evidenced by their consistent focus of enquiry into the occupation and control of territory through infrastructure and management by either party to the conflict. In the practice of the Belgian, French, Dutch and UK Courts, there is an emphasis on establishing whether specific territory is in the hands of the state or armed opposition groups.[596]

The following examples illustrate this general trend. Thus, even though there had been a worsening of the general security situation in Nassiriya, southern Iraq, since June 2014, and there were repeated attacks to the security of civilians in the context of confrontations opposing Iraqi authorities on the one hand and insurgent groups on the other, the CNDA relied on the fact that the city remained under governmental control to find there was no risk on return for the appellant.[597] The Belgian Court (Belgian Council for Alien Law Litigation, CCE/RvV) dismissed an appeal partly on the basis that the city of Kabul, like almost all provincial capitals in Afghanistan, was firmly in the hands of the government and relatively safe. Moreover, ISIS did not have a presence in Kabul and it could not be said that ISIS had a firm foothold in Afghanistan.[598]

Despite a report on the situation in Afghanistan issued by the Dutch Ministry of Foreign Affairs in 2013 stating that the security forces no longer had the security situation under control, the Dutch Council of State concluded the Iraqi government exercised authority in Iraq because state security structures were still operational, as illustrated by the large increase in the number of checkpoints operated by the Iraqi armed forces.[599] The Rb also remitted an appeal to the Secretary of State for a new decision on the basis that Baghdad did not appear to be an area that is de facto still under the daily management of the Iraqi or Kurdish authorities.[600] In relation to Kapisa Province in Afghanistan, the Rb found that the appellant had not established he originated from an area under the effective control of Anti-Government Elements.[601]

The UK FTT found that 'whilst there is a large body of reports regarding ISIS and attacks in the areas around Baghdad there does not appear to be any imminent danger of Baghdad

[596] See for example FR: CNDA 16024450/16024449 15.12.2016 (Iraq); BE: RvV 154 649 15.10.2015 (Afghanistan); UK: FTT(IAC) 31.01.2014 (Afghanistan); NL: Rb AWB 13/12607 20.12.2013 (Afghanistan); BE: RvV 101 386 22.04.2013 (Afghanistan); UK: *AK (Article 15(c)) Afghanistan* CG [2012] UKUT 00163, paras 81, 244. As above, the nature of the samples collected from the DRAB and the Spanish National High Court (Audiencia Nacional, AN) highlight that, due to the Danish and Spanish asylum systems, these questions are not being determined by their respective appellate bodies.

[597] FR: CNDA 16024450/16024449 15.12.2016 (Iraq).

[598] BE: RvV 154 649 15.10.2015 (Afghanistan).

[599] NL: RvS N° 201307429/1/V2 19.02.2014 (Iraq).

[600] NL: Rb AWB 14/12004 25.08.2014 (Iraq).

[601] NL: Rb AWB 13/12607 20.12.2013 (Afghanistan); see also a more recent decision from the Rb but in relation to the conflict in Mogadishu, Somalia, where it concluded that the appellant had not established that Mogadishu is under control of Al-Shabaab notwithstanding that Al-Shabaab is active in Mogadishu, NL: Rb NL17.14118 01.03.2018 (Somalia).

falling to ISIS'.[602] The UT, on reiterating the earlier finding by the FTT that the appellant was at risk in Kirkuk, specifically highlighted that he was not at risk because of his personal account 'but quite simply because IS forces presently control Kirkuk'.[603] In the UK's Country Guidance case on indiscriminate violence in Iraq, Islamic State of Iraq and the Levant's (ISIL's) control over certain Governorates was a prime determinant in reaching its conclusion that the threshold of violence had been met.[604] The FTT, in finding a risk of serious harm on return to the appellant's home area in Afghanistan, described Paghman district as 'insurgent-dominated',[605] Alingar district in Laghman Province as 'virtually unchallenged Taliban domain',[606] and Hisarak in Jalalabad Province as 'now effectively under insurgent control'.[607] The FTT also noted in particular 'the Taliban's extensive presence and control in Kunduz Province'.[608] The UT emphasised in the Country Guidance case on Afghanistan that 'Ghazni is the only province of the south-east where the Taliban has extensive territorial control, with insurgents having virtually full control in districts such as Andar, Moquer, Qarabagh, Giro, Gelan and Nawa.'[609]

Overall, these examples of individual cases illustrate a trend across appellate authorities whereby the effective control of territory, evidenced by infrastructure and daily management, is considered a decisive factor in the assessment of risk on return to situations of armed conflict.

4.6 Conclusion

This chapter claimed that appellate authorities in Belgium, France, the Netherlands and the UK determine the asylum appeals of persons fleeing armed conflicts predominantly from the perspective of conventional warfare and informed by a notion of territoriality. Appellate authorities in Denmark and Spain do not demonstrate a contrary practice as the specific features of their asylum systems mean that the characteristics of armed conflicts and the violence exercised in this context are simply not scrutinised at appeal. However, this territorial perspective understood as the physical control of territory enabled by armed confrontations, physical occupation, day-to-day management and infrastructure fails to acknowledge the gendered nature of violence in contemporary armed conflicts and that one of the main strategies of fighting parties is to exercise political control over territory by forcibly displacing and terrorising populations through the exercise of highly visible forms of human rights violations as discussed in Chapter 3. Although appellate authorities made rare references to these strategies, the prevailing approach was nonetheless to focus on conventional warfare and territory. An example of such practice includes the UK UT acknowledging that ISIL pursues its campaign in Baghdad by 'instilling fear within general populace and feeding off the global coverage of the incidents'[610] and that forced displacement is a militia strategy in the Baghdad belts,[611] yet concluding that there

[602] UK: FTT(IAC) 25.02.2015) (Iraq).
[603] UK: UT(IAC) 05.10.2015 (Iraq); on appeal solely on the issue of internal relocation from UK: FTT(IAC) 25.02.2015 (Iraq).
[604] UK: *AA (Article 15(c)) Iraq* CG [2015] UKUT 544, paras 102–106.
[605] UK: FTT(IAC) 31.01.2014 (Afghanistan). [606] UK: FTT(IAC) 03.06.2015 (Afghanistan).
[607] UK: FTT(IAC) 15.09.2014 (Afghanistan). [608] UK: FTT(IAC) 21.04.2016 (Afghanistan).
[609] UK: *AK (Article 15(c)) Afghanistan* CG [2012] UKUT 00163, para 81.
[610] UK: *AA (Article 15(c)) Iraq* CG [2015] UKUT 544, para 119. [611] Ibid., para 142.

is a risk on return only to areas experiencing armed confrontations between the parties to the conflict.[612] A conventional warfare perspective may explain why persons fleeing the Russian–Ukrainian conflict in 2022 were deemed in need of international protection. Albeit in the form of temporary protection rather than refugee status or subsidiary protection, the characteristics of the conflict were described by the European Council as a 'large-scale' 'Russian military aggression' and 'invasion of Ukraine'.[613] The international nature of the Ukrainian conflict fought by the Ukrainian Army against the Russian Army using conventional military technology is recognised as a 'war' by the EU, in contrast to predominantly internal conflicts involving weak states and non-state armed groups such as those taking place in Afghanistan and Iraq.

In addition, the approach of appellate authorities ignores that some insurgent groups consider themselves to be and are supported by transnational networks whose strategic logic is not dependent on territoriality,[614] and who may in any event lack the means to establish more permanent infrastructure and maintain the daily management of extensive geographical areas. In Afghanistan, insurgents are described as being 'highly mobile and not held up by any district or provincial boundaries'.[615] Giustozzi has noted that 'the growing ability of the Taliban to deploy mobile fighters, who could be deployed strategically, was perhaps the most important development of the insurgency'.[616] Insurgents fighting in Afghanistan are thus able to cross such boundaries with ease whereas their opponents, characterised by more institutionalised structures, struggle to respond to such flexibility.[617] This capability to adapt was developed from insurgents' lack of conventional military capacity to match state military forces. The broad consensus in the field of international relations and security studies that insurgency has become the principal type of warfare challenges appellate authorities' current approaches to the determination of asylum appeals related to situations of contemporary armed conflict.

Significantly, resort to asymmetrical warfare is not an indication of weakness or low impact. On the contrary, ability to adapt to the actual conditions of combat and the conflict is the main aspect of effectiveness,[618] and is generally linked to successful performance in conflict.[619] Losses incurred in ground engagements are generally the main driver of adaptation by non-state armed groups.[620] The resilience of several insurgencies suggests that the capacity to engage in continuous ground engagements in the battlefield is far from determining the outcome of armed conflicts. The Talibans' victory in Afghanistan in August 2021 is a case in point. Thus, 'higher-level' military capacity, understood as more sophisticated conventional technology, does not imply strength

612 Ibid., paras 204(2)–(3).

613 Council Implementing Decision (EU) 2022/382 of 4 March 2022 establishing the existence of a mass influx of displaced persons from Ukraine (n 279).

614 Garrett Pierman, 'The Grand Strategy of Nonstate Actors: Theory and Implications' (2015) 8 *Journal of Strategic Security* 69, 73.

615 Thomas Ruttig, 'More Violent, More Widespread: Trends in Afghan Security in 2017', *Afghanistan Analysts Network* (29 January 2018) <www.afghanistan-analysts.org/more-violent-more-widespread-trends-in-afghan-security-in-2017/> accessed 12 July 2021, 17.

616 Antonio Giustozzi, 'Counterinsurgency Challenge in Post-2001 Afghanistan' (2017) 28 *Small Wars & Insurgencies* 12, 15.

617 Ruttig, 'More Violent, More Widespread' (n 615) 17.

618 Murray, *Military Adaptation in War* (n 560) 8–9.

619 Ibid., 2-2.

620 Theo Farrell and Antonio Giustozzi, 'The Taliban at War: Inside the Helmand Insurgency, 2004–2012' (2013) 89 *International Affairs* 845, 868.

and success in conflict.[621] Hence, a situation of asymmetrical or non-conventional armed conflict due to limited resources and military capacity of non-state armed groups is not indicative of low levels or impact of violence. For example, almost half of all civilian casualties in Afghanistan between 2017 and 2019 were caused by combined improvised explosive devices (IEDs) used by armed groups, a proportion higher than civilian casualties caused by ground engagements.[622] Thus, rather than evidence of weakness in combat, the asymmetrical nature of armed conflicts demonstrates the power of insurgents, their strategic logic, and ability to adapt and be flexible, which gives them relative control over the conduct of armed conflicts. Whether displaced persons are fleeing conventional conflicts, such as Ukraine, asymmetric conflicts, such as Afghanistan and Iraq, or a combination of the two, such as Syria, is not an indication of their needs and entitlements under the Refugee Convention.

Overall, appellate authorities' understanding of ongoing conflicts in Afghanistan and Iraq through the lens of conventional warfare and territoriality does not accurately reflect the characteristics of contemporary armed conflicts. As argued in Chapter 2, adequately assessing the risk of persecution or serious harm on return to situations of armed conflict from a gender perspective as required by the general rule of interpretation in international law necessitates better understanding the realities of contemporary armed conflicts. In light of the present chapter's findings, effective protection would require a shift in assumptions and consideration of evidence that goes beyond the conventional warfare perspective currently adopted by appellate authorities. In practice, such a shift would involve an understanding and more detailed examination of the continuum of violence, the characteristics of armed groups, the parties' motivations, objectives, strategies, means and technological capacities, and the state's ability and willingness to protect through a gender lens. Chapters 5 and 6 will now evaluate how the conventional warfare perspective translates into judicial interpretation of the Refugee Convention definition.

621 Murray, *Military Adaptation in War* (n 560) 8–15.

622 UNAMA, annual reports on the 'Protection of Civilians in Armed Conflict' available at <https://unama.unmissions.org/protection-of-civilians-reports> accessed 12 July 2021.

5

Judicial Constructions of 'Well-Founded Fear of Being Persecuted' in Situations of Contemporary Armed Conflict

5.1 Introduction

Having explored how appellate authorities in the European Union (EU) conceptually consider situations of armed conflicts when determining asylum appeals in Chapter 4, this chapter examines how they interpret the first element of the Refugee Convention definition, namely the 'well-founded fear of being persecuted'. Despite general support for the proposition that the application and interpretation of the Refugee Convention definition is identical whether asylum applicants fear individual or group-based risks and that singling out is not a requirement of the Refugee Convention definition, this chapter demonstrates that appellate authorities in the EU continue to consistently interpret a 'well-founded fear of being persecuted' as requiring 'individual' risk in the sense that asylum appellants have been singled out for persecution and that this approach is tantamount to equating the standard of proof with the assessment of credibility. Appellate authorities' perception of armed conflicts through a conventional warfare lens and, consequently, that violence against civilians is indiscriminate and indirect, explored in Chapter 4, may partly explain the focus of judicial determination on past events and the assessment of credibility. However, this constitutes a major obstacle to refugee protection for persons fleeing situations of widespread violence in the context of armed conflicts, as the standard of proof is effectively conflated with the assessment of credibility.

This chapter starts by reviewing the law regarding the 'well-founded fear of being persecuted' element of the Refugee Convention definition. As persons at risk of violence in situations of armed conflict are likely to be fleeing in large numbers due to characteristics shared by many other similarly situated individuals, the discussion incorporates the notion of group-based risk of harm. Judicial misconceptions regarding the application of the Refugee Convention to persons fleeing armed conflicts is revealed as appellate authorities assess the widespread violence almost exclusively with regards to subsidiary protection rather than the Refugee Convention. In support of the proposition that the refugee definition does not require singling out, the enquiry turns to the interpretation of 'real risk' in European human rights law before setting out in more detail judicial practice of requiring singling out in the EU and more briefly how the assessment of credibility of appellants' accounts could be influenced by appellate authorities' rejection of any deviation from gender norms. Section 5.6 demonstrates how appellate authorities in the EU have unjustifiably heightened the standard of proof under the Refugee Convention by requiring appellants to meet a standard of 'concrete' risk.

5.2 'A Well-Founded Fear of Being Persecuted' and Widespread Violence

The Refugee Convention provides that a refugee is a person who,

> owing to well-founded fear of being persecuted for reasons of race, religion, nationality, membership of a particular social group or political opinion, is outside the country of his nationality and is unable or, owing to such fear, is unwilling to avail himself of the protection of that country.[623]

Zimmerman and Mahler have noted that assessing a person's fear entails a 'forward-looking expectation of risk'.[624] Although national jurisdictions define the risk test slightly differently, Hathaway and Foster suggest that there is broad agreement on the standard of proof in the Refugee Convention definition and they adopt the formulation of 'real chance'.[625] This is supported by United Nations High Commissioner for Refugees (UNHCR) that suggests persecution must be proved to be 'reasonably possible' to establish a well-founded fear of being persecuted.[626] The Court of Justice of the European Union (CJEU) has described the test as one of 'reasonable fear'.[627]

UNHCR has traditionally expressed the assessment of an asylum applicant's risk of being persecuted as both subjective (the applicant's perception of risk on return) and objective (based on the actual circumstances in the country of origin).[628] Despite this approach being adopted by many common law jurisdictions, Hathaway and Foster make the case that the concept of well-founded fear is inherently objective.[629] The European Asylum Support Office (EASO) suggested that the CJEU's approach is not to require a subjective fear in addition to the objective fear.[630] In any event, it is generally agreed that to undertake the assessment of fear there is a need to consider both the personal circumstances of the applicant and the conditions in the country of origin, including any situation of armed conflict.[631]

Furthermore, there is a broad consensus that past persecution is not required to demonstrate a well-founded fear of being persecuted because persons may be at risk on return without necessarily having been the subject of persecution in the past.[632] Nevertheless, past persecution may be relevant in demonstrating a continued fear of being persecuted.

623 Article 1A(2) Refugee Convention.

624 Andreas Zimmermann and Claudia Mahler, 'Article 1A, para. 2 (Definition of the Term Refugee)' in Zimmermann (ed), *The 1951 Convention Relating to the Status of Refugees* 341; see also UNHCR, Note on Burden and Standard of Proof in Refugee Claims, 16 December 1998, para 18.

625 For example, the terms 'reasonable possibility' (USA, Canada, South Africa), 'reasonable likelihood' (UK, Germany), 'serious possibility' (Canada), 'real chance' (Australia, New Zealand); see discussion in Hathaway and Foster, *The Law of Refugee Status* (n 20) 113–114.

626 UNHCR, Note on Burden and Standard of Proof (n 624) para 17.

627 Joined Cases C-175/08, C-176/08, C-178/08 and C-179/08 *Abdulla and others v Bundesrepublik Deutschland* [2011] QB 46, para 89; Joined Cases C-71/11 and C-99/11 *Bundesrepublik Deutschland v Y & Z* [2013] 1 CMLR 5, para 76; Joined Cases C-199/12 to C-201/12 *Minister voor Immigratie en Asiel v X, Y* and *Z v Minister voor Immigratie en Asiel* [2014] QB 1111, para 72.

628 UNHCR, *Handbook* (n 24) para 38.

629 Hathaway and Foster, *The Law of Refugee Status* (n 20) 92; Holzer also endorses this approach in Holzer, *Refugees from Armed Conflict* (n 22) 108.

630 EASO, 'Qualification for International Protection (Directive 2011/95/EU): A Judicial Analysis' December 2016 <www.easo.europa.eu/sites/default/files/QIP%20-%20JA.pdf> accessed 12 July 2021, 82. In 2022, the European Union Agency for Asylum replaced EASO with a wider mandate; see Regulation (EU) 2021/2303 of the European Parliament and of the Council of 15 December 2021 on the European Union Agency for Asylum and repealing Regulation (EU) No 439/2010.

631 Vincent Chetail, 'Armed Conflict and Forced Migration: A Systematic Approach to International Humanitarian Law, Refugee Law, and International Human Rights Law' in Andrew Clapham and Paola Gaeta (eds), *The Oxford Handbook of International Law in Armed Conflict* (OUP 2014) 722; Holzer, *Refugees from Armed Conflict* (n 22) 109.

632 UNHCR, Note on Burden and Standard of Proof (n 624) para 19.

The Qualification Directive establishes that if an asylum applicant can show that they have already been subject to persecution or serious harm or to direct threats of such persecution or such harm, this is considered 'a serious indication of the applicant's well-founded fear of persecution or real risk of suffering serious harm, unless there are good reasons to consider that such persecution or serious harm will not be repeated'.[633]

UNHCR considers that in situations of armed conflict it is more likely that entire groups are at risk of serious harm due to violence being widespread and the inability of weak states to provide protection, or due to the excessive exercise of force by states to supress the armed opposition.[634] However, the issue of whether persons fleeing from situations of armed conflict are refugees under the terms of the Refugee Convention continues to raise questions as asylum decision makers are reticent to award refugee protection to persons fleeing in large numbers.[635] Holzer has noted that decision makers frequently require individuals to be singled out for persecution and consider that fearing harm from the general conditions of violence in their country of origin does not amount to a well-founded fear of persecution.[636] As a result of this rationale, entire groups of individuals at risk in situations of widespread violence are excluded from refugee protection.[637]

However, as set out in Chapter 2, the historical development and context of international refugee law is rooted in group refugee situations and the Refugee Convention itself was adopted based on a need for protection of persons due to 'group-based risks'. Furthermore, there is a general agreement within refugee law scholarship that requiring refugees to be singled out for persecution has no basis in law. Grahl-Madsen originally articulated the proposition that the Refugee Convention definition does not require persecution to be 'individual' in the sense that the person has been personally targeted by actors of persecution, instead it merely requires a risk of sufficiently serious harm and a causal connection to a person's race, religion, nationality, membership of a particular social group or political opinion, irrespective of how many others are at risk of the same or similar measures.[638] Grahl-Madsen thus rejected the proposition which restricted the understanding of 'persecution' to 'direct' and 'individual' measures.[639]

As maintained by Hathaway, the text of the Refugee Convention in light of its context and purpose, the Convention's historical context, the logic of protection and practice in various jurisdictions do not justify such an approach.[640] The text of the Refugee Convention does not distinguish between times of peace or war and the drafters of the Convention had in mind that persons fleeing armed conflicts and violence may have a well-founded fear of being persecuted for a Convention reason.[641] The historical event preceding the adoption of the Refugee Convention was the end of the Second World War and thus persons fleeing situations of armed conflict were at the forefront of the drafters' minds.[642] The UNHCR

633 Article 4(4) Qualification Directive.
634 UNHCR, *Guidelines on International Protection No. 12* (n 5) para 19.
635 Hathaway and Foster, *The Law of Refugee Status* (n 20) 174.
636 Holzer, *Refugees from Armed Conflict* (n 22) 6.
637 Hathaway and Foster, *The Law of Refugee Status* (n 20) 174–175.
638 Grahl-Madsen, *The Status of Refugees in International Law* (n 470) 213; see also Hathaway, 'Refugee Status Arising from Generalized Oppression' (n 20); Jackson, *The Refugee Concept in Group Situations* (n 216).
639 Grahl-Madsen, *The Status of Refugees in International Law* (n 470) 213.
640 Hathaway, 'Refugee Status Arising from Generalized Oppression' (n 20).
641 UNHCR, *Summary Conclusions* (n 26) para 6.
642 Jackson, *The Refugee Concept in Group Situations* (n 216), see detailed discussion in Sections 2.3.1 and 2.3.2 in Chapter 2.

Guidelines on Claims for Refugee Status related to Situations of Armed Conflict and Violence also support an interpretation of the refugee definition which does not require persons fleeing armed conflict to be singled out or targeted for persecution. The Guidelines note that 'the fact that many or all members of particular communities are at risk does not undermine the validity of any particular individual's claim'.[643] UNHCR considers that the Refugee Convention should have an inclusive meaning in accordance with its primary purpose of providing international protection to all those who need it.[644]

Hathaway and Foster have argued that evidence of risk to persons similarly situated to an asylum claimant may be sufficient to demonstrate that the claimant has a well-founded fear of persecution.[645] They argue that once a group of persons, generally sharing racial, ethnic, religious, social or political characteristics, has been shown to suffer persecution in the claimant's country of origin, that claimant merely needs to establish inclusion in that group.[646] They thus conclude that if those two elements are established, the Refugee Convention definition does not require any additional condition, such as the claimant demonstrating a higher or differentiated risk to others similarly situated.[647] UNHCR has stressed that in a situation where many individuals may be similarly at risk, the focus of the enquiry by decision makers should remain on whether they have a well-founded fear of being persecuted for a Refugee Convention reason rather than whether a person is differentiated from the rest of those at risk.[648]

Although being singled out or individually targeted for persecution is not a condition of being recognised as a refugee, there are many instances of persons having a well-founded fear of persecution because they are personally targeted by actors of persecution. However, there are situations where entire groups of persons have a well-founded fear of persecution for a Refugee Convention reason because they share one or more personal characteristics such as sex, ethnicity, religion or political opinion without having been individually identified as a target for persecution. The former situation is described here as an 'individual risk' and the latter situation is described as one of 'group-based risk'. Nonetheless, members of groups at risk are also individually at risk in the sense of the Refugee Convention definition, meaning that each individual from the group is able to demonstrate that they are personally at risk, even if the reasons leading to the risk of harm are shared with many others and they have not personally been singled out. Thus, an individual risk of being persecuted as a precondition of refugee status is not synonymous with being singled out for persecution.

Both individual risks and group-based risks may arise in times of peace or in times of armed conflicts, although situations of widespread violence which characterise armed conflicts are likely to increase group-based risks.[649] Whether the risk of harm arises in situations of armed conflict or in times of peace thus does not alter the application and interpretation of the Refugee Convention definition although it may impact on its assessment and the type of evidence considered. More specifically, although the legal test remains the same irrespective of the conditions in the country of origin, demonstrating that one has been singled out is likely to involve evidence specific to the asylum applicant whereas the existence of a group-based risk may be established by evidence of the treatment of persons similarly

643 UNHCR, *Guidelines on International Protection No. 12* (n 5) para 17.

644 Türk, Edwards and Wouters, 'Introduction' (n 2) 21.

645 Hathaway and Foster, *The Law of Refugee Status* (n 20) 169. 646 Ibid., 170.

647 Ibid., 172. 648 Türk, Edwards and Wouters, 'Introduction' (n 2) 9.

649 UNHCR, *Guidelines on International Protection No. 12* (n 5) para 17.

situated who share the same personal characteristics such as sex, ethnicity, religion or political opinion or who are considered to share those same characteristics. Despite the general consensus within the refugee law literature that singling out is not required however, 'the circumstance(s) of persons fleeing war continues to challenge refugee law doctrine'.[650]

In the EU, the existence of a distinct subsidiary protection regime aimed at protecting civilians fleeing serious and individual threats to their life or person by reason of indiscriminate violence in situations of international or internal armed conflict has led appellate authorities to analyse the conditions in the country of origin, in particular the characteristics of armed conflict, almost exclusively under this complementary regime.[651] The limited number of cases in the sample overall in which appellate authorities considered the application of the Refugee Convention definition in light of the general situation of armed conflicts indicates that judicial misconception regarding the application of the Refugee Convention to persons fleeing armed conflicts continues to exist. As will be discussed in more detail in Section 5.4, appeals were generally fully determined under the Refugee Convention only where the assessment of the credibility of appellants' accounts led to the conclusion that they had been the subject of past persecution or experienced individual threats or targeting in the past. This trend shows that appellate authorities in the EU perpetuate the misconception that persons fleeing armed conflicts do not fall within the Refugee Convention definition in the absence of individual targeting or singling out. As large numbers of persons flee situations of armed conflicts that are characterised by widespread violence directed at particular groups sharing common characteristics but without having been singled out, this misconstruction of the Refugee Convention definition results in a failure to protect persons fleeing armed conflicts contrary to EU Member States' (MS's) obligations in international law.

5.3 Group-Based Risk of Harm in Complementary Protection

As noted, EU MS must determine an asylum application sequentially, by firstly assessing a person's entitlement to refugee status and only if this is refused, assessing whether they are eligible for subsidiary protection. Accordingly, asylum applicants generally claim that their removal from the territory of the contracting state would expose them to a risk of serious harm in addition to a risk of persecution for a Refugee Convention reason, and by extension, asylum decision makers are likely to consider different types of international protection within a single determination. The Qualification Directive provides for subsidiary protection where a person does not qualify as a refugee but in respect of whom substantial grounds have been shown for believing that the person concerned, if returned to their country of origin would face a real risk of suffering serious harm.[652] Article 15(b) of the Qualification Directive defines serious harm as 'torture or inhuman or degrading treatment or punishment of an applicant in the country of origin', which draws on EU MS's obligations under Article 3 of the European Convention on Human Rights (ECHR). Although the ECHR is relevant to international protection in a way that merely complements refugee protection,[653]

[650] Hathaway and Foster, *The Law of Refugee Status* (n 20) 177.

[651] Article 15(c) Qualification Directive.

[652] Articles 2(f) and 15 Qualification Directive.

[653] Article 2 and 3 Convention for the Protection of Human Rights and Fundamental Freedoms (adopted 4 November 1950, entered into force 3 September 1953) ETS No 005 as amended by Protocols 1 (ETS No 009), 4 (ETS No 046), 6 (ETS No 114), 7 (ETS No 117), 12 (ETS No 177), 13 (ETS No 187), 14 (STCE 194),

the jurisprudence of the European Court of Human Rights (ECtHR) is closely related to the development of international refugee law and national practice in interpreting the Refugee Convention definition. Durieux has highlighted the 'relative inter-penetration' between human rights norms and international refugee law.[654] This section explores how a real risk of serious harm has been interpreted in this jurisprudence because the test has either been considered stricter than or equivalent to the 'well-founded fear of being persecuted' and thus relevant to understand how appellate authorities in the EU are interpreting the law.

Article 3 ECHR states that 'no one shall be subjected to torture or to inhuman or degrading treatment or punishment'.[655] Article 3 ECHR has been partly incorporated into EU law as Article 15(b) Qualification Directive is closely based on Article 3 ECHR and defines 'serious harm' as 'torture or inhuman or degrading treatment or punishment of an applicant in the country of origin'. Consequently, asylum decision makers interpret international refugee law in the EU through a legal regime which incorporates different but complementary forms of protection, some of which are drawn from the ECHR, a regional human rights treaty. Any developments in the ECtHR's jurisprudence thus potentially influence how asylum decision makers apply and interpret the Refugee Convention definition. This section therefore briefly explores the legal standards established by the ECtHR in expulsion and extradition cases under Article 3 ECHR as relevant to asylum seekers and refugees, in particular regarding the requirement of 'individualised' risk of suffering treatment contrary to Article 3 ECHR on return to a person's country of origin. It concludes that the evolving jurisprudence of the ECtHR has now anchored the proposition that individuals may be able to demonstrate a risk of treatment contrary to Article 3 ECHR on return without the need to have been individually targeted or singled out. These cases generally arise where persons are fleeing widespread violence in situations of armed conflict.

National practice requiring persons to be singled out/individually targeted for persecution or to show a differential risk has led the ECtHR to consider whether the situation of armed conflict in the country of origin was such that a person would be at risk of treatment contrary to Article 3 ECHR due to their membership of a group defined by innate or fundamental characteristics or for reasons of severe levels of violence. The case of *Salah Sheekh v the Netherland* was brought before the ECtHR because the Dutch District Court (Rechtbank, Rb) applied the requirement of being singled out and thus had upheld the Dutch Immigration and Naturalisation Service's decision to refuse international protection. The Rb had found that the Somali applicant was not at risk of serious harm due to his membership of a minority clan because there was no unfavourable interest in him personally and the situation that led him to flee was due to 'the generally unstable (security) situation in Somalia, in which intimidation and insults by criminal groups regularly and arbitrarily occurred'.[656] Although the ECtHR's earlier case law required evidence that an applicant's

15 (CETS No 213) and 16 (CETS No 214) (ECHR) have been transposed into the subsidiary protection regime in the EU through Article 15(a) and 15(b) Qualification Directive.

654 Jean-François Durieux, 'Salah Sheekh Is a Refugee: New Insights into Primary and Subsidiary Forms of Protection' (2008) 49 *Refugee Studies Centre Working Paper Series* 11, 9.

655 Article 3 ECHR; for more information see Nuala Mole, *Asylum and the European Convention on Human Rights* (4th edn, Council of Europe 2007).

656 *Salah Sheekh v the Netherlands* (2007) 45 EHRR 50, para 35; see the Dutch government's submissions at para 131 of the judgment; see also analysis in Durieux, 'Salah Sheekh is a Refugee' (n 654) 11–12.

personal position was worse than the generality of other members of their community,[657] the ECtHR changed its approach in *Salah Sheekh* to ensure that the protection offered by Article 3 ECHR was not illusory.[658] The ECtHR thus established that in situations of widespread violence applicants are not required to show further distinguishing features over and above others affected by the general situation of insecurity.[659] In this case, the Court concluded that the Netherlands would breach Article 3 ECHR if it returned the applicant to Somalia because his membership of a minority clan from Somalia and the general treatment of this minority were in themselves sufficient to demonstrate a real risk on return.[660] Significantly, Durieux has pointed out that as Salah Sheekh was at risk of serious harm for reasons of his ethnicity as a minority clan member, he was in fact a refugee.[661]

In later cases where the ECtHR considered situations where certain groups may be at risk of treatment contrary to Article 3 ECHR in light of the general situation in the country of origin, the Court found that where there are 'serious reasons to believe' a group is 'systematically exposed to a practice of ill-treatment', and applicants can show membership of that group,[662] no 'further special distinguishing features are required'.[663] This group-based risk approach demonstrates that the ECtHR does not consider it a requirement of the protective scope of Article 3 ECHR that persons be individually singled out for ill-treatment.

This claim is further supported by the ECtHR's consideration of cases where applicants claim to be at risk of ill-treatment due to reasons unconnected to their personal characteristics but rather because of the situation of widespread violence that often characterises armed conflicts. Thus, the ECtHR has established that return may breach Article 3 ECHR provided it can be shown that widespread violence in the country of origin is characterised by a sufficient level of intensity.[664] The reasoning for this approach is to ensure that protection under Article 3 ECHR is not illusory and to reflect the absolute nature of the right.[665] Thus, the issue to be determined by the ECtHR remains the same in all types of cases, namely whether 'in all the circumstances of the case before it, substantial grounds have been shown for believing that the person concerned, if returned, would face a real risk of being subjected to treatment contrary to Article 3 of the Convention'.[666]

The ECtHR's jurisprudence in this area supports the proposition that if a person is a member of a group and if there is evidence of systematic human rights violations of that group's members or widespread violence is sufficiently severe in the country of origin, there is no need to show any further distinguishing personal characteristics or individual circumstances in addition to those which situate the person within that group. Indeed, Vedsted-Hansen notes that the case of *Vilvarajah* was not in fact authority for the proposition that there was ever a need for showing 'special distinguishing features' as this would be contrary to the absolute prohibition of treatment contrary to Article 3 ECHR.[667] He further suggests that *Salah Sheekh* was not a change of approach by the ECtHR but merely a reiteration of the principle set out in *Vilvarajah* which had failed on the specific facts of that case. In other

657 *Vilvarajah and Others v the United Kingdom* (1992) 14 EHRR 248, para 111.

658 *Salah Sheekh v the Netherlands* (n 656) para 148. 659 Ibid.

660 Ibid. 661 Durieux, 'Salah Sheekh Is a Refugee' (n 654) 13.

662 *N.A. v the United Kingdom* (2009) 48 EHRR 15, para 116. 663 Ibid., para 117.

664 Ibid., paras 115–116. 665 *Sufi and Elmi v the United Kingdom* (8319/07) [2011] ECHR 1045, para 217.

666 Ibid., para 218.

667 Jens Vedsted-Hansen, 'European Non-Refoulement Revisited' (2010) 55 *Scandinavian Studies in Law* 269, 276.

words, the claims brought by the applicants in *Vilvarajah* were unsuccessful not because they had not been singled out but because there was insufficient evidence of the group to which they belonged (young male Tamil returnees) being systematically ill-treated by the authorities.[668] Where there is sufficient evidence of systematic ill-treatment of a group of persons, the entire group is equally entitled to protection from *refoulement* and the legal test cannot be more onerous. Alternatively, where applicants have a number of individual characteristics, which taken by themselves do not meet the required threshold of real risk but do when considered cumulatively in the context of widespread violence in situations of armed conflict, the standard may be met. The need to place appropriate weight to the general situation in the country of origin is derived from the obligation to take into account all relevant circumstances.[669] Where the general situation of violence in the country of origin is not such that anyone is at risk or members of particular groups are systematically ill-treated, it is likely that an individual will be required to show more specific proof that they are individually at risk.[670] However, this does not entail a requirement of singling out per se.

There are relatively few cases which the ECtHR has decided based on the general situation of violence and insecurity in the country of origin. Even fewer cases have been decided in relation to whether a person is at risk of gender-based violence on return due to the situation of widespread violence. In 2010, the ECtHR considered the general situation of women in Afghanistan. The ECtHR referred to the objective evidence which demonstrated that 80 per cent of women in Afghanistan were affected by domestic violence and that a recent law, although not yet implemented, requires women to comply with their husbands' sexual requests and to obtain permission to leave the home except in emergencies. The ECtHR referred to the lack of state protection because seeking protection from public authorities was itself likely to lead to ill-treatment from their families.[671] The ECtHR thus noted:

> That there are no specific circumstances in the present case substantiating that the applicant will be subjected to such treatment by X, but the Court cannot ignore the general risk indicated by statistic and international reports.[672]
>
> Women are at particular risk of ill-treatment in Afghanistan if perceived as not conforming to the gender roles ascribed to them by society, tradition and even the legal system.[673]

Thus, this case demonstrates that under the ECHR if the risk of serious harm cannot be established by reference to the individual circumstances of the applicant alone, consideration of the general conditions in the country of origin becomes the main context of analysis. In this case, the applicant's status as a woman was sufficient to demonstrate a real risk of treatment contrary to Article 3 ECHR. This contrasts with appellate authorities' application of the Refugee Convention definition to group-based risks, including women as a group at risk, which will be discussed in Chapter 6.

[668] Ibid., 278.

[669] *Sufi and Elmi v the United Kingdom* (n 665) para 130; see discussion in Section 2.3 in Chapter 2.

[670] See the typology proposed by Tsourdi as follows: (i) where levels of violence are so high that *anyone* is at risk on return; (ii) where the general situation is such that particular groups are systematically exposed to ill-treatment, it is sufficient to show membership in that group; and (iii) other situations may require applicants to show that they are personally at risk, Tsourdi, 'What Protection for Persons Fleeing Indiscriminate Violence?' (n 352) 280–282.

[671] *N v Sweden* [2011] Imm AR 38, para 57. [672] Ibid., para 58. [673] Ibid., para 55.

In 2015, the ECtHR considered for the third time whether the general situation in Mogadishu was characterised by violence of such intensity that anyone in that city would face a real risk of treatment contrary to Article 3 ECHR.[674] Despite finding that the general security situation in Mogadishu remained serious and fragile, the ECtHR did not consider the situation had deteriorated since September 2013 when it had last considered the general security situation and thus not everyone returned there would be at risk of treatment contrary to Article 3 ECHR.[675] The ECtHR recognised, however, that the applicant in the present case had different personal characteristics as she was a woman born in 1988 who had left Somalia aged seventeen and the applicant in the earlier case was a man born in 1960.[676] Looking at the general treatment of women in Somalia, the ECtHR concluded 'that a single woman returning to Mogadishu without access to protection from a male network would face a real risk of living in conditions constituting inhuman or degrading treatment under Article 3 of the Convention'.[677] Although reliance on non-state actors of protection when women fear gender-based violence has been criticised,[678] the ECtHR is consistent in its approach to group-based risk, in this case the group being defined by sex, in light of the general situation in the country of origin, including that society's gender norms.

The case law of the ECtHR discussed demonstrates that *non-refoulement* under the ECHR is not dependent on the applicant being singled out/individually targeted or demonstrating a risk over and above other similarly situated persons. Provided substantial grounds have been shown for believing that the person concerned, if returned, would face a real risk of being subjected to treatment contrary to Article 3 ECHR, *refoulement* is prohibited even if large groups of persons are ill-treated because of shared characteristics such as sex or where there is a situation of widespread violence in the context of armed conflicts placing everyone at risk. European human rights law in this respect supports the proposition that singling out or individual targeting is not a requirement to be recognised as a refugee under the Refugee Convention. Although state practice varies regarding whether the standard of proof is the same under the Refugee Convention and international human rights instruments, no jurisdiction is adopting a stricter test under the Refugee Convention.[679] Moreover, there is scholarly support from authors such as Gorlick, McAdam and Mariño Menéndez for the

[674] *R.H. v Sweden* (2018) 67 EHRR 22. [675] *K.A.B. v Sweden* [2014] Imm AR 371.

[676] *R.H. v Sweden* (n 674) para 69. [677] Ibid., para 70.

[678] Christel Querton, 'The Role of the European Court of Human Rights in the Protection of Women Fleeing Gender-Based Violence in their Home Countries' (2017) 7 *Feminists @ Law*. <https://journals.kent.ac.uk/index.php/feministsatlaw/article/view/425> accessed 18 March 2023; Christel Querton, 'Non-State Actors of Protection and the Sliding Scale of Protection for Refugee Women' (2022) 41(3) *Refugee Survey Quarterly* 444.

[679] For UK practice establishing that the standard of proof is the same under both legal regimes, see STARRED *Kacaj (Article 3, Standard of Proof, Non-State Actors) Albania* [2001] UKIAT 00018, para 10 (although the decision was successfully appealed this was on the basis of the assessment of facts rather than any issue with the legal findings, see *Kacaj v Secretary of State for the Home Department* [2002] EWCA Civ 314; the findings were also endorsed in *Dhima v Immigration Appeal Tribunal* [2002] EWHC 80). For practice in Canada and the USA where the 'well-founded fear' test under the Refugee Convention is deemed lower than the 'personal, real and foreseeable risk' test of Article 3 CAT, see the discussion in Jane McAdam, 'Australian Complementary Protection: A Step-by-Step Approach' (2011) 33 *Sydney Law Review* 687, 719–720. McAdam claims that the subsidiary protection standard of proof in the Qualification Directive is higher than the 'well-founded fear' test, see McAdam, *Complementary Protection in International Refugee Law* (n 8) 62; Hathaway and Foster, however, claim that the standard of proof under the Refugee Convention, expressed in slightly different forms in the USA, Canada, South Africa, the UK, Germany, Australia and New Zealand, are largely interchangeable, see Hathaway and Foster, *The Law of Refugee Status* (n 20) 113.

proposition that the test is and should be the same.[680] Hence, there is no suggestion in state practice or academic opinion that the standard of proof in the Refugee Convention definition is more onerous than under other complementary forms of protection. Accordingly, if singling out is not a requirement under the ECHR, it cannot logically be applied in the interpretation of the Refugee Convention definition, which has a similar or lower standard of proof. Applying this perspective implies that evidence that members of a group sharing common characteristics are being exposed to sufficiently serious harm should serve as a satisfactory indication that a member of that group has a well-founded fear of being persecuted for a Refugee Convention reason without the need for further personal distinguishing characteristics or individual instances of direct confrontations with actors of persecution. This would demonstrate that there is a real chance that the individual concerned has a well-founded fear of being persecuted on return to their country of origin.[681]

5.4 The Requirement of Singling Out in the Judicial Practice of EU MS

This study demonstrates that the issue of the differential risk approach, namely a requirement of being at risk over and above those who are similarly situated in a situation of widespread violence, is not explicitly raised. In other words, there were no instances where appellate authorities acknowledged that all members of a particular group sharing common characteristics were at risk yet required that appellants demonstrate a risk over and above other members of the group. However, asylum appellate authorities consider it necessary that appellants demonstrate individual targeting or singling out by actors of persecution in order to be recognised as refugees. In effect, this means that there may be cases where a group-based risk exists based on that group's actual or perceived characteristic(s), yet members of that group are refused refugee status if they have not been singled out. The requirement of singling out was confirmed in judicial practice in Belgium, Denmark, France and the UK, and in a less explicit way in the Netherlands and Spain.

As noted, developments in the EU subsidiary protection regime influence the application and interpretation of the Refugee Convention definition where persons are fleeing from armed conflicts. Hence, the CJEU's jurisprudence regarding Article 15(c) will to some extent implicitly influence judicial interpretation of the refugee definition, in particular since both refugee protection and subsidiary protection are considered as part of a single determination. Although, the CJEU in *Elgafaji* used the terminology of being 'specifically targeted' when it concluded that the application of Article 15(c) is 'not subject to the condition that that applicant adduce evidence that he is *specifically targeted* by reason of factors particular to his personal circumstances',[682] the case is not authority for the proposition that by juxtaposition, refugees must be specifically targeted. The CJEU was concerned there with explaining the apparent tension between the notions of 'individual threat' and 'indiscriminate

[680] Brian Gorlick, 'Human Rights and Refugees: Enhancing Protection through International Human Rights Law' (2000) 69 *Nordic Journal of International Law* 117, 154; McAdam, 'Australian Complementary Protection' (n 679); Fernando M. Mariño Menéndez, 'Recent Jurisprudence of the United Nations Committee against Torture and the International Protection of Refugees' (2015) 34 *Refugee Survey Quarterly* 61, 67–68.

[681] As per the characterisation of the well-founded fear of being persecuted test adopted by Hathaway and Foster in *The Law of Refugee Status* (n 20) 114.

[682] *Elgafaji v Staatssecretaris van Justitie* (n 435) para 43 (emphasis added).

violence' and the language used merely indicates that beneficiaries of subsidiary protection do not need to demonstrate any particular reasons for the risk of serious harm. Indeed, in later cases concerning refugee protection, the CJEU does not refer to any notion of being targeted. In a preliminary reference ruling concerning cessation of refugee status under the Qualification Directive,[683] the CJEU reiterated the definition of a refugee as set out in Article 2(c) Qualification Directive and noted that 'the national concerned must therefore, on account of circumstances existing in his country of origin, have a well-founded fear of being *personally the subject of persecution* for at least one of the five reasons listed in the Directive and the Geneva Convention'.[684] The personal element of the well-founded fear, in other words the individual risk, is here again linked to the reasons for persecution. Thus, there is a difference between a requirement of targeting or singling out and a requirement of persecution on discriminatory grounds as defined in the Refugee Convention reasons for persecution. The practice of appellate authorities suggests, however, that the CJEU's jurisprudence may have been read as an indication of the former rather than the latter.

In France, the jurisprudence of the highest court, the Council of State (Conseil d'État, CE), sets out that to meet the requirements of the refugee definition a person must have a current and personal fear in relation to persecution of a certain severity.[685] Judicial practice in France can explicitly be traced back to the CJEU's ruling in *Elgafaji*. Initially, the CE adopted word for word the CJEU's interpretation of Article 15(c) that an applicant for subsidiary protection does not need to show that he is 'specifically targeted by reason of factors particular to his personal circumstances'.[686] Thus, in the case of *Baskarathas*, the CE set out that 'the existence of a serious, direct and individual threat to the life or person of an applicant for subsidiary protection is not subject to the condition that the applicant demonstrates that he is specifically targeted because of factors related to his personal situation'.[687] In turn, the wording of *Baskarathas* is invariably repeated by the French National Asylum Court (Cour Nationale du Droit d'Asile, CNDA) in its judgments after it dismisses appeals under the Refugee Convention because the personal account of past persecution or instances of conflict with actors of persecution is found not credible. In this construction of its written judgments and its emphasis on the absence of the need to be 'specifically targeted' under Article 15(c) Qualification Directive, the CNDA is creating a dichotomy between establishing whether appellants have been singled out, failing which entitlement to subsidiary protection is considered.

The Danish Refugee Appeals Board's (Flygtningenævnet, DRAB's) approach in determining asylum appeals is to enquire whether there has been a particular confrontation putting

[683] The CJEU set out the first preliminary reference question as 'whether Article 11(1)(e) of the Directive is to be interpreted as meaning that refugee status ceases to exist if the circumstances which justified the refugee's fear of persecution for one of the reasons referred to in Article 2(c) of the Directive, on the basis of which refugee status was granted, no longer exist and the refugee has no other reason to fear being "persecuted" within the meaning of Article 2(c) of the Directive', *Abdulla and others v Bundesrepublik Deutschland* (n 627) para 55.

[684] *Abdulla and others v Bundesrepublik Deutschland* (n 627) paras 56–57 (emphasis added); see also Case C–472/13 *Shepherd v Germany* [2015] QB 799, para 24.

[685] CE, Les Dossiers Thématiques du Conseil d'État: Le Judge Administratif et le Droit d'Asile, January 2016 <www.conseil-etat.fr/ressources/etudes-publications/dossiers-thematiques/le-juge-administratif-et-le-droit-d-asile> accessed 12 July 2021, 13–14.

[686] *Elgafaji v Staatssecretaris van Justitie* (n 435) para 43; see also para 30.

[687] France (FR): CE, *Office Français de Protection des Réfugiés et Apatrides c/M. Baskarathas*, N° 320295, 03.07.2009.

appellants personally in conflict with actors of persecution or serious harm. The focus of the Board's investigation on past facts reveals that a risk of persecution or serious harm will arise only in cases where appellants have been in direct conflict with actors of persecution or serious harm leading to their identification and singling out by those actors. Where appellants claim to be at risk from the authorities, an analysis of the Board's decisions shows that there is a requirement to be of particular interest to the authorities in order to demonstrate a well-founded fear of individual persecution.[688] For example, the Board dismissed the appeal of a Syrian woman who had received a threatening letter from Shabiha at her office where she worked as a school guidance councillor. The Board noted that irrespective of the threatening letter left at her office, the appellant had not established that the threat was directed against her personally.[689] In another case, the Board concluded that despite her son's work as an ambulance driver who had helped the rebels, the appellant had not personally had any problems with the authorities or non-state actors in Syria.[690] The Board also refused the appeal of a young Afghan orphan as it concluded that there was no risk of forced recruitment from the Taliban because he had not had any conflict with the Taliban.[691]

The Board's practice in relation to upgrade appeals where appellants were granted Temporary Protection Status indicates how it conceptualises the difference between refugee status and complementary protection. In these cases, determination by the Board entails a consideration of whether there have been specific individual instances of conflict between appellants and actors of persecution, failing which appellants retain their Temporary Protection Status. Furthermore, the practice of the Board shows that persons belonging to a group, of whose members many have been persecuted, is insufficient to be awarded refugee status and individuals must demonstrate that they will 'most likely personally be subjected to persecution'.[692] Equally, where appellants based their asylum claim on the high level of widespread violence, the Board required them to have been singled out by actors of persecution.[693] As an example, the Board dismissed the upgrade appeal brought by a Kurdish Yazidi man from Aleppo on the basis that his spouse and children lived in Aleppo where there were a lot of Kurds and where his sons could get a job because the family was not individually pursued in Aleppo.[694]

The UK First-Tier Tribunal (FTT) adopts a similar approach whereby it juxtaposes 'general' risks with 'direct' risks that arise only if there has been any singling out.[695] Thus, the FTT concluded that an appellant from Kirkuk was not at risk on return as it was not accepted

[688] In Danish the term used is '*i myndigheders søgelys*', the literal translation of which is 'in the authorities' searchlight'. In Pia Lynggaard Justesen, 'Denmark' in Jean-Yves Carlier et al. (eds), *Who Is a Refugee? A Comparative Case Law Study* (Kluwer Law International 1997) 306, it is described as 'the limelight of the authorities'; see for example Denmark (DK): DRAB 02.10.2015 (Syria); or 'the limelight' of various non-state actors DK: DRAB 07.06.2016 (Syria): YPG; DK: DRAB 12.08.2013 (Syria): Shabiha.

[689] DK: DRAB 12.08.2013 (Syria). [690] DK: DRAB 25.09.2013 (Syria).

[691] DK: DRAB 20.05.2014 (Afghanistan).

[692] Justesen, 'Denmark' (n 688) 305, although she continues by stating that 'on the other hand, it is not required that the asylum seekers be "singled out" for persecution'. However, it is difficult to see how a person must show that they will personally be at risk without also needing to show that they have been 'singled out'.

[693] See for example DK: DRAB 25.02.2016 (Syria); DK: DRAB 12.08.2013 (Syria).

[694] DK: DRAB February 2016 in DRAB Annual Report 2016, p 121; see also DK: DRAB 28.06.2013 (Syria).

[695] UK: FTT(IAC) 08.11.2016 (Syria); UK: FTT(IAC) 14.12.2013 (Iraq); UK: FTT(IAC) 22.07.2013 (Iraq).

that 'he is under threat from Daesh or ISIS. He never personally encountered any difficulty with or from Daesh.'[696] Although accepting that a Kurdish appellant originated from Fallujah which was occupied by the Islamic State of Iraq and Syria (ISIS) and characterised as a 'contested area', the FTT did not deem his account of ISIS approaching his family to recruit him credible and thus concluded that he 'had no direct contact with ISIS and had no problems with them directly. His fear on which he based his claim for asylum, is a general one and is based on the fear of that organisation and its barbarity in general.'[697] His appeal was therefore dismissed under the Refugee Convention.

The Spanish National High Court (Audiencia Nacional, AN) also appears to require particular instances of (recent) past persecution to meet the criteria of the refugee definition. It required appellants to demonstrate a particular (political) profile and accordingly dismissed the appeal of a Syrian national on the basis that he had merely alleged a 'feeling of displeasure and humiliation' as a Kurd, in relation to poverty, racism and the political situation, but he had not been detained a second time and there were no other facts that could put him at risk.[698] In refusing appeals on safe third-country grounds, the AN noted that the general situation in Syria meant that 'despite not having suffered persecution in the required terms by the Convention' the grant of subsidiary protection was appropriate. The AN concluded that the appellants' cases were to be distinguished from the jurisprudence of the Supreme Court leading to the grant of refugee status because they had left Syria before the start of the conflict to look for work and had not therefore been the 'object of persecution'.[699] In summarising the principles established by the CJEU in *Shepherd*, the AN notes, amongst other criteria, that 'there must be a situation of persecution regarding the applicant'.[700] Thus, in cases where Syrian appellants had left Syria prior to the start of the conflict and lived in a third country such as Morocco or Algeria before seeking international protection in Spain, the Court noted that 'the allegations made are generic and imprecise and there has been no proof of a risk of persecution to the applicants so that they may fear for their lives or for the free exercise of their fundamental rights'.[701] In the appeal of an Afghan Hazara who expressed a fear of persecution by the Taliban, the AN concluded that he had provided no evidence of being attacked by the Taliban when he refused to tell them who in his village was keeping weapons.[702]

As discussed in Section 5.3, it was the Dutch practice of requiring singling out as a condition of the Refugee Convention definition which resulted in Mr Salah Sheekh's application before the ECtHR. According to this approach, the general situation of widespread violence in Somalia was insufficient to meet the test for refugee protection.[703] Although the ECtHR rejected this approach,[704] the Dutch government continues to require the individual

[696] UK: FTT(IAC) 06.10.2016 (Iraq). [697] UK: FTT(IAC) 14.10.2016 (Iraq).

[698] Spain (ES): AN SAN 3336/2013 15.07.2013 (Syria).

[699] ES: AN SAN 3492/2016 19.09.2016 (Syria) – Algeria as safe third country; ES: AN SAN3235/2016 06.07.2016 (Syria) – Morocco as safe third country; see also ES: AN SAN 4350/2016 18.11.2016 (Syria); ES: AN SAN 4395/2016 17.11.2016 (Syria); ES: AN SAN 4083/2016 25.10.2016 (Syria); ES: AN SAN 3937/2016 17.10.2016 (Syria); ES: AN SAN 3839/2016 17.10.2016 (Syria) – citing at length the judgment in ES: AN SAN 3235/2016 06.07.2016 (Syria) – Morocco as safe third country.

[700] ES: AN SAN 4083/2016 25.10.216 (Syria); ES: AN SAN 3837/2016 17.10.2016 (Syria); ES: AN SAN 3839/2016 17.10.2016 (Syria); see discussion of *Shepherd* (n 1208).

[701] ES: AN SAN 4433/2016 29.11.2016 (Syria). [702] ES: AN SAN 5686/2013 26.12.2013 (Afghanistan).

[703] *Salah Sheekh v the Netherlands* (n 656) para 131.

[704] Ibid., para 148; see also *N.A. v the United Kingdom* (n 662) paras 116–117.

targeting of asylum claimants. For example, despite accepting that teachers in Iraq are in a risk category, the Secretary of State noted this was insufficient by itself to demonstrate a well-founded fear of persecution.[705] Although the Rb did not explicitly state the requirement, practice showed that where appellants' account of events in their country of origin was found not credible, the Court did not consider that appellants' personal characteristics such as ethnicity, religion or being wealthy were sufficient on their own to create a well-founded fear of being persecuted.[706] For example, the Court found that the Secretary of State had sufficiently motivated its decision when it found that the appellant had not demonstrated he would actually be sought out by the Syrian authorities.[707] Hence, although the approach was not as explicit as in the judicial practice of other EU MS discussed in this section, the approach of the Rb does suggest a similar expectation of individual targeting and singling out.[708]

The trend identified reflects the imposition of a requirement that individual appellants have been personally singled out by actors of persecution, which does not reflect an interpretation of the Refugee Convention in accordance with international refugee law or EU law. In effect, as appellate authorities' determination of asylum appeals under the Refugee Convention ended when accounts of individual instances of interactions with actors of persecution were found not credible, refugee protection was closely related with the assessment of credibility. However, an appropriate application and interpretation of the Refugee Convention would necessitate further examination of whether, irrespective of negative credibility findings, evidence regarding the treatment of persons sharing the same personal characteristics (as established or attributed) demonstrates a well-founded fear of being persecuted for reasons of race, religion, nationality, membership of a particular social group or political opinion. Section 5.5 briefly explores the particular problems that arise from the overlap of gender norms and the assessment of credibility.

5.5 Credibility and Gendered Norms in Situations of Armed Conflict

Chapter 3 highlighted how both men and women are subject to expectations of gender conformist behaviour and that this is linked to violence in situations of armed conflict. Appellate authorities display some awareness of these gender dynamics. Whereas at first sight this may suggest that appellate authorities are alert to the relevance of gender in situations of armed conflict, those gendered expectations are applied rigidly such that departure from these norms will generally result in the individual account being considered not credible. Two examples of gendered expectations are explored in this section.

The gendered expectation that boys and young men follow the political inclinations of their fathers, uncles or other male relatives is addressed first. Provided that appellants' accounts of events are accepted, appellate authorities are prepared to find that a political opinion will be imputed to sons or male relatives, resulting in a risk of persecution. Thus, 10 per cent of appeals resulting in refugee protection were linked to the Refugee Convention

705 The Netherlands (NL): Rb AWB 14/12004 25.08.2014 (Iraq).

706 NL: Rb AWB 15/18833 19.11.2015 (Iraq); NL: Rb AWB 14/12313, AWB 14/12311 20.06.2014 (Iraq); NL: Rb AWB 13/24160, AWB 13/24159 11.10.2013 (Iraq); NL: Rb AWB 13/21790, AWB 13/21789 13.09.2013 (Iraq).

707 NL: Rb AWB 16/9070, AWB 16/9066 25.05.2016 (Syria).

708 See for an explicit example NL: Rb AWB 16/11308 21.10.2016 (Afghanistan).

reason of imputed political opinion because 'political opinion will commonly be imputed from one's father's opinion' as young men and boys are supposed to follow their fathers' decisions in respect of their political involvement.[709] However, where individual accounts differed from those gendered dynamics, namely where younger male generations refused to align themselves with their male relatives' political preferences, appellate authorities found their accounts not credible on the basis of those expectations. Thus, appellate authorities made negative credibility assessments on the basis that appellants' accounts were not consistent with the expectation that young boys and men usually follow their fathers' political alignment.[710]

Another illustration of gendered expectations relates to women living in countries where women's rights are limited, including not having access to any form of property. Thus, where women had fled their country of origin by accessing funds or property, this was considered by appellate authorities as an indication that they had the support of their family and hence that their account of serious harm from family members was not credible.[711] There was nonetheless an example of good practice where the Rb allowed an appeal because it was unreasonable for the Secretary of State to conclude that an Afghan woman taking the initiative to start an extramarital relationship was implausible due to the harsh penalties.[712]

Although both these types of cases demonstrate that appellate authorities may be aware of the existence of gendered norms in societies where appellants come from, these norms are considered fixed. Considering gender-related norms as inflexible means that any gender-diverging behaviour (for example boys and young men adopting different political views to their male family members or women having access to funds) is considered by appellate authorities as constituting evidence that the account is not credible and results in the Refugee Convention appeal being dismissed. The approach of appellate authorities in these cases illustrates the interplay between their reliance on fixed expectations of male or female behaviour in situations of armed conflict and the requirement of appellants having been personally singled out by actors of persecution.

Practice across EU MS has thus erroneously elevated evidence of being singled out into a legal criterion for the existence of a well-founded fear of being persecuted. Although previous work has shown this was an issue, the methodological approach to this study demonstrates that the practice continues to prevail in the EU. As a result, unless persons seeking international protection have previously experienced personal instances of conflict with actors of persecution in their country of origin, they are unlikely to be awarded refugee status, particularly if they have fled from situations of armed conflict characterised by widespread violence. The 'well-founded fear of being persecuted' test has become conflated with the assessment of credibility, which itself can be highly gendered. Accordingly, the standard of proof under the Refugee Convention is heightened, contrary to international refugee law.

[709] UK: FTT(IAC) 15.09.2014 (Afghanistan); see also FR: CNDA 12034053 09.04.2013 (Afghanistan); FR: CNDA 15007217/15007216 15.07.2015 (Iraq); UK: FTT(IAC) 24.11.2016 (Afghanistan); UK: FTT(IAC) 03.10.2013 (Afghanistan).

[710] UK: FTT(IAC) 21.04.2016 (Afghanistan); UK: FTT(IAC) 14.12.2013 (Iraq).

[711] UK: FTT(IAC) 12.09.2016 (Iraq): appellant able to save her wages; UK: FTT(IAC) 19.02.2015 (Iraq): appellant had access to money and gold from her dowry (first marriage); see also DK: DRAB 13.05.2016 (Afghanistan).

[712] NL: Rb AWB 16/7907, AWB 16/7908 30.05.2016 (Afghanistan).

5.6 A Heightened Standard of Proof: The Requirement of Concrete Risk in the Judicial Practice of EU MS

The analysis of judicial approaches to the 'well-founded fear of being persecuted' indicates that appellate authorities apply a higher standard of proof than is warranted under the Refugee Convention when determining the asylum appeals of persons fleeing armed conflicts. As noted earlier, the 'well-founded fear' element of the refugee definition denotes an objective test understood as a forward-looking expectation of risk, and past persecution is not a requirement of meeting the test although it is an indicator of future risk.

The study reveals that appellate authorities consistently use the term 'concrete' in assessing the risk and fear of persecution on return,[713] suggesting a standard of proof higher than the low standard warranted in international refugee law. When determining the appeals of persons fleeing armed conflicts, appellate authorities invariably connect the term 'concrete' to past instances of persecution or threats of persecution and evidence but also more generally the future risk and fear of persecution on return. In this way, the 'well-founded fear of being persecuted' criterion in the Refugee Convention definition is equated to a concrete risk of persecution. The *Cambridge English Dictionary* defines the adjective 'concrete' as 'clear and certain, or real and existing in a form that can be seen or felt' and the *Thesaurus* gives the term 'certainty' as a synonym.[714] There is a clear difference between a requirement of a concrete risk of persecution and the need to show that persecution is 'reasonably possible'.[715] Thus, the practice of appellate authorities in the EU in appeals brought by persons fleeing armed conflicts demonstrates the application of a higher standard of proof than warranted under international refugee law. Yet rather than making a claim under the Refugee Convention less likely, the impact of widespread violence in situations of armed conflict may increase the risk of persecution and serious harm and the lack of state protection.[716]

In the jurisprudence of the Belgian Court (Belgian Council for Alien Law Litigation, CCE/RvV), regular references are made to the appellant not having had 'concrete problems' in the country of origin,[717] to the conclusion that the appellant did not have a 'concrete and individual fear' on return,[718] there were no 'concrete indications' that the appellant would be personally targeted,[719] the appellant must show 'in concrete terms' that they personally run a risk of forced recruitment,[720] the fear of persecution must be demonstrated in 'concrete terms',[721] the risk must be demonstrated 'in concrete',[722] the fear of persecution or real risk of serious harm must be demonstrated 'in concrete',[723] and the fear of persecution must be shown 'in concrete terms'.[724] The French Court (CNDA) also referred regularly to the test amounting to a concrete risk of persecution when it noted

[713] FR: CNDA 16024450/16024449 15.12.2016 (Iraq); FR: CNDA 15027724 11.04.2016 (Iraq); Belgium (BE): RvV 165 409 08.04.2016 (Afghanistan); BE: RvV 154 649 15.10.2015 (Afghanistan); BE: RvV 147 398 08.06.2015 (Afghanistan); BE: RvV 142 056 27.03.2015 (Syria); BE: RvV 131 607 17.10.2014 (Afghanistan); BE RvV 122 391 11.04.2014 (Afghanistan); BE: RvV 116 849 14.01.2014 (Afghanistan); BE: RvV 114 377 25.11.2013 (Afghanistan); ES: AN SAN 5539/2013 12.12.2013 (Syria); ES: AN SAN 2221/2013 22.05.2013 (Syria).

[714] *Cambridge Advanced Learner's Dictionary and Thesaurus* <https://dictionary.cambridge.org/dictionary/english/concrete> accessed 12 July 2021.

[715] UNHCR, Note on Burden and Standard of Proof (n 624) para 17.

[716] Türk, Edwards and Wouters, 'Introduction' (n 2) 9; UNHCR, *Summary Conclusions* (n 26) para 8.

[717] BE: RvV 163 585 08.03.2016 (Syria).

[718] BE: RvV 142 056 27.03.2015 (Syria).

[719] BE: RvV 165 409 08.04.2016 (Afghanistan).

[720] BE: RvV 147 398 08.06.2015 (Afghanistan).

[721] BE: RvV 116 849 14.01.2014 (Afghanistan).

[722] BE: RvV 154 640 15.10.2015 (Afghanistan).

[723] BE: RvV 131 607 17.10.2014 (Afghanistan).

[724] BE: RvV 114 377 25.11.2013 (Afghanistan).

that the appellant did not 'concretely present the threats' directed at them,[725] and that the appellant's account lacked any 'concrete element'.[726] In Denmark, DRAB found that there was no 'concrete risk' of being exposed to serious harm because the appellant had not received any further threats since leaving Iraq,[727] the appellants had not established that on return there would be a concrete and individual risk of persecution,[728] there was a 'concrete and individual risk of persecution' as the appellant had been issued a military book,[729] and the appellant had not established that they would be at risk of persecution due to 'individual and concrete conditions'.[730] In Denmark, the requirement of demonstrating a 'concrete and individual risk' has long been part of DRAB's practice,[731] and is applied whether the claim concerns gender-based violence or not.[732]

In Spain, judicial practice disclosed evidence of the term 'concrete' also being used and similar expectations of concrete evidence to establish a personal risk. Accordingly, the AN regularly refers to the Supreme Court jurisprudence from 1998 regarding the standard of proof in asylum cases, stating

> it is necessary that, at least, circumstantial evidence exists, otherwise every citizen of a country experiencing serious social disruption, with the death of civilians and the absence of protection of basic human rights, would automatically be entitled to the granting of asylum, which is not the purpose of asylum protection.[733]

The AN also cited the established jurisprudence of the Supreme Court that,

> the situation of generalised internal conflict in a country, even with the weakening of state powers and the emergence of uncontrolled groups that may put people's most basic human rights at risk, is not by itself a ground giving rise to the recognition of refugee status, which requires, not only the general risk, common for all, inherent to such a situation but also that this risk has been translated and become a concrete instance of persecution, or in a well-founded fear of persecution, towards the asylum seeker, either individually or because of their belonging to a group and for reasons of race, religion, nationality, belonging to a particular social group or political opinion.[734]

The AN also required that the account of the appellant

> must have a level of specificity that allows identifying a true persecution, not being sufficient for that purpose a vague and generic account that could be applicable to practically

[725] FR: CNDA 15027724 11.04.2016 (Iraq). [726] FR: CNDA 14037272 26.06.2015 (Syria).
[727] DK: DRAB 13.03.2013 (Iraq).
[728] DK: DRAB 09.11.2016 (Afghanistan); DK: DRAB 07.06.2016 (Syria); DK: DRAB 02.10.2015 (Syria); DK: DRAB 12.08.2013 (Iraq); DK: DRAB 06.02.2013 (Afghanistan).
[729] DK: DRAB 09.11.2015 (Syria). [730] DK: DRAB 05.04.2016 (Syria).
[731] Jens Vedsted-Hansen, '"Konkret og individuelt": Et Kriteriums forvandling fra Kvalifikation til Eksklusion' in Annette Møller-Sørensen and Anette Storgaard (eds), *Jurist uden Omsvøb: Festskrift til Gorm Toftegaard Nielsen* (Christian Ejlers 2007) 599–616.
[732] Jesper Lindholm, *Danske Asylafgørelser: Baggrund, Kontekst, Analyse* (Jurist- og Økonomforbundets Forlag 2014) 342.
[733] ES: AN SAN 4854/2016 24.11.2016 (Iraq); ES: AN SAN 1202/2015 01.04.2015 (Syria); ES: AN SAN 5686/2013 26.12.2013 (Afghanistan).
[734] ES: AN SAN 2156/2015 11.06.2015 (Syria) – successfully appealed to ES: TS STS 1182/2016 16.03.2016 (Syria), citing ES: TS RC 3933/2009 10.10.2011.

> anyone from the same country as the appellant, or who lacks elements of contrast and verification that allow to appreciate its verisimilitude.[735]

The AN noted that an appellant had 'not alleged any concrete reasons for persecution'[736] or that 'the situation of civil conflict in the country of origin is not sufficient to meet the criteria of an asylum application if it is not accompanied by evidence that the applicant will suffer personal and concrete persecution' for a Convention reason.[737] Significantly, the AN applied a decision of the Supreme Court noting that a situation of civil confrontation cannot on its own lead to asylum if it is not accompanied by an account or exposure to concrete repercussions from this general climate of confrontation for the person and this account must also be concrete and coherent to a minimum degree.[738]

Although there were no explicit statements of the risk of persecution test in judicial practice in the Netherlands due to the limited judicial review grounds in asylum appeals, a high standard of proof is nonetheless applied, requiring extensive documentary evidence.[739] For example, in an appeal remitted by the Court to review the security situation in Iraq, the Secretary of State had argued that a teacher finding a bullet in his home was insufficient evidence of risk because the appellant had not established that it was intended for him.[740] Finally, although the UK FTT did not make references to a 'concrete' risk of persecution, instead generally referring to a 'risk of persecution' or 'real risk of persecution',[741] the requirement of singling out and individual targeting as discussed in Section 5.4 nonetheless demonstrates that in practice a higher standard of proof is applied by the FTT.

Overall, judicial practice in EU MS is to consistently require 'concrete' evidence of a well-founded fear of being persecuted, a standard of proof which appellate authorities are satisfied is met only when personal instances of conflict with or persecution by actors of persecution has been accepted as credible. The additional requirement that appellants be specifically targeted or individually singled out for persecution illustrates this heightened standard of proof. The trend across EU MS has erroneously elevated this element into a legal requirement for the existence of a well-founded fear of being persecuted. As a result, unless persons seeking international protection have previously experienced personal instances of conflict with actors of persecution in their country of origin, they are generally refused refugee protection, particularly if they have fled from situations of armed conflict characterised by widespread violence.

5.7 Conclusion

This chapter set out how appellate authorities in Belgium, Denmark, France, the Netherlands, Spain and the UK require that persons fleeing armed conflicts be singled out by actors of persecution in order to be recognised as refugees under the Refugee Convention

735 ES: AN SAN 4433/2016 29.11.2016 (Syria); ES: AN SAN 4395/2016 17.11.2016 (Syria), citing ES: TS RC 678/2008 17.05.2011.

736 ES: AN SAN 3336/2013 15.07.2013 (Syria). 737 ES: AN SAN 5539/2013 12.12.2013 (Syria).

738 ES: AN SAN 2221/2013 22.05.2013 (Syria), citing ES: TS STS 6252/2004 15.02.2008.

739 See for example NL: Rb AWB 16/9070, AWB 16/9066 25.05.2016 (Syria); NL: Rb AWB 14/12313, AWB 14/12311 20.06.2014 (Iraq); NL: Rb AWB 13/23795, AWB 13/23792 03.10.2013 (Afghanistan).

740 NL: Rb AWB 14/12004 25.08.2014 (Iraq).

741 See for example UK: FTT(IAC) 14.11.2016 (Iraq); UK: FTT(IAC) 01.11.2016 (Iraq); UK: FTT(IAC) 15.09.2014 (Afghanistan); UK: FTT(IAC) 31.01.2014 (Afghanistan).

in practice. In other words, the concept of 'well-founded fear of being persecuted' is being interpreted as requiring 'individual' persecution in the sense of being personally targeted. Although the condition was not stated explicitly, the existence of this added legal requirement is apparent as most appellants were refused refugee status when appellate authorities did not find their account of past persecution or having experienced personal instances of conflict with actors of persecution credible. Furthermore, this chapter briefly set out how the assessment of credibility of appellants' accounts could be influenced by appellate authorities' rejection of any deviation from gender norms.[742] In their legal reasoning, appellate authorities translate the absence of singling out or individual targeting into the failure to meet a standard of 'concrete' risk, thereby elevating the standard of proof under the Refugee Convention. Although it is clear that past persecution or past instances of conflict with actors of persecution may act as an indicator of a future risk and well-founded fear, it nonetheless does not constitute a legal requirement of the Refugee Convention definition. In this sense, the standard of proof is being conflated with the assessment of credibility of appellants' account of events in their country of origin. This is not in accordance with the generally agreed interpretation of the standard of proof in international refugee law.

Consequently, the general conditions of violence in the country of origin are rarely, if ever, assessed from an interdisciplinary perspective contrary to states' obligations in international refugee law. Appellate authorities' perspective of armed conflicts through a conventional warfare lens and consequent perception that violence against civilians is random and indiscriminate explains the focus of judicial determination on past events and subsequently on the assessment of credibility. Overall, the failure of appellate authorities in EU MS to engage with the Refugee Convention unless an appellant's account of having been singled out for persecution is considered credible acts as a barrier to the protection of persons fleeing armed conflicts in breach of states' duties under international refugee law. Although temporary protection in the EU for persons fleeing 'areas of armed conflict or endemic violence'[743] is not hampered by the same obstacles to interpretation discussed in this chapter, it still does not entitle its beneficiaries to the same length of residence as refugee status. Temporary Protection may be administratively convenient for EU MS due to the grant of group protection, yet its use contributes to the displacement of the Refugee Convention as the cornerstone of international protection.

The implication for international refugee law is that the application of the Refugee Convention and development of jurisprudence regarding the interpretation of the Refugee Convention definition in the cases of persons fleeing armed conflicts in the EU is constrained. The general conditions in the country of origin are rarely examined by appellate authorities with a view to understanding and evaluating the nature of violence and strategic actions of parties to the conflicts. Large numbers of persons fleeing armed conflicts and seeking international protection in the EU are thus being denied a full examination of their claim under the Refugee Convention, in particular where persons are at risk of persecution for reasons of their membership of a group or where fighting parties impute certain characteristics to groups defined as opponents in armed conflicts through identity politics.

The effective protection in international law of persons fleeing widespread violence in situations of armed conflict requires asylum decision makers to interpret the

[742] Although full exploration of this issue is beyond the scope of this study, it is highlighted as creating a need for further research.

[743] Article 2(c) Temporary Protection Directive.

Refugee Convention definition in light of the social reality of contemporary armed conflicts. Applying the knowledge acquired in feminist and security studies scholarship when interpreting the Refugee Convention definition highlights that violence in situations of armed conflict is rarely targeted against single individuals but rather that it is directed against similarly situated individuals on the basis of identity politics. More specifically, parties to the conflict exercise violence strategically by targeting entire groups of persons sharing actual or imputed characteristics in order to terrorise the population and thereby control large parts of the territory. As demonstrated in Chapter 4, appellate authorities perceive the dynamics of violence against civilians as an unfortunate effect of conventional warfare rather than the product of gendered fighting strategies aimed at terrorising groups of persons distinguished by real or perceived characteristics. Instead, it is suggested that enquiring into the means and tactics of parties to conflict locates a logic in the choice of violence, leading to highly visible forms of human rights violations. This allows the conceptualisation of particular incidents, such as kidnappings or sexual violence at checkpoints to control freedom of movement, as strategic choices of violence rather than criminal by-products of conflict. This perspective supports an interpretation of the Refugee Convention reasons for persecution in a manner that better responds to the realities of contemporary armed conflicts and is discussed in Chapter 6.

6

Judicial Constructions of the Refugee Convention Reasons for Persecution in Situations of Contemporary Armed Conflict

6.1 Introduction

Although the different elements of the Refugee Convention definition, such as the well-founded fear of being persecuted and the reasons for persecution, are often addressed separately, both in the literature and by asylum decision makers, they are closely interconnected. Therefore, the manner in which one of these elements is interpreted influences how the remaining elements are interpreted. Broadly, this chapter demonstrates how asylum appellate authorities' conceptualisation of violence in situations of armed conflict, discussed in Chapter 4, impacts not only their interpretation of a 'well-founded fear of being persecuted', which was analysed in Chapter 5, but also the application and interpretation of the Refugee Convention reasons for persecution. The Refugee Convention defines a refugee as a person who has a well-founded fear of being persecuted in the absence of state protection but only where the risk is for reasons of 'race, religion, nationality, membership of a particular social group or political opinion'. This chapter thus examines the impact of a conventional warfare perspective and the requirement of singling out on the application and interpretation of the Refugee Convention reasons for persecution by appellate authorities in the European Union (EU).

So far, this book has argued that appellate authorities' understanding of armed conflicts through the lens of conventional warfare explains the assumption that violence in situations of armed conflict arises predominantly from armed confrontations between fighting parties. As a consequence of this understanding, violence experienced by persons who do not take part in armed confrontations is perceived as 'collateral' or an unfortunate consequence of the general situation of conflict in the country of origin. In other words, a perspective of conventional warfare entails a corollary assumption that violence against civilians is not a specific objective of parties to the conflict.

In contrast, the analysis of how the Refugee Convention reasons for persecution should be applied and interpreted in the cases of persons fleeing armed conflicts is informed by the conceptual framework proposed in Chapter 3 that drew on security and gender studies. This perspective challenges the perception that most violence in situations of armed conflict arises in sites of armed confrontations directed against opposing parties to the conflict and that this form of violence is the most severe. Instead, it demonstrates that violence is motivated by identity politics on the basis of real or imputed characteristics, such as sex, ethnicity, race, religion, political opinion or membership of a particular social group, in highly gendered ways which distinguishes parts of the population and frames them as opponents in conflicts. Chapter 3 set out how political identities are constructed then fixed, and used as a justification for violence in situations of armed conflict. The current chapter will argue that these dynamics directly relate to the Refugee Convention ground of (imputed) political opinion. Significantly, this framework also robustly contests the notion that violence exercised by parties to the conflict is felt indiscriminately by civilians. On the contrary, the strategies of armed groups are highly gendered and targeted against civilians in order to control populations and, by extension, territory.

This chapter claims that appellate authorities' perception that violence in situations of armed conflict is more severe and arises predominantly in the context of confrontations between parties to the conflict and that violence against civilians is thus mainly an unfortunate consequence of armed conflicts has significantly restricted judicial consideration of the Refugee Convention reasons for persecution. As a consequence of appellate authorities' perspective of violence in armed conflicts and the requirement of singling out and heightened standard of proof, discussed in Chapters 4 and 5 respectively, there is limited judicial engagement with applying and interpreting the Refugee Convention reasons in light of widespread violence in the context of armed conflicts. Instead, the Refugee Convention reasons for persecution are applied solely in light of the individual circumstances of appellants where these are considered to amount to singling out. Accordingly, there is a general failure to adequately consider actual or imputed Refugee Convention reasons for persecution.

As the primary difference between the scope of subsidiary protection and refugee protection in the EU is whether violence and serious harm is discriminatory on the basis of distinguishing characteristics, the lack of engagement with the general conditions of violence as actual or imputed Refugee Convention reasons fails to ensure the effective protection of refugees fleeing armed conflicts. This chapter concludes that the failure to consider the nature of violence and the characteristics of contemporary armed conflicts under the Refugee Convention obscures the increasing significance of imputed Refugee Convention grounds in situations of armed conflict. Furthermore, there is a significant gap in the application and interpretation of the Refugee Convention reasons for persecution by appellate authorities in EU Member States (MS) despite the wealth of knowledge acquired in feminist and security studies scholarship.

The chapter firstly considers how the requirement of an interdisciplinary approach to interpretation of the Refugee Convention definition in light of scholarship on gender and security studies set out in Chapter 2 justifies an interpretation of the Refugee Convention reasons for persecution that takes into account the dynamics of violence in contemporary armed conflicts. Section 6.3 proposes an understanding of the Refugee Convention reason of (imputed) political opinion drawing on the notion of discrimination inherent in the Refugee Convention, which better reflects the nature of violence in situations of armed conflict that is motivated by constructed political identities. Section 6.4 provides an empirical account of judicial practice in respect of the Refugee Convention reasons for persecution. This section starts by analysing the Refugee Convention reasons identified by appellate authorities where appellants originate from Afghanistan, Iraq and Syria. The analysis reveals that where appellants had been singled out, judicial determination of the Refugee Convention reason(s) is relatively straightforward such that there is little legal analysis of this element of the Refugee Convention definition. Section 6.4.2 then explores how appellate authorities take into account distinguishing characteristics as risk factors in respect only of subsidiary protection and explains how those factors are relevant to the Refugee Convention reasons for persecution. Section 6.4.3 reviews how appellate authorities apply and interpret the law where women are at risk of gender-based violence in situations of armed conflict. Finally, judicial practice with respect to widespread violence in the context of armed conflicts is analysed and consideration is given to how the conceptual framework set out in Chapter 3 provides an explanatory lens for revisiting the application and interpretation of the Refugee Convention reasons for persecution.

6.2 Existing Perspectives on Violence in Situations of Armed Conflict and Reasons for Persecution

Türk, Edwards and Wouters claim that continued misconceptions regarding the application of the Refugee Convention to persons fleeing armed conflicts can be explained by the perception held by decision makers that violence in situations of armed conflict is indiscriminate rather than motivated by one or more of the Refugee Convention grounds.[744] They argue instead that violence has more profound underlying justifications or objectives,[745] and that the motivations pursued by actors in armed conflicts remain predominantly related to race/ethnicity, religion, political opinion and social group.[746] They have also claimed that most contemporary conflicts are rooted in political, ethnic, religious or social divisions such that the Refugee Convention grounds are applicable.[747] In its Guidelines, the United Nations High Commissioner for Refugees (UNHCR) has recommended that the question to guide decision makers is whether 'the reasons for the person's feared predicament, within the overall context of the country, relate to a Convention ground'.[748] In particular, the Guidelines state that:

> Situations of armed conflict and violence may be rooted in, motivated or driven by, and/or conducted along lines of race, ethnicity, religion, politics, gender or social group divides, or may impact people based on these factors. In fact, what may appear to be indiscriminate conduct (i.e. conduct whereby the persecutor is not seeking to target particular individuals), may in reality be aimed at whole communities or areas whose inhabitants are actual or perceived supporters of one of the sides in the situation of armed conflict and violence. Rarely are modern-day situations of armed conflict and violence characterised by violence that is not in one way or another aimed at particular populations, or which does not have a disproportionate effect on a particular population, establishing a causal link with one or more of the Convention grounds. Who belongs to or is considered or perceived to be affiliated with, a particular side in a situation of armed conflict and violence, is often interpreted broadly by actors during such situations – and may include a range of people, including family members of fighters as well as all those who belong to the same religious or ethnic groups or reside in particular neighbourhoods, villages or towns. A Convention ground is regularly imputed to groups of people based on their family, community, geographic or other links.[749]

Whereas UNHCR's Guidelines provide an essential starting point for the analysis of reasons for persecution in situations of armed conflict and how to interpret the Refugee Convention

744 Türk, Edwards and Wouters, 'Introduction' (n 2) 7; see also UNHCR, *Guidelines on International Protection No. 12* (n 5) para 33.
745 Türk, Edwards and Wouters, 'Introduction' (n 2) 8.
746 Ibid., 5; see also UNHCR, *Guidelines on International Protection No. 12* (n 5) paras 1, 35, 39.
747 Türk, Edwards and Wouters, 'Introduction' (n 2) 10.
748 UNHCR, *Guidelines on International Protection No. 12* (n 5) para 32.
749 Ibid., para 33.

grounds for persecution, they do little to engage with the field concerned with understanding armed conflicts. As discussed in Chapter 3, there is a wealth of relevant knowledge on the dynamics of violence in situations of armed conflict in the field of security studies. However, as mentioned in that chapter, the engagement to date of scholars with the value of an interdisciplinary approach in international refugee law has been limited to broad macro-level studies regarding the causes of armed conflicts rather than the dynamics of violence in the context of contemporary armed conflicts. Thus, although Lambert, Farrell and Schmitt have relied on interdisciplinary knowledge in their work, in particular the greed or grievance theory proposed by the economists Collier and Hoeffler, they have not explicitly considered literature critical of this model.[750] For example, it has been said that Collier and Hoeffler's model is too simplistic, gives credence to economic factors and thus implies that violence in situations of contemporary armed conflict lacks political purpose.[751] Kalyvas, amongst others, argues that the greed or grievance model proposed by Collier and Hoeffler is based on a dichotomy which conceptualises armed groups as either bandits/criminals or political dissidents.[752] Kalyvas considers that this model makes generalisations based on incomplete and biased evidence, originating mostly from journalistic and political elite sources and fails to give proper weight to insurgents' own claims regarding the purpose of their movement.[753]

Kalyvas suggests instead that armed groups' ideological motivations remain central to the waging of conflicts and that they often have a 'sophisticated political understanding of their own participation' aiming to 'develop a complex apparatus of rule in the areas they control'.[754] Indeed, there is a growing body of scholarship on 'rebel governance', defined broadly as 'organizing civilians for a public purpose'.[755] As was discussed in Chapter 3 and will be explored further in this chapter, the reasons for the exercise of violence are inherently political in character as it is motivated by political gains. In conflict situations, individuals are generally expected to take sides and, if not, will in any event be categorised as supporters of one side or another on the basis of certain characteristics including race, ethnicity, religion, family ties and residence.[756] Consequently, these perspectives challenge the notion of violence in situations of armed conflict as indiscriminate or an unfortunate consequence of war for the purpose of applying and interpreting the Refugee Convention reasons for persecution.

Contrary to this perspective of violence, Lambert adopts as a starting point the assumption that many victims of conflict fall outside the scope of the Refugee Convention definition in her article exploring the potential for expanding protection in Europe for victims of armed conflict which is accordingly limited to subsidiary protection.[757] This gap in

[750] Lambert and Farrell, 'The Changing Character of Armed Conflict' (n 6); Lambert, 'The Next Frontier' (n 6); Farrell and Schmitt, *The Causes, Character and Conduct of Armed Conflict* (n 163). As endorsed by Wouters in 'Conflict Refugees' (n 5) 816.

[751] See for example Cristina Bodea and Ibrahim A. Elbadawi, *Riots, Coups and Civil War: Revisiting the Greed and Grievance Debate* (World Bank, 2007).

[752] Stathis Kalyvas, '"New" and "Old" Civil Wars: A Valid Distinction?' (2001) 54 *World Politics* 99, 102.

[753] Ibid., 103. [754] Ibid., 104–105.

[755] See for example Nelson Kasfir, 'Rebel Governance – Constructing a Field of Inquiry: Definitions, Scope, Patterns, Order, Causes' in Ana Arjona, Nelson Kasfir and Zachariah Mampilly (eds), *Rebel Governance in Civil War* (CUP 2015) 21.

[756] UNHCR, *Guidelines on International Protection No. 12* (n 5) para 33.

[757] She notes '[this article] tackles a true reality: in the many cases where victims of conflict and indiscriminate violence find themselves falling outside the scope of article 1A(2), the automatic default option is that offered by article 15c', Lambert, 'The Next Frontier' (n 6) 211.

refugee law scholarship is significant because, as claimed in this book, the application of an interdisciplinary approach as a means to explain the dynamics of violence in situations of armed conflict and uncover the motivations of fighting parties allows an interpretation of the Refugee Convention reasons for persecution that ensures the effective protection of persons fleeing armed conflicts. The following section highlights the notion of discrimination inherent in the Refugee Convention and its relationship to the Refugee Convention reasons for persecution, in particular the ground of political opinion in the context of armed conflicts.

6.3 Discrimination and the Nature of Political Violence

At the heart of the Refugee Convention is a concern with ensuring the protection of persons against persecution based on protected characteristics. These characteristics include factors inherent to individuals that they cannot or should not be expected to forego such as race, ethnicity, nationality, religion, political opinion, sex and sexual orientation.[758] A real risk of persecution or serious harm for reasons not covered by the Refugee Convention does not result in refugee status but rather subsidiary protection in EU law.[759] The concept of a refugee is therefore of a person with a well-founded fear of being persecuted for discriminatory reasons, or more specifically a person who is at risk of serious harm because of unequal treatment based on (perceived) individual distinguishing characteristics as defined in the Refugee Convention definition. Thus, discrimination in matters affecting fundamental rights and freedoms is central to the understanding of the Refugee Convention.[760] The preamble to the Refugee Convention which refers to the United Nations (UN) Charter and the Universal Declaration of Human Rights (UDHR) supports this proposition.[761] The UN Charter sets out the purposes of the UN including 'to achieve international co-operation [...] in promoting and encouraging respect for human rights and for fundamental freedoms for all without distinction as to race, sex, language, or religion'.[762] The principle of equality between all human beings is also enshrined in the UDHR, which applies 'without distinction of any kind, such as race, colour, sex, language, religion, political or other opinion, national or social origin, property, birth or other status'.[763]

[758] Ethnicity being encompassed within the Convention grounds of race or nationality and sex and sexual orientation being encompassed within the Convention grounds of religion, political opinion or particular social group.

[759] Alternatively, the EU may decide to activate the Temporary Protection Directive, which removes the need to establish the existence of any Refugee Convention reasons. As noted, this was done for persons fleeing the Ukrainian conflict in March 2022, Council Implementing Decision (EU) 2022/382 of 4 March 2022 establishing the existence of a mass influx of displaced persons from Ukraine (n 279).

[760] *Islam v Secretary of State for the Home Department Immigration Appeal Tribunal and Another, Ex Parte Shah, R v* [1999] 2 AC 629, per Lord Hoffmann.

[761] The preamble to the Refugee Convention states that 'Considering that the Charter of the United Nations and the Universal Declaration of Human Rights approved on 10 December 1948 by the General Assembly have affirmed the principle that human beings shall enjoy fundamental rights and freedoms without discrimination'; as per Lord Steyn in *Islam v Secretary of State for the Home Department Immigration Appeal Tribunal and Another, Ex Parte Shah, R v* [1999] 2 AC 629.

[762] Article 1(3) UN Charter. [763] Articles 1–2 UDHR.

Although some scholars claim that gender-related persecution was not in the drafters' mind,[764] Lord Steyn in the UK House of Lords stated that 'it would have been remarkable if the draftsmen had overlooked other forms of discrimination' particularly in light of the non-discrimination clause in the UDHR.[765] The absence of explicit reference to sex or gender could be explained by the historical context as the drafters of the Refugee Convention explicitly listed 'the most apparent forms of discrimination then known' in the circumstances of the aftermath of the Second World War and persecution by the Nazis.[766] However, where violence is gender-based it is often rooted in discriminatory treatment, both in relation to the motivation of the perpetrators and the lack of state protection. Wallace has stated that 'gender-based persecution stems from discrimination, but often deeply embedded, cultural practices which themselves can be traced to structural inequalities which leave some members of society more vulnerable to exploitation and hindered from availing available protection'.[767] Hence, although the Refugee Convention does not explicitly refer to sex or gender as one of the protected characteristics in its refugee definition,[768] or in its non-discrimination provision,[769] it is suggested that the context of the Convention in light of its object and purpose is such that discrimination based on sex is equally protected.[770] Interpreting the Refugee Convention reasons for persecution by reference to the concept of discrimination inherent in the Convention ensures the effective protection of persons fleeing armed conflicts.

In order to adequately apply the Refugee Convention reasons for persecution in the context of violence in situations of armed conflict, it is necessary to engage with the notion of political violence. Farrell and Schmitt argue that contemporary armed conflicts include political, criminal and interpersonal violence and note that these factors have implications for the determination of who obtains the benefit of international protection.[771] However, these terms are not explained even though the authors previously criticised these traditional notions of violence under international law for failing to adequately encompass the complexities of armed conflict.[772] It is suggested here that the notion of political violence must be interpreted through the conceptualisation of refugee protection as international protection from discrimination, in the sense of differential treatment based on (perceived) individual characteristics.[773] In situations of armed conflict, the ways in which political identities are imagined and constructed, invoked and pushed to the extreme were explored in Chapter 3 and directly relate to the Refugee Convention ground of (imputed) political opinion.[774]

The prevailing judicial approach in defining the Refugee Convention ground of political opinion is to adopt a broad rather than a narrow viewpoint.[775] Jurisprudence in Australia

764 Indra, 'Gender' (n 66) 3; Alice Edwards, 'Transitioning Gender: Feminist Engagement with International Refugee Law and Policy 1950–2010' (2010) 29 *Refugee Survey Quarterly* 21, 23.

765 *Islam v Secretary of State for the Home Department Immigration Appeal Tribunal and Another, Ex Parte Shah, R v* [1999] 2 AC 629.

766 Ibid., per Lord Steyn.

767 Rebecca Wallace, 'Internal Relocation Alternative in Refugee Status Determination: Is the Risk/Protection Dichotomy Reality or Myth? A Gendered Analysis' in Satvinder Singh Juss and Colin Harvey (eds), *Contemporary Issues in Refugee Law* (Edward Elgar Publishing 2013) 299.

768 Article 1A(2) Refugee Convention.

769 Article 3 Refugee Convention provides that 'the Contracting States shall apply the provisions of this Convention to refugees without discrimination as to race, religion or country of origin'.

770 Article 31 VCLT.

771 Farrell and Schmitt, *The Causes, Character and Conduct of Armed Conflict* (n 163) 54.

772 Ibid., 26. 773 See also Section 2.2.2 in Chapter 2. 774 See Section 3.5 in Chapter 3.

775 Hathaway and Foster, *The Law of Refugee Status* (n 20) 407.

and the USA support the contention that a risk of persecution on account of 'political opinion' properly encompasses those who actively oppose or refuse to abide by legal or socio-cultural norms. The element of 'political opinion' need not be limited to party politics,[776] and may include behaviour and action in sites such as the community or the home. This Refugee Convention ground does not refer to the term political 'activity' but explicitly uses the term 'opinion' which suggests that the concept is much wider than traditional understandings of what is political.[777] Thus, a person may be at risk of persecution for reasons of political opinion as provided for in the Refugee Convention without ever having officially engaged in political activity or even having a political opinion or belief where the motivation of the persecutor is based on a political attribution.[778] Significantly, this attribution of political opinion may be made by the state or by non-state actors. In further support of this approach is the notion that persons should not be expected to suppress or conceal their political opinion in order to avoid persecutory treatment.[779] State and non-state actors of persecution may attribute political opinions to persons who engage in activities implying an adverse political opinion such as a rejection of gender-conformist behaviour.[780]

To adequately understand and determine whether certain behaviour, acts or inaction may be considered to be an expression of political opinion, it is necessary to give careful attention to the broader societal context,[781] including social structures.[782] UNHCR has endorsed this approach and advised that behaviour may be considered political where it is perceived as contrary to the policies of those in power:

> The 1951 Convention ground of political opinion needs to reflect the reality of the specific geographical, historical, political, legal, judicial, and socio-cultural context of the country of origin. In certain contexts, expressing objections to the activities of gangs or to the State's gang-related policies may be considered as amounting to an opinion that is critical of the methods and policies of those in power and, thus, constitute a 'political opinion' within the meaning of the refugee definition.[783]

This UNHCR Guidance draws on a 2008 decision from the New Zealand Refugee Status Appeals Authority which considered that the concept of 'honour' in Turkish society 'is about the distribution and exercise of power' and that it 'reflects the gendered inequality of power in that society'. Thus 'the claimant's assertion of her right to life and of her right to control her life and her challenge to inequality and the structures of power which support it, was plainly "political" as that term is used in the Refugee Convention'.[784] Guidelines from UNHCR, the USA, Canada and the UK and jurisprudence in Austria, Germany and Canada have recognised that a refusal to comply with traditional expectations of behaviour associated with gender may result in political opinion being attributed and therefore come within the scope of the Refugee Convention,[785] although the notion does not reflect

[776] See jurisprudence from USA and Australia cited in ibid., 405.

[777] The term must be interpreted in accordance with its ordinary meaning, Article 31(1) VCLT.

[778] Hathaway and Foster, *The Law of Refugee Status* (n 20) 406.

[779] Ibid., 408. [780] Ibid., 411. [781] Ibid., 412.

[782] Ian Macdonald and Ronan Toal, *Immigration Law and Practice in the United Kingdom* (9th edn, LexisNexis 2014) 842.

[783] UNHCR, 'Guidance Note on Refugee Claims Relating to Victims of Organized Gangs' (31 March 2010) www.refworld.org/docid/4bb21fa02.html, accessed 12 July 2021, para 46.

[784] *Refugee Appeal No. 76044*, New Zealand: Refugee Status Appeals Authority, 11 September 2008.

[785] Hathaway and Foster, *The Law of Refugee Status* (n 20) 421.

a universal approach.[786] The relevant issue for asylum decision makers therefore is not so much the individual behaviour/activity determinative of a 'profile', such as refusing to wear the veil or organising a demonstration as an active opposition party member, but rather the meaning ascribed to this behaviour/activity by those in power, whether within the institutions of the state or within armed groups, the wider community or the family. Inequality and discrimination are considered part of the wider distribution of power within a given society.

Violence in the home is part of a broader social, political and economic process which is influenced by state policies, public institutions and the global economy.[787] This highlights the relation between violence by non-state actors, which is regularly considered private and apolitical by asylum decision makers, and institutional inequality translated into discriminatory legislative measures or societal discrimination. Legislative measures are considered to be political manifestations of structural discrimination where men and women are treated unequally by law or where the law applies equally on its face but is applied unequally in practice. It is often this context which permits non-state actors to inflict serious harm with impunity. In order to fully determine the context and causes of violence in situations of armed conflict it is necessary to understand the gendered politics that allow it to occur and continue.[788] This conceptualisation suggests that the public/private distinction permeating international law is not an accurate representation of how violence is exercised and motivated in practice.[789]

In the context of situations of armed conflict, UNHCR has specifically noted in its Guidelines that fighting parties often aim violence at certain areas or particular neighbourhoods 'whose inhabitants are actual or perceived supporters of one of the sides in the situation of armed conflict and violence'.[790] Having regard to the patterns of violence exercised by the fighting parties in Aleppo through country of origin information could provide an indication of the reasons and rationale for the use of violence.[791] More specifically, UNHCR has found that

> A particular and deepening feature of the conflict is that different parties to the conflict frequently impute a political opinion to larger groups of people, including families, tribes, religious or ethnic groups or whole towns, villages or neighbourhoods, by association. As such, members of a larger entity, without individually being singled out, become the targets for repercussions by different actors, including government forces, ISIS, and anti-government armed groups, for reason of real or perceived support to another party to the conflict. According to consistent reports, whole communities which are perceived to be holding a particular political opinion or affiliation in relation to the conflict are targeted by aerial bombardments, shelling, siege tactics, suicide attacks and car bombs, arbitrary arrest, hostage-taking, torture, rape and other forms of sexual violence, and extra-judicial executions. The perception of sharing a political opinion or affiliation in relation to the conflict is often based on little more than an individual's physical presence

[786] See for example *Islam v Secretary of State for the Home Department Immigration Appeal Tribunal and Another, Ex Parte Shah, R v* [1999] 2 AC 629, Lord Steyn rejected reliance by the appellant on the ground of political opinion as 'unsustainable' although this was said *obiter* and in light of the particular facts of the case of Mrs Islam.

[787] Giles and Hyndman, 'Introduction' (n 389) 4. [788] Ibid., 4.

[789] Conaghan describes the public/private distinction as a conceptual tool in maintaining women's formal exclusion, Conaghan, *Law and Gender* (n 69) 83.

[790] UNHCR, *Guidelines on International Protection No. 12* (n 5) para 33.

[791] See for example Amnesty International, 'Syria: Armed Opposition Groups Committing War Crimes in Aleppo City' (13 May 2016) <www.amnesty.org/en/latest/news/2016/05/syria-armed-opposition-groups-committing-war-crimes-in-aleppo-city/> accessed 12 July 2021.

> in a particular area (or the fact that he/she originates from a particular area), or his/her ethnic, religious or tribal background.[792]

Thus, the Guidelines suggest that entire groups of persons, in this case whole communities, are being attributed a political opinion in the context of an armed conflict. The targeting of civilians for reasons of real or imputed political opinion based on their residence in a particular neighbourhood was already identified by UNHCR in December 2012:

> The methods of warfare observed in Syria include the shelling of or other forms of attacks on whole neighbourhoods, purportedly for reason of real or perceived support to the other party, as well as more recent reports of bulldozing of residences. These actions, together with consistent and reliable reports of human rights violations committed by all parties to the conflict, indicate that substantial numbers of Syrian civilians are likely to have fled Syria because of a well-founded fear based on a real or imputed political opinion.[793]

Blanche Tax has argued that the case of the armed conflict in Syria demonstrates that very large groups of persons may be at risk of persecution for reasons of imputed political opinion where anti-government or government forces perceive them as supporters of the other party.[794] This political opinion may be imputed due to persons' places of residence or their origin disclosed on their ID cards.[795] Thus, mere physical presence in an area may be sufficient for a party to the conflict to associate a person with the other side to the conflict. Where, as a result, a party to the conflict attacks this area, the risk of persecution arises for reasons of Refugee Convention grounds even though persons are not personally targeted.[796]

Thus the concept of 'political opinion' cannot be interpreted through 'excessive formalism' in order to determine whether circumstances, characteristics, actions or behaviour in a particular society may be considered as amounting to a political opinion.[797] What may be perceived as political in asylum seekers' countries of origin may not appear political from the perspective of decision makers in Europe,[798] but asylum claims should always be assessed in the context of conditions in the country of origin. Effective and inclusive asylum decision-making therefore requires up-to-date country of origin information and independent country-specific expert opinion to assist decision makers in the determination of asylum claims.[799]

6.4 Judicial Practice in EU MS

Overall, where appellants were considered to have a well-founded fear of being persecuted on return to Afghanistan, Iraq or Syria, the judicial determination of the Refugee Convention

[792] UNHCR, 'International Protection Considerations with Regard to People Fleeing the Syrian Arab Republic Update IV', November 2015, HCR/PC/SYR/01, para 17.

[793] UNHCR, 'International Protection Considerations with Regard to People Fleeing the Syrian Arab Republic, Update I', December 2012, footnote 26.

[794] Blanche Tax, 'Refugee by Association' (2014) *Forced Migration Review* (47) 26–27, 26.

[795] Ibid. [796] Ibid., 27; for a discussion of singling out see Chapter 5.

[797] Hathaway and Foster, *The Law of Refugee Status* (n 20) 412, rely on a decision of the Australian High Court, *Guo* (1997) 191 CLR 559.

[798] Ibid., 412.

[799] See for example Anthony Good and Tobias Kelly, 'Best Practice Guide: Expert Country Evidence in Asylum and Immigration Cases in the United Kingdom' (The University of Edinburgh, July 2013) <www.ein.org.uk/sites/default/files/Expert%20Country%20Evidence%20BPG.pdf> accessed 12 July 2021.

grounds was generally dealt with summarily with little analysis.[800] However, as demonstrated in Chapter 5, this required appellants to demonstrate that they had been singled out for persecution. Thus, unless past persecution or personal circumstances amounting to being singled out were found credible, refugee status was generally refused. Consequently, Belgian, Danish, French and UK appellate authorities considered that where appellants had not been singled out but shared personal characteristics that increased the risk of harm, this was generally only considered in relation to subsidiary protection.[801] In the UK, individual characteristics were also often considered in the assessment of the reasonableness of internal flight alternatives rather than as a source of risk in itself.[802] In other words, innate or fundamental characteristics held by some appellants, including age, sex, ethnicity and religion which appellate authorities accepted increased the risk of harm, were nonetheless not examined as potential Refugee Convention reasons for persecution.[803] Furthermore, there was an almost complete absence of consideration of actual or imputed Refugee Convention reasons for persecution in light of the general conditions of violence.[804] This approach fails to take into consideration the dynamics of violence in situations of armed conflict and ignores the possibility that fighting parties motivate and justify the use of violence through identity politics whereby the identities of different sides to the conflict are amplified in a mutually reinforcing manner, as was discussed in Chapter 3. The sample revealed a trend by appellate authorities not to engage with any actual or imputed Refugee Convention grounds in their assessments of international protection claims unless appellants were singled out. The implications of this additional yet unfounded requirement are significant, in particular where persons flee contemporary armed conflicts, because persons fleeing situations of widespread violence are less likely to have been singled out for persecution.

Section 6.4.1 explains how appellate authorities apply and interpret the Refugee Convention reasons for persecution in the cases of persons fleeing armed conflicts. Section 6.4.2 then discusses appellate authorities' treatment of accepted distinguishing characteristics held by appellant as 'risk factors' of relevance to subsidiary protection rather than refugee protection. Section 6.4.3 scrutinises how appellate authorities applied and interpreted the law where women were at risk of gender-based violence in situations of armed conflict. Section 6.4.4 sets out the very few instances where the proposition that widespread violence in the context of armed conflicts may satisfy the Refugee Convention definition was explicitly addressed.

6.4.1 *Judicial Constructions of the Refugee Convention Reasons for Persecution*

Where appellants had been singled out, appellate authorities determined the issue of the existence of any Refugee Convention reasons in a relatively straightforward manner, meaning that there was little judicial discussion of this element of the Refugee Convention definition. In addition, where appeals were allowed but remitted to the administrative decision maker for a new decision there was no substantive judicial engagement with the Refugee Convention reasons for persecution.[805] Hence, although remitted asylum appeals are an important part of the asylum

[800] See Section 6.4.1.

[801] As noted, due to the nature of asylum appeals in Spain and the Netherlands, this particular trend could not be explicitly confirmed in those jurisdictions.

[802] UK: FTT(IAC) 22.09.2016 (Iraq). [803] See Sections 6.4.2–6.4.3. [804] See Section 6.4.4.

[805] Twenty-seven appeals – Belgium (BE): CCE 169 451 09.06.2016 (Iraq); BE: CCE 165 620 12.04.2016 (Iraq); BE: RvV 163 585 08.03.2016 (Syria); BE: CCE 161 404 04.02.216 (Syria); BE: RvV 147 883 16.06.2015 (Syria); BE: RvV 146 522 27.05.2015 (Syria); BE: RvV 142 056 27.03.2015 (Syria); BE: RvV 106 246 03.07.2013 (Iraq); BE: RvV

appeal process when first-instance decisions are deficient, the practice does not contribute to the development of international refugee law, in particular with respect to interpreting the Refugee Convention reasons for persecution where persons are fleeing widespread violence in situations of armed conflict. Accordingly, although 32 per cent of all appeals were allowed, only forty-three cases (13.5 per cent of the total sample) led to refugee status recognition. Thus, it was only in a very small number of cases that appellate authorities actually engaged with the Refugee Convention reasons for persecution. Furthermore, there were large disparities in the number of appeals leading to the grant of refugee status between the EU MS selected for this study. There were twenty-one grants of refugee status in the UK compared with two in Belgium, three in Spain,[806] and five in Denmark. The rate of refugee status grant by the French National Asylum Court (Cour Nationale du Droit d'Asile, CNDA) was somewhere in the middle, with twelve cases. Although there were none in the Netherlands this is partly due to the scope of judicial review in asylum appeals before the Dutch District Court (Rechtbank, Rb).

Disaggregating those cases according to appellants' countries of origin demonstrated that only sixteen Afghan appeals (16.3 per cent of the Afghan sample) were successful under the Refugee Convention, predominantly in the UK and France but also in Denmark.[807] Appellate authorities recognised these Afghan appellants as refugees because it was considered they had a well-founded fear of persecution for reasons of imputed political opinion (eight),[808] particular social group (five),[809] or religion (three).[810]

103 003 16.05.2013 (Afghanistan); Denmark (DK): DRAB 20.10.2016 (Iraq); Spain (ES): AN SAN 4783/2016 21.12.2016 (Syria); ES: AN SAN 4854/2016 24.11.2016 (Iraq); ES: AN SAN 3456/2013 18.07.2013 (Afghanistan); ES: AN SAN 1445/2013 01.04.2013 (Afghanistan); the Netherlands (NL): Rb AWB 15/14760 26.08.2016 (Syria); NL: Rb AWB 16/3148 18.08.2016 (Afghanistan); NL: Rb AWB 16/13578 13.07.2016 (Afghanistan); NL: Rb AWB 16/7907; AWB 16/7908 30.05.2016 (Afghanistan); NL: Rb AWB 16/2729 16.03.2016 (Afghanistan); NL: Rb AWB 14/25106 09.07.2015 (Syria); NL: Rb AWB/ROE 13/14625 26.03.2015 (Afghanistan); NL: Rb AWB 14/12004 25.08.2014 (Iraq); NL: Rb AWB 13/7303 30.06.2014 (Afghanistan); NL: Rb AWB 14/1431; AWB 14/1433 19.03.2014 (Afghanistan); NL: Rb AWB 13/3622; AWB 12/34815 11.06.2013 (Iraq); NL: Rb AWB 12/15471, AWB 12/15473 29.03.2013 (Afghanistan); NL: Rb AWB 12/24673 01.02.2013 (Iraq).

806 Note that these three appeals are from the Supreme Court (Tribunal Supremo, TS) rather than the National High Court (Audiencia Nacional, AN), see Section 1.2.3 in Chapter 1.

807 UK: 10; France (FR): 5; DK: 1.

808 FR: CNDA 16018188 22.09.2016 (Afghanistan): perceived by both Taliban and government of supporting opposition; FR: CNDA 12016495 06.12.2013 (Afghanistan): perceived by insurgents of supporting opposition; FR: CNDA 12001368 22.05.2013 (Afghanistan): perceived by insurgents as supporter of international forces due to work as driver for foreign company; FR: CNDA 12034053 09.04.2013 (Afghanistan): perceived by Taliban of supporting opposition due to father's political activities and brother's work for Afghan forces; UK: FTT(IAC) 24.11.2016 (Afghanistan): perceived supporter of Afghan government and enemy of Taliban as brother worked for British Army and father was tribal leader; UK: FTT(IAC) 15.09.2014 (Afghanistan): risk from Taliban on basis of father's work with Afghan government and refusal to join the Taliban; UK: FTT(IAC) 15.10.2013 (Afghanistan): risk from Taliban due to family members' criminal activities when Taliban in power; UK: FTT(IAC) 03.10.2013 (Afghanistan): risk from Taliban who had previously targeted and killed his father.

809 FR: CNDA 13029815 25.11.2014 (Afghanistan): lesbian woman; UK: FTT(IAC) 21.12.2016 (Afghanistan): risk of forced child recruitment by Taliban in home area; UK: FTT(IAC) 25.06.2015 (Afghanistan): family member of wealthy individuals (sons); UK: FTT(IAC) 31.01.2014 (Afghanistan): unaccompanied children with no family support; UK: FTT(IAC) 26.11.2013 (Afghanistan): family member of person involved in land dispute (father).

810 DK: DRAB 26.01.2015 (Afghanistan): Christianity; UK: FTT(IAC) 28.06.2016 (Afghanistan): Sikhism; UK: FTT(IAC) 05.05.2016 (Afghanistan): Sikhism.

With respect to Iraqi appeals, only nine (9 per cent of the Iraqi sample) were successful under the Refugee Convention, again primarily in the UK and France but also in Denmark.[811] The appellants were recognised as refugees on the basis of a well-founded fear of persecution for reasons of religion (three),[812] particular social group and imputed political opinion (three),[813] imputed political opinion (one),[814] political opinion and religion (one),[815] or imputed political opinion and religion (one).[816]

Only eighteen Syrian appeals (15 per cent of the Syrian sample) were allowed under the Refugee Convention in all the EU MS selected except the Netherlands.[817] These appeals were allowed on the basis of a well-founded fear of persecution for reasons of imputed political opinion (twelve),[818] political opinion (one),[819] religion (one),[820] particular social group (one),[821] race and political opinion (one),[822] imputed political opinion and particular social group (one),[823] or imputed political opinion and religion (one).[824]

Overall, the breakdown of Refugee Convention reasons for persecution across the entire sample is set out in Table 6.1.[825]

The Refugee Convention reason for persecution of imputed political opinion stands out as the ground most often invoked across the entire sample with more than half of all refugee status appeals (54 per cent). This could be an indication of adherence to an understanding of the dynamics of violence in situations of armed conflict where parties to conflicts generally attribute political identities to 'others' in order to justify existing and motivate continued violence against those portrayed as the opposition. However, the individual facts of these imputed political opinion appeals indicate that most involved the attribution of a political

811 UK: 5; FR: 3; DK: 1.

812 DK: DRAB 11.05.2015 (Iraq): Mandaeism; FR: CNDA 14031526 02.06.2015 (Iraq): Shia woman married to Sunni man; UK: FTT(IAC) 11.05.2015 (Iraq): Yazidi.

813 UK: FTT(IAC) 22.11.2016 (Iraq): unaccompanied child at risk of forced recruitment by Islamic State of Iraq and Syria (ISIS); UK: FTT(IAC) 22.09.2016 (Iraq): single woman at risk from ISIS who could not relocate. In the final case the Refugee Convention ground was unclear, UK: FTT(IAC) 14.11.2016 (Iraq): man at risk of arrest and detention further to false rape allegation.

814 UK: FTT(IAC) 01.11.2016 (Iraq): working in media.

815 FR: CNDA 15027551 31.10.2016 (Iraq): politically active Sunni man.

816 FR: CNDA 15007217/15007216 15.07.2015 (Iraq): Sunni brothers whose father had worked under Saddam Hussein and had been killed.

817 BE: 2; DK: 3; FR: 4; ES: 3 (TS); UK: 6.

818 BE: RvV 122 130 04.04.2014 (Syria): exclusion decision, draft evader; ES: TS STS 1182/2016 16.03.2016 (Syria): Syrian airline pilot perceived as supporting opposing side; all DK appeals on basis of failure to perform military service – DK: DRAB 09.11.2015 (Syria); DK: DRAB 28.05.2015 (Syria); DK: DRAB 18.11.2013 (Syria); FR: CNDA 16010669 31.10.2016 (Syria): son recognised as refugee for his political activities against the regime; all UK appeals on basis of detention on return to Syria (see UK: UT(IAC) *KB (Failed asylum seekers and forced returnees)* [2012] UKUT 426 (20.12.2012) – UK: FTT(IAC) 08.11.2016 (Syria); UK: FTT(IAC) 06.10.2015 (Syria); UK: FTT(IAC) 31.07.2015 (Syria); UK: FTT(IAC) 07.07.2015 (Syria); UK: FTT(IAC) 02.06.2015 (Syria); UK: FTT(IAC) 11.03.2014 (Syria).

819 FR: CNDA 13013741 19.12.2013 (Syria): politically active against regime.

820 FR: CNDA 14.03.6897/14037197 07.05.2015 (Syria): Christianity.

821 BE: CCE 176 477 18.10.2016 (Syria): Particular Social Group (PSG) as family member (daughter) of draft evader.

822 FR: CNDA 12033689 03.05.2013 (Syria): Kurdish member of Democratic Union Party (Partîya Yekîtî ya Dêmokrat, PYD).

823 ES: ST STS 569/2016 19.02.2016 (Syria): civil servant perceived as supporter of one or other side to the conflict.

824 ES: TS STS 5211/2015 10.12.2015 (Syria): Sunni human rights defender.

825 Where more than one Refugee Convention ground was identified in a given case, they were counted separately.

Table 6.1 *Refugee Convention reasons for persecution in sample*

Refugee Convention reason for persecution	Number	Percentage of all Refugee Convention reasons
Imputed political opinion	27	54%
Religion	13	26%
Particular social group	7	14%
Political opinion	3	6%
Race	1	2%

opinion as a result of appellants' own or their family members' specific activities and past experiences in their country of origin. In this sense, any finding of imputed political opinion reasons for persecution were closely related to appellants' personal circumstances rather than the general dynamics of violence in situations of armed conflict.[826] The judicial analysis in the Afghan appeals for example demonstrated that appellate authorities in the UK and France were alert to the fact that there was a risk of persecution by the Taliban, and by the Afghan government to a lesser extent, as a result of individuals' professions or the political activities and professions of their family members.[827] To a lesser extent, this trend was also reflected in the practice of appellate authorities in the UK and France with respect to Iraqi appeals.[828]

The trends were slightly different in the Syrian sample as exemplified by the more even spread of refugee status recognition across the EU MS surveyed, as described. Most Syrian appellants were recognised as refugees on the basis of imputed political opinion resulting from draft evasion, including being a family member of a draft evader, and having sought asylum abroad. In addition, all but one of the cases of recognised Syrian refugees in the sample concerned a well-founded fear of being persecuted by the Syrian state. The only exception was a Kurdish Christian couple at risk from ISIS in the absence of state protection.[829]

Although Chapter 5 briefly highlighted how appellate authorities sometimes rigidly relied on expectations of gender norms to reject the credibility of appellants' accounts,[830] judicial engagement with the Refugee Convention reasons for persecution demonstrates that most imputed political opinion cases concerned male appellants being attributed political opinions due to their own or their male relatives' opinions, activities or professions. Alternatively, the cases concerned draft evaders, another gendered aspect of armed conflict, where male appellants were recognised as refugees for refusing to join the Syrian armed forces. This is in contrast to appellate authorities' approach in appeals where women had experienced gender-based violence in the context of armed conflict in their country of origin but the circumstances were considered not to fall within the Refugee Convention definition.[831]

[826] As noted in Chapter 5, most appeals that were rejected were refused on the basis of a lack of credibility in relation to appellants' accounts of events or past instances of conflicts with actors of persecution in their home country.

[827] See n 808.

[828] FR: CNDA 15007217/15007216 15.07.2015 (Iraq): Sunni brothers whose father had worked under Saddam Hussein and had been killed; UK: FTT(IAC) 01.11.2016 (Iraq): working in media.

[829] FR: CNDA 14.03.6897/14037197 07.05.2015 (Syria): Christianity.

[830] Such as sons following their fathers or other male relatives' political persuasions or women not having access to funds and property, see Section 5.5 in Chapter 5.

[831] This is discussed in Sections 6.4.2–6.4.3.

Although there were a few cases demonstrating judicial consideration of women's position in the country of origin,[832] it is claimed here that in general the Refugee Convention ground of political opinion is interpreted through excessive formalism and too narrowly. In asylum appeals concerning flight from armed conflicts, appellate authorities mostly link the Refugee Convention reasons for persecution to fighting between parties, including risks relating to joining the state armed forces or armed groups and being perceived as actively supporting one side or other of the conflict. The focus of judicial constructions of the Refugee Convention reasons for persecution is on political activity or opinion directly related to the fighting of the conflict and less on how gendered norms and institutional discrimination are intensified in situations of armed conflict. Hence, appellate authorities are more attentive to how situations of armed conflict impact men, in particular the institutional requirements and social expectations that they have to take part in the fighting, and consequently, male appellants fleeing armed conflicts are more likely to be recognised as refugees.

Whereas Chapter 5 demonstrated that appellate authorities in the EU generally require appellants to be singled out for persecution under the Refugee Convention, there were a few instances where appeals were allowed and appellants granted refugee status despite not having been singled out. In such cases, the risk on return was determined in light of their individual characteristics and the general conditions in the country of origin. These appeals were successful purely on the basis that appellants belonged to a group that experienced persecution in the country of origin. They included a lesbian[833] and a Sikh[834] from Afghanistan, a westernised Shia woman married to a Sunni foreigner with Sunni children returning as a single woman to Iraq,[835] a Yazidi family[836] and an unaccompanied child from Iraq,[837] and the daughter of a draft evader from Syria.[838] In the last case, the Belgian Court (Belgian Council for Alien Law Litigation, CCE/RvV) cited the UNHCR *Handbook*, establishing that 'these considerations need not necessarily be based on the applicant's own personal experience. What, for example, happened to his friends and relatives and other members of the same racial or social group may well show that his fear that sooner or later he also will become a victim of persecution is well-founded.'[839] Furthermore, where appellants' Syrian nationality was accepted, the UK First-Tier Tribunal (FTT) applied the Upper Tribunal (UT) Country Guidance case concluding that 'it is likely that a failed asylum seeker or forced returnee would, in general, on arrival face a real risk of arrest and detention and of serious mistreatment during that detention as a result of imputed political opinion. That is sufficient to qualify for refugee protection.'[840] Thus, in these cases, the appellants were likely to be detained and consequently be persecuted, unless they 'be perceived as a supporter of the Assad regime'.[841]

Overall, there were few appeals where appellate authorities considered the Refugee Convention reasons for persecution. In total, only 13.5 per cent of cases in the sample contained any engagement with this element of the Refugee Convention definition. Furthermore, the Refugee Convention ground of imputed political opinion was relied on in more than half of

[832] FR: CNDA 16010669 31.10.2016 (Syria); UK: FTT(IAC) 22.09.2016 (Iraq); FR: CNDA 14031526 02.06.2015 (Iraq); FR: CNDA 13029815 25.11.2014 (Afghanistan).
[833] FR: CNDA 13029815 25.11.2014 (Afghanistan). [834] UK: FTT(IAC) 28.06.2016 (Afghanistan).
[835] FR: CNDA 14031526 02.06.2015 (Iraq). [836] UK: FTT(IAC) 11.05.2015 (Iraq).
[837] UK: FTT(IAC) 22.11.2016 (Iraq). [838] BE: CCE 176 477 18.10.2016 (Syria).
[839] UNHCR, *Handbook* (n 24) para 43.
[840] *KB (Failed asylum seekers and forced returnees)* [2012] UKUT 426 (20.12.2012).
[841] UK: FTT(IAC) 08.11.2016 (Syria); UK: FTT(IAC) 06.10.2015 (Syria); UK: FTT(IAC) 31.07.2015 (Syria); UK: FTT(IAC) 07.07.2015 (Syria); UK: FTT(IAC) 02.06.2015 (Syria); UK: FTT(IAC) 11.03.2014 (Syria).

all successful refugee appeals. Those cases predominantly concerned requirements of military service, forced recruitment into armed groups and political opinion attributed to men in light of their fathers' or male relatives' prior political activities and opinions. In this sense, the analysis of the Refugee Convention reasons for persecution by appellate authorities related to more 'traditional' forms of political activity in the context of armed conflicts that were limited to active fighting or engagement in the conflicts. As a result, the exercise of violence in situations not directly related to fighting by parties to the conflict was not examined by appellate authorities to determine if it occurred for reasons of race, religion, nationality, membership of a particular social group or political opinion. Judicial interpretation thus had highly gendered effects such that men fleeing armed conflicts were more likely to be recognised as refugees. Section 6.4.2 discusses appeals where appellants held certain individual characteristics that put them at higher risk than others in the country of origin but nonetheless resulted in the denial of refugee status and instead the grant of complementary protection.[842]

6.4.2 *Judicial Constructions of Distinguishing Characteristics as 'Risk Factors'*

There was an important number of cases where appellate authorities considered that although the level of violence was not such that a person's mere presence in the country/region of origin created a risk on return,[843] it was nonetheless accepted that there was an increased risk for some appellants because of certain characteristics warranting the grant of complementary forms of protection. As appellate authorities consider that these particular characteristics constitute 'risk factors' and thereby increase the risk of harm, appellate authorities must have implied some element of causation between the serious harm and the personal characteristics. Accordingly, the only distinction in those cases between the grant of refugee status and subsidiary protection is the identification of Refugee Convention reasons for persecution. These cases therefore provide a robust evidence base to examine how appellate authorities in the EU (fail to) apply and interpret the Refugee Convention reasons for persecution in situations of armed conflict.

The jurisprudence of the European Court of Human Rights (ECtHR) and Court of Justice of the European Union (CJEU) on the risk to individuals from countries experiencing widespread violence illustrates how individuals who might reasonably have been recognised as refugees due to distinguishing characteristics instead have their cases considered under complementary forms of protection only. Durieux has previously noted that Mr Salah Sheekh, who brought a claim before the ECtHR to prevent his removal to Somalia,[844] is a refugee because he feared persecution for reason of his ethnicity as a member of the Ashraf minority.[845] This aspect of his asylum claim, however, was barely examined by the Dutch administrative and appellate authorities because 'he had not made himself known as an opponent to local rulers, nor had he been politically active'.[846] This case, which eventually contributed to an important development in the jurisprudence of the ECtHR regarding group-based risk of treatment contrary to Article 3 European Convention on Human Rights (ECHR) on return to situations of widespread violence, demonstrates that the practice by

842 Subsidiary protection under Article 15(a), (b) Qualification Directive or (c) or Section 7(2)–(3) Aliens Act in Denmark.

843 Under Article 15(c) Qualification Directive or Article 15(b) Qualification Directive/Article 3 ECHR; for a discussion of the latter see Section 5.3 in Chapter 5.

844 See discussion of this case in Section 5.3 in Chapter 5.

845 Durieux, 'Salah Sheekh is a Refugee' (n 654) 13. 846 Ibid., 12.

Dutch asylum decision makers to require singling out was already operating in 2003. However, the ECtHR found that there was a risk on return to Somalia as a result of the general situation of violence and Mr Salah Sheekh was at risk because he belonged to a minority clan. Yet, in the absence of the ECtHR's jurisdiction to determine cases under the Refugee Convention, Mr Salah Sheekh was never recognised as a refugee.[847]

The personal circumstances of the appellants in the *Elgafaji* case, where the CJEU was asked to determine the difference, if any, between Article 15(c) of the Qualification Directive and Article 3 ECHR, could also reasonably have been interpreted within the ambit of the Refugee Convention reason for persecution of imputed political opinion. The male appellant had worked as a security agent in Baghdad for a British security firm to ensure personnel transport between the airport and the Green Zone. His uncle who worked for the same company had been killed by the militia and a few days later a threatening letter had been fixed to the appellant's door calling for 'death to collaborators'.[848] It does not appear that the Dutch Secretary of State for Justice found the account not credible, rather the claim was refused as the standard of proof had not been met in light of the documents provided and the lack of official documents.[849] Thus, the circumstances of Mr Elgafaji's asylum case were that individual threats had been issued against him because of his employment for a British security firm that militias considered to constitute collaboration with the international forces in Iraq. The UNHCR Eligibility Guidelines for Iraq issued at the time stated 'individuals working for certain entities in Iraq are perceived by the insurgency as supporting the US-led invasion of Iraq and its "occupation" by the MNF. These individuals are thus targeted by elements of the insurgency.'[850] Hence, perceived collaborators in Iraq were at risk for reasons of imputed political opinion,[851] yet Mr Elgafaji was not considered a refugee.

In the same manner as the *Salah Sheekh* and *Elgafaji* cases demonstrate, the analysis of the sample collected for this study shows that appellate authorities in all of the EU MS surveyed regularly take into consideration the particular characteristics of persons fleeing armed conflicts but only with respect to appellants' entitlement to subsidiary protection under Article 3 ECHR/Articles 15(a)–(b) or Article 15(c) Qualification Directive. The individual characteristics included matters such as sex, age, ethnicity and religion.[852]

In Belgian jurisprudence relating to Iraqi appellants, the Court explicitly stated that Sunnis were at higher risk from Shia militias. However, this finding was generally not explored under the scope of the Refugee Convention. Generally, the Belgian Court considered that

[847] Ibid., 8. [848] *Elgafaji v Staatssecretaris van Justitie*, Opinion of AG Poiares Maduro, para 6.

[849] Ibid., para 7.

[850] The Guidelines also added 'Individuals include those Iraqis who are working for the [Multi-National Forces], foreign embassies, foreign companies, the former Coalition Provisional Authority (CPA), the United Nations (UN), the International Committee of the Red Cross (ICRC) as well as other humanitarian and human rights organizations.' UNHCR, 'Eligibility Guidelines for Assessing the International Protection Needs of Iraqi Asylum-Seekers', August 2007, 12.

[851] See also *NS (Iraq: perceived collaborator: relocation) Iraq* CG [2007] UKAIT 00046 para 40.

[852] BE: RvV 175 087 21.09.2016 (Iraq): religion; BE: RvV, 116 849 14.01.2014 (Afghanistan): age; FR: CNDA 15035416 04.04.2016 (Syria): sex; FR: CNDA 15007928 31.08.2015 (Iraq): sex, ethnicity, religion; FR: CNDA 14009621 23.07.2014 (Afghanistan): age; FR: CNDA 13028715 22.04.2014 (Afghanistan): age; FR: CNDA 13019800 07.03.2014 (Afghanistan): age, isolation, lack of family ties; NL: Rb AWB 16/11308 21.10.2016 (Afghanistan): ethnicity; NL: Rb AWB 16/2368 03.03.2016 (Iraq): religion; NL: Rb AWB 14/12313, AWB 14/12311 20.06.2014 (Iraq): Western lifestyle; NL: Rb AWB 13/12607 20.12.2013 (Afghanistan): age and ethnicity; NL: Rb AWB 13/21790, AWB 13/21789 13.09.2013 (Iraq): religion; NL: Rb AWB 12/27332, AWB 12/27333 21.08.2013 (Afghanistan): ethnicity; UK: FTT(IAC) 14.12.2013 (Iraq): religion.

the nature of the violence in Iraq was now targeted at certain specific groups and minorities but only Article 15(c) was applied to this analysis of the armed conflict.[853] Similarly, the CNDA often identified distinguishing characteristics, such as age, religion or profession, as 'risk factors' but only in the context of Article 15(c) and not under the Refugee Convention. Hence, the Court found that appellants sharing those distinguishing characteristics were at risk of indiscriminate violence despite the conclusion that the degree of indiscriminate violence was not such that everyone was at risk on return.[854] As discussed in Chapter 5, the reasoning of the Court was to conclude that the criteria for refugee status were not met because the appellants' accounts of past threats or persecution were found not to be credible. However, the Court did not proceed to examine whether accepted individual circumstances of relevance to the Refugee Convention grounds of race, religion, membership of a particular social group or political opinion would cause a risk of persecution in light of evidence of treatment of similarly situated persons.

In Spain, the AN displayed similar reasoning in a number of Syrian cases where the administrative authorities had already granted the appellants subsidiary protection. More specifically, despite appellants having distinguishing characteristics, such as being a human rights defender[855] or a civil servant,[856] and the acceptance that there was a risk of serious harm on return, the Court concluded their circumstances did not meet the Refugee Convention definition because their accounts were very generic and based on the situation of conflict in Syria. Even where the appellant's account of being a civil servant (Syrian airline pilot) was not disputed, the AN found that the risk of serious harm was not due to political opinion but had 'to do with the situation of conflict generated in the country, from which nobody is free and which is at the origin of the millions of displaced outside of Syria'.[857]

There were numerous cases where the Danish Refugee Appeals Board (Flygtningenævnet, DRAB) accepted that there was a risk on return on the basis of appellants' individual circumstances. However, these appeals resulted in the grant of Protection Status rather than refugee status. The cases included an interpreter from Iraq,[858] a Syrian civil servant,[859] an Afghan United States Agency for International Development (USAID) employee,[860] and an Afghan police officer,[861] types of cases that are generally recognised as falling within the Refugee Convention definition by other EU MS. Alternatively, distinguishing characteristics considered to increase the risk of harm but leading to complementary protection only included matters such as ethnicity[862] and sex.[863]

[853] BE: RvV 175 087 21.09.2016 (Iraq); BE: RvV 94 655 09.01.2013 (Iraq). However, this was examined (and dismissed) in BE: RvV 161 304 03.02.2016 (Iraq).

[854] In light of the 'sliding-scale' approach developed by the CJEU in *Elgafaji v Staatssecretaris van Justitie* (n 435); FR: CNDA 15027724 11.04.2016 (Iraq); FR: CNDA 15007928 31.08.2015 (Iraq): the CNDA noted the appellant had not raised a current and personal risk of persecution as she referred only to the general security situation; FR: CNDA 14009621 23.07.2014 (Afghanistan); FR: CNDA 13028715 22.04.2014 (Afghanistan); FR: CNDA 130019800 07.03.2014 (Afghanistan).

[855] ES: AN SAN 1202/2015 01.04.2015 (Syria) – successfully appealed to ES: TS STS 5211/2015 10.12.2015 (Syria).

[856] ES: AN SAN 2859/2015 16.07.2015 (Syria) – successfully appealed to ES: TS STS 569/2016 19.02.2016 (Syria).

[857] ES: AN SAN 2156/2015 11.06.2015 (Syria) – successfully appealed to ES: TS STS 1182/2016 16.03.2016 (Syria).

[858] DK: DRAB 03.12.2013 (Iraq).

[859] DK: DRAB 27.08.2015 (Syria).

[860] DK: DRAB 14.06.2013 (Afghanistan).

[861] DK: DRAB 20.09.2016 (Afghanistan).

[862] DK: DRAB 20.12.2016 (Afghanistan): Hazara; DK: DRAB 06.01.2016 (Syria): Turkmen; DK: DRAB 12.06.2013 (Iraq): Faili-Kurd.

[863] DK: DRAB 09.02.2016 (Afghanistan); DK: DRAB 07.08.2013 (Afghanistan).

The analysis in this section demonstrates that appellate authorities generally identify appellants' individual characteristics that contribute to, or in other words increase, the risk of serious harm in the country of origin. However, as discussed, these increased 'risk factors', such as religion, ethnicity, profession and sex, are usually only taken into account in the determination of entitlement to subsidiary protection rather than refugee protection. Where appellate authorities concluded that there was a real risk of serious harm in the absence of state protection, whether under Article 3 ECHR/Article 15(b) Qualification Directive or Article 15(c) Qualification Directive, it is not clear why it was considered that the requirements of the Refugee Convention were not met.

6.4.3 *Gender-Based Violence and Persecution of Women as a Group*

Where female appellants feared gender-based violence in situations of armed conflict, appellate authorities' application and interpretation of the Refugee Convention definition resulted in the finding that such cases were not considered to come within the ambit of the Refugee Convention.[864] As these cases nonetheless resulted in the grant of subsidiary protection, appellate authorities must have considered that the harm was sufficiently serious to justify the grant of international protection.[865] In fact, Storey notes that the human rights-based approach to interpretation of persecution means that it is generally equated with serious harm.[866] As illustrated by the discussion in this section, it is thus possible to conclude that appellate authorities refuse refugee protection for women at risk of gender-based violence because it is considered that no Refugee Convention reasons for persecution apply.

In the French sample, a case concerning the risk of gender-based violence in the context of an armed conflict was viewed as not coming within the scope of the refugee definition.[867] Thus, the CNDA found that the appellant's account of having to engage in forced sexual encounters with Free Syrian Army members at checkpoints in order to access hospital treatment in an area controlled by the government and being threatened by them that they would sell her to ISIS did not engage the Refugee Convention, notwithstanding her being isolated and vulnerable due to her health.[868] Most of the judicial analysis centred on the risk to the appellant deriving from her brothers' political activities and whether or not they had been granted refugee status in other EU MS. Having found that this part of the appellant's account had not been established and thus there was no risk of persecution as a result of any imputed political opinion, the CNDA explicitly stated that even if she had been

[864] DK: DRAB 07.08.2013 (Afghanistan): domestic violence, attempted rape and fear of honour killing was not a basis for refugee protection; DK: DRAB 08.04.2013 (Afghanistan): domestic violence did not reach a sufficient level of intensity for protection status; FR: CNDA 150035416 04.04.2016 (Syria): sexual violence not within the ambit of the Refugee Convention.

[865] The Qualification Directive includes in its definition of acts of persecution 'acts of sexual violence' and 'acts of a gender-specific nature', Articles 9(2)(a), (f). The UK House of Lords for example has equated persecution and serious harm provided serious harm is accompanied by a lack of state protection, see *Islam v Secretary of State for the Home Department Immigration Appeal Tribunal and Another, Ex Parte Shah, R v* [1999] 2 AC 629, per Lord Hoffmann.

[866] Storey, 'Persecution' (n 290) 514.

[867] FR: CNDA 15035416 04.04.2016 (Syria): account of family members' political activities had not been found credible.

[868] FR: CNDA 15035416 04.04.2016 (Syria).

forced to have sex with Free Syrian Army members to get through checkpoints from the outskirts of Damascus into the city centre for hospital treatment, this violence was covered by subsidiary protection.

Lindholm considers that the practice of the DRAB regarding gender-based violence is to apply a restrictive interpretation of the refugee definition.[869] The analysis here supports the proposition made by Lindholm that it is unclear why cases of gender-based violence are granted subsidiary protection by the Board and not refugee status.[870] Looking at the Board's decision-making from a gender perspective suggests that the Board requires at least some state involvement in the serious harm to constitute persecution leading to the grant of refugee status. Thus, female appellants fearing gender-related violence such as forced marriage,[871] domestic violence,[872] and honour-based violence or killings by non-state actors in the absence of state protection were granted Protection Status and not Refugee Convention status.[873] The Board often categorically stated that these claims did not satisfy the requirements for refugee protection although no further legal reasoning was provided. Equally, however, where male appellants feared serious harm by non-state actors such as armed groups, the Board also granted subsidiary protection rather than refugee status.[874]

These cases demonstrate that appellate authorities in the EU generally do not consider gender-based violence by itself to occur for reasons of (imputed) political opinion or other Refugee Convention reasons for persecution in situations of armed conflict as discussed.[875] Accordingly, it is possible to conclude that appellate authorities in general fail to acknowledge or recognise the relevance of gender in understanding the dynamics of violence in situations of armed conflicts as set out in Chapter 3.

In a few instances, appellate authorities examined whether women as a group had a well-founded fear of being persecuted for a Refugee Convention reason. However, the definition of the group at risk itself was limited to single women, meaning that examination of whether there was a group-based risk on return to the country of origin was preceded by an assessment of credibility with respect to appellants' account that they had no family support. By limiting the definition of the group at risk, or in other words the 'risk category', the determination of risk on return shifts from a forward-looking assessment to a more onerous determination of the credibility of appellants' accounts of personal circumstances and past events.[876]

869 Lindholm, *Danske Asylafgørelser* (n 732) 340.

870 Ibid 342. 871 DK: DRAB 07.08.2013 (Afghanistan).

872 DK: DRAB 09.02.2016 (Afghanistan); DK: DRAB 07.08.2013 (Afghanistan).

873 DK: DRAB 09.02.2016 (Afghanistan); DK: DRAB 21.01.2013 (Syria).

874 DK: DRAB 20.12.2016 (Afghanistan); DK: DRAB 20.09.2016 (Afghanistan); DK: DRAB 03.12.2013 (Iraq); DK: DRAB 14.06.2013 (Afghanistan); although two cases of female appellants at risk of serious harm from non-state actors but for reasons of religion resulted in refugee status, as discussed in Section 6.4.1.

875 See Section 6.3. Section 6.4.1 discussed the few instances where appellants at risk of gender-based violence were granted refugee status, see UK: FTT(IAC) 14.11.2016 (Iraq): man at risk of arrest and detention following false rape allegation; UK: FTT(IAC) 22.09.2016 (Iraq): single woman who had been raped at risk from ISIS; FR: CNDA 13029815 25.11.2014 (Afghanistan): lesbian woman at risk of forced marriage.

876 For a more detailed analysis of how the use of narrow risk categories by various asylum actors impact the protection of refugee women, see Querton, 'Non-State Actors of Protection' (n 678).

On a few occasions, the French Court took the view that single women were particularly vulnerable on return to Iraq[877] or Syria,[878] without explicitly recognising them as refugees for the mere fact of being women. Thus, in these two cases, the female appellants were recognised as refugees because other Refugee Convention reasons for persecution applied, such as religion and political opinion. The DRAB, however, explicitly concluded that the circumstances of being a single woman was insufficient in itself to lead to a risk of persecution for a Refugee Convention reason on return to in Iraq[879] or Afghanistan,[880] including where the appellant was the sole carer of her children.[881] These appeals were all dismissed by the Board as the individual circumstances of the cases were not considered to fall within the refugee protection provisions of the Aliens Act. This further supports the conclusion in Section 6.4.1 that appellate authorities are more likely to recognise refugees who accounted for a risk of persecution for additional reasons, such as formal political activity or religion.

6.4.4 Judicial Constructions of Widespread Violence in Situations of Armed Conflict as Refugee Convention Reasons for Persecution

Appellate authorities generally fail to consider how widespread violence in the context of the armed conflicts in Afghanistan, Iraq and Syria may result in the attribution of Refugee Convention reasons for persecution as a consequence of their conventional warfare perspective and the requirement of singling out. More specifically, appellate authorities do not always consider the existence of actual or imputed Refugee Convention grounds where fighting parties in situations of armed conflicts may construct and attribute political identities to the (perceived) opposition based on racial, ethnic, religious, national or gender characteristics. However, irrespective of negative credibility findings, it is necessary to assess whether there is a well-founded fear of persecution on the basis of accepted facts and distinguishing characteristics.[882] In the context of the Syrian conflict for example, this means examining whether fighting parties broadly associate residence in a particular area with the opposition, hence those who live there become a target for violence.[883]

In very few instances, appellate authorities addressed the proposition that widespread violence in the context of armed conflict may satisfy the Refugee Convention definition. On one occasion, the Belgian Court merely stated that the general situation in Syria was not such that there existed a well-founded fear of persecution.[884] In the only instance where the

877 It is not entirely clear if the Court was referring to a risk of persecution or that internal relocation was unreasonable; the Court noted that 'reinstallation in Iraq as a single woman does not appear feasible', FR: CNDA 14031526 02.06.2015 (Iraq).

878 Although the Court found a risk of persecution due to her son's political activities, it also noted that 'isolated women are a particularly vulnerable group in the context of the Syrian conflict', FR: CNDA 16010669 31.10.2016 (Syria).

879 The Board described this single Faili Kurd woman as 'entirely un-profiled', DK: DRAB 12.06.2013 (Iraq).

880 The Board described this elderly and single woman as 'entirely without profile', DK: DRAB 18.12.2013 (Afghanistan).

881 DK: DRAB 14.03.2014 (Afghanistan).

882 UNHCR, *Guidelines on International Protection No. 12* (n 5) para 33; see also BE: RvV 122 129 04.04.2014 (Syria).

883 UNHCR, 'Key Considerations of the Court: BE: RvV 122 129 04.04.2014 (Syria)' <www.refworld.org/cgi-bin/texis/vtx/rwmain/opendocpdf.pdf?reldoc=y&docid=582068d64> accessed 12 July 2021.

884 BE: RvV 106 838 16.07.2013 (Syria).

Belgian Court actually examined the characteristics of the Syrian conflict in the context of the Refugee Convention it found that the government's air strikes against a particular area did not suggest it considered its inhabitants to support the opposition.[885] More specifically, the Belgian Court found that the Syrian regime was carrying out air strikes in areas under the control of the opposition and that civilians were purposefully targeted but the evidence did not establish that inhabitants of the appellant's village were perceived by the Syrian regime as supporting the opposition and were punished for that reason. The Court said that although there was evidence of air strikes against this village and resulting civilian casualties at the end of 2013, its residents were not targeted by the Syrian authorities, rather the risk emanated from fighting between opposition groups. In conclusion, the Belgian Court found that the mere fact of living in a village controlled by the opposition did not establish the existence of an imputed political opinion by the Syrian regime.[886] Thus, overall the Belgian Court did not follow UNHCR's Guidelines that the excessive bombing of certain neighbourhoods associated with the opposition by the Syrian state could constitute an indication of the regime's imputation of a political opinion to all who resided in that geographical area.[887] Instead, the perspective was that violence experienced by the residents was indiscriminate and a by-product of the fighting between the parties to the conflict.

6.5 Conclusion

This chapter examined the intersection of the Refugee Convention reasons for persecution and the dynamics of violence in situations of armed conflict. The chapter set out how knowledge regarding the characteristics of violence in contemporary armed conflicts and the strategic use of violence by all parties to conflicts first explored in Chapter 3 provides an explanatory framework for interpreting the Refugee Convention reasons for persecution where the well-founded fear of being persecuted arises in situations of armed conflict. Hence, better understanding the dynamics of violence and the aims of parties to conflicts may demonstrate that the constitution of political identities based on racial, ethnic, religious, national, sex or gender characteristics justify and maintain the exercise of violence around times of armed conflict.[888] The case was also made for the particular relevance of the Refugee Convention ground of imputed political opinion. This perspective provides a useful lens to identify the relevant Refugee Convention reasons for persecution and highlights the increasing significance of imputed Refugee Convention grounds in situations of contemporary armed conflict.

The review of judicial practice with respect to this element of the refugee definition was then set out and the impact of appellate authorities' perspective of conventional warfare and requirement of singling out, discussed in Chapter 4 and 5 respectively, on the application and interpretation of the Refugee Convention reasons for persecution in situations of armed conflict was discussed. In the small proportion of cases where reasons for persecution were considered because appellants had been singled out, there was little judicial analysis.

885 BE: RvV 123 550 05.05.2014 (Syria). 886 BE: RvV 123 550 05.05.2014 (Syria) para 2.4.

887 UNHCR, 'International Protection Considerations with Regard to People Fleeing the Syrian Arab Republic, Update II' 22 October 2013, para 14 and sources cited in footnote 56, para 16 Risk Profiles II and III; see also UNHCR, *Guidelines on International Protection No. 12* (n 5) para 33; see also Section 6.2.

888 See in particular Sections 3.5–3.6 in Chapter 3.

A trend was also identified whereby appellate authorities in the EU do not generally consider the application of the Refugee Convention definition to persons who share personal characteristics with groups of persons similarly situated but who have not experienced individual instances of conflict with actors of persecution or whose account of such events was found not credible. In practice, the determination of a person's appeal under the Refugee Convention was thus cursorily completed where no personal instances of contact with actors of persecution were raised or ended as soon as the account indicating having been singled out was rejected. Subsequently, this chapter demonstrated that there was little to no consideration by appellate authorities of the relevance of the Refugee Convention reasons for persecution to the general conditions of widespread violence.

The pervasive practice by appellate authorities in the EU is stilting the development of international refugee law in this respect, even though persons fleeing armed conflicts represent the majority of persons seeking international protection globally. Instead, persons fleeing armed conflicts are either granted subsidiary or temporary protection status with lesser rights or refused protection entirely. In practice few are returned, however, due to the practical difficulties of returns to zones of conflict.[889]

Significantly, the findings in this chapter support the proposition that appellate authorities do not take into account the gender-differentiated impact of armed conflicts, thereby failing to effectively protect women fleeing violence in contemporary armed conflicts. This conclusion fills an important gap in the literature, particularly as it is based on a comparative and systematic analysis of judicial interpretation in EU MS. Overall, violence exercised by non-state actors, such as armed groups, against men was considered by appellate authorities to be for reasons of (imputed) political opinion whereas violence experienced by women at the hands of non-state actors fell outside the Refugee Convention reasons for persecution.

As set out in Chapter 3, contemporary armed conflicts are characterised by the rise of non-state actors. Despite the fact that asylum claims based on a fear of persecution at the hands of non-state actors have traditionally faced obstacles, appellate authorities were generally alert to the risks faced by male appellants of being forcibly recruited by armed groups in situations of armed conflicts. On the one hand, appellate authorities in France and the UK in particular demonstrated an understanding of these gendered norms with respect to the attribution of political opinion to male appellants. On the other hand, there was little to no consideration of the gendered dynamics of violence arising outside the context of fighting in contemporary armed conflicts. As a result, appeals by women at risk of gender-based violence from armed groups were rarely considered as coming within the ambit of one of the Refugee Convention reasons for persecution. The DRAB consideration of risks of serious harm from non-state actors as outside the scope of the Refugee Convention is noteworthy.[890] Overall, appellate

[889] See for example Kurdistan 24, 'Baghdad Rejects Efforts by European Nations to Forcibly Deport Iraqi Refugees' (29 January 2018) <www.kurdistan24.net/en/news/ce115375-001b-46ea-810e-65e5c480267a> accessed 12 July 2021; ECRE, 'No Reason for Returns to Afghanistan' (February 2019) <www.ecre.org/wp-content/uploads/2019/02/Policy-Note-17.pdf> accessed 12 July 2021; EU External Action, 'The EU and the Crisis in Syria' (20 September 2019) <eeas.europa.eu/headquarters/headquarters-Homepage/59417/eu-and-crisis-syria_en> accessed 12 July 2021.

[890] DK: DRAB 20.12.2016 (Afghanistan): at risk from the Kuchi people; DK: DRAB 20.09.2016 (Afghanistan): at risk from Taliban; DK: DRAB 09.02.2016 (Afghanistan): at risk from family and in-laws; DK: DRAB 03.12.2013 (Iraq): at risk from the Mahdi Militia; DK: DRAB 07.08.2013 (Afghanistan): at risk from husband and uncle; DK: DRAB 14.06.2013 (Afghanistan): at risk from Taliban; see also ES: AN SAN 5686/2013 26.12.2013 (Afghanistan): feared the Taliban; see Sections 6.4.2–6.4.3.

authorities' perspective of conventional warfare helps explain how risks relating to taking part in fighting, generally faced by men, are more readily considered as falling within the Refugee Convention reasons for persecution than the gendered dynamics of violence experienced by women.

Applying and interpreting the Refugee Convention to determine whether the definition of a refugee encompasses persons fleeing armed conflicts requires an understanding of the Refugee Convention reasons for persecution in situations of armed conflicts and this, in turn, requires an understanding of the dynamics of violence in contemporary armed conflicts. Acquiring this understanding necessitates consideration of the historical causes of armed conflicts, the fighting parties' motivations in conflict and the objectives and strategies of parties to the conflict. Ensuring that those who apply and interpret international refugee law are able to undertake this assessment in line with international law will require access to up-to-date and objective information regarding the nature of violence in contemporary armed conflicts, some of which is already widely available in the feminist security studies field. Country of origin information collected by terms of reference or questions guided by a conventional warfare perspective is unlikely to provide the relevant evidence required to interpret the Refugee Convention definition in light of present-day conditions. Thus, conflict-related asylum decision-making in line with states' international obligations is dependent on evidence going to the core of violence in contemporary armed conflicts. This suggests further research into the assumptions made regarding armed conflicts in the process of collecting objective evidence and country of origin information and highlights the need for further guidance and training in this area.

7

Conclusion

7.1 Research Objective and Contribution

The book contributes to existing debates regarding the continued relevance of the Refugee Convention by engaging with the misconception that persons fleeing armed conflicts do not come within the scope of the Refugee Convention definition. It addressed the international protection of persons fleeing armed conflicts in the European Union (EU) from a gender perspective. The issue is relevant because the number of displaced persons globally is the highest ever recorded today and most refugees are fleeing countries experiencing protracted armed conflicts. Thus, refugees often flee situations characterised by a material level and spread of violence. The increase in persons fleeing contemporary armed conflicts is a trend observed in the EU as well. There was a surge in asylum applications in the period from 2015 to 2016 and although the numbers have dropped since, almost 30 per cent of asylum applicants in the EU originate from just three countries, namely Syria, Iraq and Afghanistan. The research thus contributes to existing debates regarding the continued relevance of the Refugee Convention in the context of persons fleeing armed conflicts.

The principal legal instrument for the protection of refugees is the Refugee Convention but the EU legal order also provides for subsidiary protection status specifically aimed at providing protection for persons fleeing indiscriminate violence in situations of armed conflict, a status that entails a lesser set of rights than refugee status, or temporary protection status in the case of a mass influx of displaced persons fleeing areas of armed conflict or endemic violence. The question of how international protection provisions are applied and interpreted in the EU is significant because the proportion of persons originating from the same countries of origin recognised as refugees or as beneficiaries of subsidiary protection varies widely amongst EU Member States (MS).[891] These divergences are less readily justified where a large proportion of persons flee the objective circumstances of widespread violence exercised in situations of protracted armed conflicts.

An aspect of refugee protection in the context of persons fleeing armed conflicts that has not received much attention in the literature, and which this book sought to address, is the generally accepted claim within security studies that the nature of armed conflicts has changed since the early 1990s. Although there may be some disagreements regarding the precise differences between 'old' and 'new' conflicts, there is a general agreement that the characteristics of and the nature of violence in contemporary armed conflicts have changed. More specifically, the rise of non-state actors, their relative control over the conduct of hostilities, the weakening of state institutions, gendered identity politics as drivers

[891] There are of course no divergences in respect of temporary protection because the decision to grant this status is taken at EU level rather than an individual MS level.

of violence and the strategic logic of violence are all fundamental characteristics of contemporary armed conflicts. Accordingly, the original starting point of the book was the recognition of the changed characteristics of contemporary armed conflicts and the conceptual distinction between violence and conflicts. Although other scholars have researched the interpretation of the Refugee Convention in the cases of refugees fleeing armed conflicts, none have set this enquiry into the wealth of knowledge existing in feminist and security studies scholarship or conducted a study based on a systematic probability sampling method allowing for the making of generalisations about judicial practice in the EU. Moreover, whereas some scholars have looked to some extent at the changing characteristics of armed conflicts, their focus of enquiry was on subsidiary protection status in the EU rather than on the Refugee Convention as the cornerstone of international protection. Therefore, the book examined the extent to which appellate authorities in Europe take into account the changing nature of contemporary armed conflicts, including its gender-differentiating impact, and explored how the Refugee Convention may be interpreted in a manner that better responds to the changed nature of contemporary armed conflicts from a gender perspective.

7.2 Research Findings

Chapter 2 made the case that the definition of a refugee in the United Nations (UN) Refugee Convention encompasses groups of persons fleeing across borders for reasons related to widespread violence in situations of armed conflict. Although there is an increase in groups of persons displaced across borders as a result of violence in situations of armed conflict, this reason for flight is not new. The research has shown how the concept of refugee protection originated in mechanisms set up by the international community to recognise as refugees groups of persons fleeing a number of specific events, including war and widespread violence. Furthermore, although the adoption of the Refugee Convention in 1951 marked a shift in the framework for international protection in general, this change concerned only the inclusion of a definition of general application, not linked to specific countries of origin, rather than the normative concept of a refugee. Finally, regional frameworks for refugee protection were never devised with a view to fill a perceived gap in the application of the Refugee Convention definition to persons fleeing situations of armed conflict.

Chapter 2 also argued that an interpretation of the Refugee Convention definition that complies with the Law of Treaties requires taking account of the characteristics of contemporary armed conflicts and the dynamics of violence in situations of widespread human rights violations as set out in feminist and security studies scholarship. An interpretation of the Refugee Convention definition that ignores this knowledge will fail to provide effective protection to persons fleeing contemporary armed conflicts.

Accordingly, Chapter 3 set out how an understanding of the nature of violence in contemporary armed conflicts is relevant to the interpretation of the Refugee Convention definition. The conceptual framework developed for this book highlights the importance of distinguishing between armed conflicts and violence as conceptually distinct notions. More specifically, it challenges appellate authorities' conflation of asymmetrical warfare with lower levels of violence and less serious forms of violence, contrary to knowledge in the field of feminist and security studies indicating that non-conventional armed conflicts are in fact characterised by armed groups' relative control over the exercise of strategic violence, as discussed in Chapter 4. This perspective and subsequent approach to interpretation means that the effectiveness of refugee protection in the EU is lacking, as persons fleeing contemporary armed conflicts who meet the Refugee Convention criteria, when examined through the lenses of gendered perspectives of contemporary armed conflicts are not recognised as refugees. Instead, the book demonstrates that the interpretation of the Refugee Convention definition in accordance with the general rule of treaty interpretation and in light of the characteristics of contemporary armed conflicts and the nature of violence therein brings under the protective scope of the Refugee Convention the circumstances of their flight.

The analysis in Chapter 4 of the 320 asylum appeal judgments collected for this study revealed that appellate authorities conceive of the conflicts in Afghanistan, Iraq and Syria predominantly from the perspective of conventional warfare and through a territorial lens. Broadly, this perspective amounts to conceptualising armed conflicts as conducted mainly by means of conventional warfare whereby the different sides to the conflict have equal capacity to engage in ground combats using heavy weaponry in a manner reminiscing of interstate wars. The focus on territoriality involves an assumption that control over territory is achieved by successful armed confrontations and subsequent physical occupation through day-to-day management and infrastructure. This territorial perspective fails to acknowledge that one of the main strategies of fighting parties is to exercise political control over territory by forcibly displacing and terrorising populations through the exercise of highly visible and gendered forms of human rights violations.

Using the analytical framework developed in Chapter 3, the claim was made in Chapter 4 that appellate authorities in EU MS fail to take into account the changing nature of contemporary armed conflicts when interpreting the Refugee Convention definition in the asylum appeals of persons fleeing armed conflicts. Thus, judicial understanding and conceptualisation of contemporary armed conflicts does not reflect the wealth of knowledge existing in the field of feminist and security studies. More specifically, appellate authorities' conventional warfare approach does not align with evidence demonstrating that asymmetrical or non-conventional warfare is the principal mode of fighting in contemporary armed conflicts because armed groups are generally unable to match the military capacity of the state.

However, and most importantly in the context of asylum determination, this inability is not synonymous with relative weakness in the broader conflict. On the contrary, the capability of armed groups to adapt to and endorse different fighting strategies renders them increasingly resilient and effective in conflicts, such that armed groups now generally control and determine the conduct of hostilities. Therefore, armed conflicts characterised by asymmetrical or non-conventional modes of fighting are not indicative of low levels or lesser impact of violence. Thus, Chapter 4 concluded that appellate authorities do not take into consideration the current circumstances of violence in armed conflicts in a manner that reflects this contemporary phenomenon, meaning that the effective protection of persons fleeing armed conflicts is not guaranteed. Not only do appellate authorities fail to view contemporary conflicts in accordance with the wealth of knowledge in this field, they make contrary assumptions with regards to the relationship between the characteristics of armed conflict and the nature of violence. Accordingly, appellate authorities fail to consider the gendered and strategic logic of violence exercised by parties to armed conflicts.

In addition, appellate authorities in the EU rarely examine whether the Refugee Convention definition applies in individual appeals in light of the objective conditions of contemporary armed conflicts. Although EU law requires appellate authorities to firstly consider whether appellants are Convention refugees and only if the answer is negative consider whether they may be entitled to subsidiary forms of protection, the study found that appellate authorities rarely examined the objective circumstances of armed conflicts when applying and interpreting the Refugee Convention and almost always considered these solely in relation to Article 15(c) Qualification Directive. Hence, the potential repercussions of appellate authorities' conventional warfare perspective for their interpretation of the Refugee Convention definition were discussed in Chapters 5 and 6. Broadly, the research found that appellate authorities adopt a conventional warfare perspective that imbues their interpretation of the international protection provisions in EU law in a way that does not ensure the Refugee Convention's *effet utile*.

Chapter 5 discussed the finding of a general trend across appellate authorities in the EU to interpret a 'well-founded fear of being persecuted' as requiring individuals to have been singled out for persecution contrary to an interpretation of the Refugee Convention definition in line with the general rule of treaty interpretation. Overall, judicial analysis of appellants' personal characteristics and circumstances focuses on past events and, consequently, the assessment of risk is equated with an assessment of credibility of appellants' personal accounts of events occurring in their country of origin prior to flight. There is thus a failure to determine whether the objective evidence demonstrates that similarly situated persons are experiencing persecution. Furthermore, there are indications that the assessment of credibility is highly gendered in the sense that any personal account that deviates from gender norms is considered as lacking in credibility. This suggestion is critical in light of the finding that appellate authorities conflate the 'well-founded fear of being persecuted' element of the Refugee Convention definition with the assessment of credibility. This issue can be identified as requiring further research.

Chapter 5 also discussed how appellate authorities in the EU heighten the standard of proof from a reasonable likelihood of being persecuted to a concrete risk of being persecuted. This practice is likely to impact persons fleeing armed conflicts more severely because they are more likely to be fleeing violence without having been singled out, when in fact widespread violence in situations of armed conflict generally increases the risk of persecution and serious harm and the lack of state protection. As appellate authorities' assessment of appellants' entitlement to refugee status ends when the account of personal events or circumstances in the country of origin is considered not credible, Chapter 5 concluded that this pervasive practice is contrary to the need to interpret the Refugee Convention definition in light of the realities of contemporary armed conflicts. An enquiry into the nature of violence in contemporary armed conflicts and the application of knowledge acquired in the fields of feminist and security studies would bring the gendered and strategic logic of violence motivated by identity politics to the fore. Interpreting the meaning of a 'well-founded fear of persecution' in the context of flight from armed conflicts requires taking into account this knowledge to ensure the effective protection of persons fleeing countries such as Afghanistan, Iraq and Syria.

Chapter 6 argued that appellate authorities do not generally consider whether actual or imputed Refugee Convention reasons for persecution exist in light of the nature of violence in contemporary armed conflicts, thereby stilting the development of international refugee law. Chapter 6 examined how appellate authorities in the EU construct the Refugee Convention grounds for persecution and argued that the nature of violence in contemporary armed conflicts is generally motivated by reasons encompassed by the Refugee

Convention definition. The chapter further argued that appellate authorities' conception of violence, namely that it is more severe and arises predominantly during armed confrontations between parties to the conflicts, and the consequent perception that violence against civilians is merely indiscriminate significantly hamper the jurisprudential development of the Refugee Convention reasons for persecution in the context of armed conflicts.

In practice, where appellants' account of personal circumstances and past events is accepted by appellate authorities, judicial consideration of the Refugee Convention reasons for persecution is generally straightforward with little legal analysis and discussion. As a consequence of appellate authorities' requirement of appellants being singled out, personal characteristics that are considered to increase the risk of harm on return are only examined in relation to complementary protection. Furthermore, there is an almost complete absence of consideration of how the general conditions of violence in Afghanistan, Iraq and Syria may be seen as engaging any actual or imputed Refugee Convention reasons for persecution. In light of the dynamics of violence in contemporary armed conflicts, including the drive for violence through gendered identity politics, this approach fails to effectively examine all the relevant facts of the case, such that the interpretation of the Refugee Convention definition is not undertaken in accordance with EU MS's obligations in international law.

Chapter 6 also concluded that appellate authorities' interpretation of the Refugee Convention ground of political opinion is too narrow and fails to acknowledge women's experiences of gendered violence. The research found that few appeals lead to the grant of refugee status and that most of those cases are allowed on the basis that the risk of persecution arises for reason of imputed political opinion. Although this finding may be explained by the fact that violence in contemporary armed conflicts is frequently motivated on the basis of attributed political identities, the decisions are justified by reference to appellants' personal circumstances and past experiences in their countries of origin. More specifically, on the one hand, most of the cases concern male appellants who have a well-founded fear of being persecuted because of an imputed political opinion resulting from their own or other male relatives' opinions, activities or professions, draft evasion or forced recruitment.

On the other hand, appellate authorities generally do not consider that women who have experienced gender-based violence have a well-founded fear of being persecuted for a Refugee Convention reason. In the limited instances where this was considered, appellate authorities did not find that women or women without family support constitute a group at risk of persecution on return to Afghanistan, Iraq or Syria. The chapter thus concluded that appellate authorities interpret the Refugee Convention ground of political opinion with excessive formalism and too narrowly. This trend reflects their perspective of violence arising from conventional warfare in a manner such that the gendered dynamics of violence against men in armed conflicts are acknowledged whereas those experienced by women are not. In general, gender-based violence against women is not considered as coming within the scope of the Refugee Convention reasons for persecution.

Drawing on the conceptual framework developed in Chapter 3, Chapter 6 further developed the claim that the realities of contemporary armed conflicts indicate that risk on return is increasingly linked to actors of persecution attributing political identities to groups of persons, in order to distinguish and target them for acts of violence. Overall, appellate authorities' failure to consider the gendered dynamics of violence in armed conflicts is stilting the development of international refugee law even though persons fleeing armed conflicts represent the majority of persons seeking international protection globally.

7.3 Future Research Implications

Focusing on the nature of violence in situations of armed conflict, rather than the notion of armed conflict, to determine entitlement to refugee protection, as argued in this book, leaves open the exploration of the concept of political violence in other situations of armed conflict not discussed here, such as internal conflicts involving drug cartels and organised gangs.[892]

Another of the wider practical implications of this study relates to efforts to improve the harmonisation of asylum decisions across the EU. In particular, the European Union Agency for Asylum (EUAA), with its recent additional powers,[893] is playing an increasing role in ensuring a harmonised approach to the interpretation of the Refugee Convention definition of a refugee in EU law. The EUAA Regulation creates an obligation on EU MS to 'take into account' its Country Guidance 'when examining applications for international protection, without prejudice to their competence to decide on individual applications for international protection',[894] in order to foster convergence in applying the assessment criteria established in the Qualification Directive.[895] Accordingly, the approach to interpretation of international protection provisions endorsed by the Agency and the underlying perspective of armed conflicts adopted in its guidance documents may have a substantial impact on the future protection of refugees fleeing armed conflicts in the EU.

Furthermore, a ramification of the research concerns the collection and use of country of origin information and evidence to support asylum decision-making in the EU. This evidence may be based on sources of information that focus on the macro-level causes of armed conflict rather than the micro-level dynamics of violence in situations of armed conflict. Thus, using the former information as evidence in the refugee status determination process may inescapably and unjustifiably maintain appellate authorities' perspective of violence through a conventional warfare lens. Future research and advocacy efforts should be informed by the conceptual framework set out in Chapter 3 and implemented throughout this book.

892 For works on the protection needs of persons fleeing cartels and criminal gangs, see for example Nicolas Rodriguez Serna, 'Fleeing Cartels and Maras: International Protection Considerations and Profiles from the Northern Triangle' (2016) 28 *International Journal of Refugee Law* 25; Jillian N. Blake, 'Gang and Cartel Violence: A Reason to Grant Political Asylum from Mexico and Central America' (2012) 38 *Yale Journal of International Law Online* 31. See also UNHCR, 'Guidance Note on Refugee Claims Relating to Victims of Organized Gangs' (n 783) paras 45–51.

893 Formerly the European Asylum Support Office, EUAA Regulation.

894 Article 11(3) EUAA Regulation.

895 Article 11(1) EUAA Regulation Christel Querton, 'Country Guidance, Country of Origin Information, and the International Protection Needs of Persons Fleeing Armed Conflicts' (2023) 42(3) *Refugee Survey Quarterly*, see https://academic.oup.com/rsq/advance-article/doi/10.1093/rsq/hdad003/7091824.

APPENDICES

Appendix A

Overview of International Protection Legislation and Asylum Procedures

	Belgium	Denmark	France	Spain	The Netherlands	United Kingdom
First-instance decision-making authority	Commissioner General for Refugees and Stateless Persons (CGRS)[896]	Danish Immigration Service (DIS)[897]	Office for the Protection of Refugees and Stateless Persons (OFPRA)[898]	Office of Asylum and Refuge (OAR)[899]	Immigration and Naturalisation Service (IND)[900]	UK Visas and Immigration (UKVI)

[896] Commissariat Général aux Réfugiés et aux Apatrides (CGRA)/Commissariaat-generaal voor Vluchtelingen en Staatlozen (CGVS).
[897] Udlændingestyrelsen. [898] Office Français de Protection des Réfugiés et Apatrides. [899] Oficina de Asilo y Refugio. [900] Immigratie en Naturalisatiedienst.

Legislation transposing Art. 1A(2) Refugee Convention	Article 48/3(1) Aliens Act 1980[901]	Section 7(1) Aliens Act 1983[902]	Article L511-1 Code of Entry and Residence of Foreigners and of the Right to Asylum (CESEDA)[903]	Article 3 Law 12/2009 of 30 October 2009, regulating the Law of Asylum and Subsidiary Protection (Asylum Act)[904]	Article 29(1)(a) Aliens Act 2000[905]	Regulation 2 of The Refugee or Person in Need of International Protection (Qualification) Regulations 2006[906]
Legislation transposing Art. 15(c) Qualification Directive	Article 48/4(1)-(2) Aliens Act 1980	N/A Protection Status: s. 7(2) Aliens Act as amended[907] Temporary Protection Status: s. 7(3) Aliens Act as amended[908]	Article L512-1(c) CESEDA[909]	Article 4 Asylum Act	Article 29(1)(b)(3) Aliens Act 2000	Para. 339C-339CA(iv) Immigration Rules[910]

901 Loi du 15 décembre 1980 sur l'accès au territoire, le séjour, l'établissement et l'éloignement des étrangers/Wet van 15 december 1980 betreffende de toegang tot het grondgebied, het verblijf, de vestiging en de verwijdering van vreemdelingen (Aliens Act 1980) <www.ejustice.just.fgov.be/cgi_loi/change_lg.pl?language=fr&la=F&cn=1980121530&table_name=loi> accessed 12 July 2021.

902 Udlændingeloven: Lov nr. 226 af 8 juni 1983, Lovtidende A 1983, S. 549–550 as amended <www.retsinformation.dk/eli/lta/2021/1910> accessed 12 July 2021.

903 Code de l'Entrée et du Séjour des Etrangers et du Droit d'Asile (CESEDA) <www.legifrance.gouv.fr/affichCode.do?cidTexte=LEGITEXT000006070158&dateTexte=20130416> accessed 12 July 2021 (former Article L711-1).

904 Ley 12/2009, de 30 de octubre, reguladora del derecho de asilo y de la protección subsidiaria BOE núm. 263, de 31 de octubre (Asylum Act) <www.interior.gob.es/web/servicios-al-ciudadano/normativa/leyes-ordinarias/ley-12-2009-de-30-de-octubre> accessed 12 July 2021.

905 Vreemdelingenwet 2000 (Vw 2000) as amended <https://wetten.overheid.nl/BWBR0011823/2021-07-01#Hoofdstuk3_Afdeling4> accessed 12 July 2021.

906 Until 28 June 2022 <www.legislation.gov.uk/uksi/2006/2525/made> accessed 12 July 2021. Now Sections 30–35 Nationality and Borders Act 2022 <www.legislation.gov.uk/ukpga/2022/36/contents/enacted> accessed 26 July 2022.

907 Beskyttelsesstatus.

908 Midlertidig beskyttelsesstatus; Lov om ændring af udlændingeloven: Lov nr. 153 af 18 februar 2015, Lovtidende A 2015.

909 Former Article L712-1(c) CESEDA.

910 Statement of Changes in Immigration Rules (HC395) May 1994 as amended <www.gov.uk/guidance/immigration-rules/immigration-rules-part-11-asylum> accessed 12 July 2021.

	Belgium	Denmark	France	Spain	The Netherlands	United Kingdom
RS Residence Permit Length	5 years[911]	2 years[912]	10 years[913]	5 years[914]	5 years[915]	5 years[916]
SP Residence Permit Length	1 year followed by 2 years on renewal[917]	PS: 1 year followed by 2 years on renewal TPS: 1 year for first 3 years followed by 2 years[918]	4 years (since March 2019)[919]	5 years[920]	5 years[921]	5 years[922]
Family Reunification	Same conditions for beneficiaries of RS and SP[923]	Same conditions for beneficiaries of RS and PS TPS: After 3 years only[924]	Same conditions for beneficiaries of RS and SP[925]	Same conditions for beneficiaries of RS and SP[926]	Same conditions for beneficiaries of RS and SP	Same conditions for beneficiaries of RS and SP

911 Article 49(1) Aliens Act 1980.

912 Ny i Danmark, 'Voksen Asylansøger' <https://nyidanmark.dk/da/Du-vil-ans%C3%B8ge/Asyl/Voksen-asylans%C3%B8ger> accessed 12 July 2021.

913 Article L424-1 CESEDA (former Article L.314-11(8)).

914 Article 34(3) Royal Decree 557/2011 of 20 April approving the regulation implementing Law 4/2000 on rights and liberties of aliens in Spain and their social integration (Real Decreto 557/2011, de 20 de abril, por el que se aprueba el Reglamento de la Ley Orgánica 4/2000, sobre derechos y libertades de los extranjeros en España y su integración social, tras su reforma por Ley Orgánica 2/2009) (Aliens Regulation).

915 Article 28(2) Aliens Act 2000. 916 Para. 339Q(i) Immigration Rules. 917 Article 49/2(1)-(2) Aliens Act 1980. 918 Ny i Danmark (n 887).

919 Article L424-9 CESEDA (former Article L.313-25, inserted by Article 1 Law n. 2018-778 of 10 September 2018). Prior to 2019, the length was 1 year followed by 2 years on renewal (former Article L.313-13(1) CESEDA).

920 Article 34(3) Aliens Regulation. 921 Article 28(2) Aliens Act 2000. 922 Para. 339Q(ii) Immigration Rules.

923 Article 10(1)(4) Aliens Act 1980.

924 Spouses must both be at least 24 years old. S. 9(1)(c)-(d), s. 9(2)(c)-(d) and s. 9(3)(c)-(d) Aliens Act as amended by Lov om ændring af udlændingeloven: Lov nr. 102 af 3 februar 2016, Lovtidende A 2016.

925 Article L561-2 CESEDA. 926 Article 41 Asylum Act.

Appellate Authority	Council of Alien Law Litigation (CCE/RvV)[927]	Danish Refugee Appeals Board (DRAB)[928]	National Asylum Court (CNDA)[929]	National High Court (AN)[930]	District Court (Rb)[931]	First Tier Tribunal, Immigration and Asylum Chamber (FTT (IAC))
Type of Appellate Procedure	Judicial, asylum and immigration law specialism	Administrative (quasi-judicial procedures), asylum law specialism	Judicial, asylum law specialism	Judicial, administrative law specialism	Judicial, administrative law specialism	Judicial, immigration and asylum law specialism
Appellate Authority Jurisdiction	• Allow and grant RS/SP • Dismiss • Annul CGRS decision and remit	• Allow and grant RS/PS/TPS • Dismiss • Annul DIS decision and remit	• Allow and grant RS/SP • Dismiss • Annul OFPRA decision and remit	• Allow and grant RS/SP • Dismiss • Annul OAR decision and remit	• No appeal from grant of SP[932] • Allow and grant RS/SP • Dismiss • Annul IND decision and remit	• Allow and grant RS/SP • Dismiss • Annul UKVI decision and remit (until 2016)

927 Conseil du contentieux des étrangers (CCE)/Raad voor Vreemdelingenbetwistingen (RvV).
928 Flygtningenævnet. 929 Cour Nationale du Droit d'Asile. 930 Audiencia Nacional. 931 Rechtbank. 932 NL: RvS No. 20010591481 28.03.2002.

	Belgium	Denmark	France	Spain	The Netherlands	United Kingdom
Availability of Decisions	All decisions are published on website database[933]	Summary of most decisions on website database[934] and of relevant decisions in DRAB annual reports[935]	Summary of relevant decisions in annual and thematic CNDA reports published on website[936]	All decisions are published on website database[937]	Some decisions are published on website database[938]	Not publicly available
Deadline to appeal (regular procedure)	30 days	Automatic[939]	1 month[940]	2 months[941]	1 week	14 days
Suspensive effect	Yes	Yes[942]	Yes	Not automatically	Not automatically	Yes (unless certified)
Onward Appeal	Council of State[943] on point of law only	Not available[944]	Council of State[945] on point of law only	Supreme Court,[946] can remake decision[947]	Council of State[948]	Upper Tribunal, Immigration and Asylum Chamber (UT (IAC)); Court of Appeal; Supreme Court

933 RvV/CCE, 'Arrêts' (undated) <www.rvv-cce.be/fr/arr> accessed 12 July 2021. 934 DRAB, 'Praksis' (undated) <www.fln.dk/da/Praksis.aspx> accessed 12 July 2021.
935 DRAB, 'Beretninger' (undated) <www.fln.dk/da/Publikationer/Publikationer/Beretninger.aspx> accessed 12 July 2021.
936 CNDA, 'Recueils de jurisprudence' (undated) <www.cnda.fr/Ressources-juridiques-et-geopolitiques/Recueils-de-jurisprudence> accessed 12 July 2021.
937 Consejo General del Poder Judicial, 'Centro de Documentación Judicial' (undated) <www.poderjudicial.es/search/indexAN.jsp> accessed 12 July 2021.
938 Rechtspraak, 'Uitspraken' (undated) <https://uitspraken.rechtspraak.nl/> accessed 12 July 2021.
939 S. 53a(2) Aliens Act. 940 Article L532-1 CESEDA. 941 Article 29(2) Asylum Act. 942 S. 53a(2) Aliens Act. 943 Conseil d'Etat/Raad van State (CE/RvS).
944 Article 56(8) Aliens Act. 945 Conseil d'Etat (CE). 946 Tribunal Supremo (TS). 947 Article 29(2) Asylum Act.
948 Afdeling Bestuursrechtspraak Raad van State (RvS).

Appendix B

Asylum Statistics in the EU

All the tables in this appendix were compiled from Eurostat statistics.[949]

Table B.1 *First-instance decisions and outcome by sex in the EU, 2013–2016*

Year	First-instance decisions	Refugee status	%	Subsidiary protection status	%
2013	314,925	49,675	15.77	45,435	14.43
M	208,050	29,435	14.15	29,630	14.24
F	106,810	19,940	18.67	15,645	14.65
2014	367,435	95,390	25.96	56,295	15.32
M	246,565	62,330	25.28	39,485	16,01
F	120,795	32,890	27.23	16,695	13.82
2015	597,125	229,460	38.43	54,900	9.19
M	416,495	161,680	38.32	38,655	9.28
F	180,410	67,670	37.51	16,235	9
2016	1,106,770	366,475	33.11	255,440	23.08
M	738,525	238,760	32.33	161,955	21.93
F	367,405	127,395	34.67	93,300	25.39

Table B.2 *Final decisions and outcome by sex in the EU, 2013–2016*

Year	Final decisions	Rejections	Rejections%	Refugee status	RS%	Subsidiary protection status	SP%
2013	134,885	110,210	81.71	14,845	11%	5,350	3.97%
M	88,075	72,465	82.28	9,595	10.85	3,365	3.82
F	46,770	37,705	80.62	5,245	11.21	1,985	4.24
2014	136,405	110,200	80.79	15,990	11.72	5,415	3.97
M	88,370	71,600	81.02	10,285	11.64	3,560	4.03
F	47,855	38,425	80.29	5,700	11.91	1,850	3.86

949 Eurostat, 'First instance decisions on applications by citizenship, age and sex Annual aggregated data (rounded) [migr_asydcfsta]' <https://ec.europa.eu/eurostat/web/asylum-and-managed-migration/data/database> accessed and compiled 1 April 2019.

Table B.2 *(cont.)*

Year	Final decisions	Rejections	Rejections%	Refugee status	RS%	Subsidiary protection status	SP%
2015	179,480	153,060	85.28	18,110	10.09	4,640	2.58
M	114,285	96,925	84.81	12,020	10.52	3,185	2.79
F	65,140	56,085	86.1	6,090	9.35	1,455	2.23
2016	231,190	188,540	81.55	23,660	10.23	8,275	3.58
M	152,860	122,845	80.36	15,935	10.42	6,050	3.96
F	78,160	65,530	83.84	7,720	9.88	2,225	2.85

Table B.3 *Afghanistan: Final decisions and outcome by sex in the EU, 2013–2016*

Year	Final decisions	Rejections	%	Refugee status	%	Subsidiary protection status	%
2013	9,650	5,195	53.83	2,055	21.29	900	9.33
M	7,375	4,330	58.71	1,310	17.76	745	10.1
F	2,275	865	38.02	745	32.75	155	6.81
2014	8,205	3,465	42.23	2,415	29.43	1,305	15.09
M	6,560	2,965	45.2	1,690	25.76	1,170	17.83
F	1,645	500	30.39	725	44.07	135	8.21
2015	6,395	2,195	34.32	2,260	35.34	1,195	18.69
M	5,080	1,845	36.32	1,610	31.69	1,115	21.95
F	1,315	355	27	650	49.43	80	6.08
2016	9,630	6,175	64.12	1,795	18.64	840	8.72
M	7,280	4,820	66.21	1,200	16.48	710	9.75
F	2,345	1,350	57.57	590	25.16	130	5.54

Table B.4 *Iraq: Final decisions and outcome by sex in the EU, 2013–2016*

Year	Final decisions	Rejections	Rejections%	Refugee status	RS%	Subsidiary protection status	SP%
2013	4,385	3,385	77.19	525	11.97	185	4.22
M	2,845	2,215	77.85	320	11.25	130	4.57
F	1,540	1,170	75.97	205	13.31	55	3.57
2014	3,550	2,175	61.27	900	25.35	215	6.06
M	2,400	1,560	65	540	22.5	155	6.46
F	1,145	615	53.71	360	31.44	60	5.24
2015	2,575	1,150	44.66	1,070	41.55	225	8.74
M	1.810	840	46.40	730	40.33	165	9.12
F	765	310	40.52	340	44.44	60	7.84
2016	6,800	5,005	73.6	1,155	16.98	470	6.91
M	4,810	3,575	74.32	780	16.21	335	6.96
F	1,990	1,430	71.86	370	18.59	135	6.78

Table B.5 *Syria: Final decisions and outcome by sex in the EU, 2013–2016*

Year	Final decisions	Rejections	Rejections%	Refugee status	RS%	Subsidiary protection status	SP%
2013	4,140	1,295	31.28	1,110	26.81	1,725	41.67
M	2,660	810	30.45	760	28.57	1,085	40.79
F	1,480	485	32.77	350	23.65	640	43.24
2014	4,175	1,030	24.67	2,010	48.14	1,110	26.59
M	2,725	715	26.24	1,325	48.62	675	24.77
F	1,445	315	21.8	680	47.06	440	30.45
2015	4,875	895	18.36	3,390	69.54	515	10.56
M	3,555	640	18	2,530	71.17	340	9.56
F	1,320	255	19.32	860	65.15	175	13.25
2016	8,905	1,260	14.15	6,150	69.06	1,075	12.07
M	6,250	870	13.92	4,495	71.92	645	10.32
F	2,650	390	14.72	1,650	62.26	430	16.23

Table B.6 *Afghanistan: Final decisions – Proportion of refugee status in select EU MS, 2013–2016*

Afghanistan RS%	2013	2014	2015	2016
Belgium	0.97	1.12	0	1.3
Denmark	7.79	7.69	21.43	9.61
Spain	0	0	0	N/A[950]
France	14.54	16.95	17.39	21.74
The Netherlands	22.22	25.92	12.5	16
UK	41.52	32.64	61.73	57.21

Table B.7 *Afghanistan: Final decisions – Proportion of subsidiary protection status in select EU MS, 2013–2016*

Afghanistan SP%	2013	2014	2015	2016
Belgium	0.97	0	1.67	0
Denmark	25.97	23.08	10.71	15.38
Spain	0	0	0	N/A
France	54.54	59.32	43.48	39.13
The Netherlands	20.99	25.92	37.5	24
UK	2.34	1.39	0.61	0.5

950 N/A has been used where there were no final decisions for this group of appellants.

Table B.8 *Iraq: Final decisions – Proportion of refugee status in select EU MS, 2013–2016*

Iraq RS%	2013	2014	2015	2016
Belgium	1.45	3.85	2.86	6.75
Denmark	6.67	0	12.5	0
Spain	0	N/A	N/A	N/A
France	14.28	20	33.33	11.11
The Netherlands	25	16.67	20	5.55
UK	30.88	42.31	36.71	35.33

Table B.9 *Iraq: Final decisions – Proportion of subsidiary protection status in select EU MS, 2013–2016*

Iraq SP%	2013	2014	2015	2016
Belgium	0	0	2.86	1.23
Denmark	0	9.09	0	11.76
Spain	0	N/A	N/A	N/A
France	28.57	40	33.33	22.22
The Netherlands	31.82	29.17	20	47.22
UK	0	0	7.59	11.38

Table B.10 *Syria: Final decisions – Proportion of refugee status in select EU MS, 2013–2016*

Syria RS%	2013	2014	2015	2016
Belgium	0	12.5	28.57	10
Denmark	33.33	9.09	26.67	50
Spain	0	0	N/A	60.87
France	55.55	45.83	45	45.16
The Netherlands	0	0	19.23	25.92
UK	56.25	33.33	42.86	44.12

Table B.11 *Syria: Final decisions – Proportion of subsidiary protection status in select EU MS, 2013–2016*

Syria SP%	2013	2014	2015	2016
Belgium	20	12.5	0	0
Denmark	37.5	18.18	3.33	0
Spain	0	0	N/A	0
France	11.11	8.33	2.5	0
The Netherlands	66.66	50	69.23	66.66
UK	3.12	0	0	2.94

BIBLIOGRAPHY

Books

Ashe F, *The New Politics of Masculinity: Men, Power and Resistance* (Routledge 2011)

Aust A, *Handbook of International Law* (2nd edn, Cambridge University Press 2010)

Barkawi T, *Globalization and War* (Rowman & Littlefield 2006)

Betts A, Loescher G and Milner J, *The United Nations High Commissioner for Refugees (UNHCR): The Politics and Practice of Refugee Protection* (2nd edn, Routledge 2012)

Bjørge E, *The Evolutionary Interpretation of Treaties* (Oxford University Press 2014)

Brownmiller S, *Against Our Will: Men, Women and Rape* (Penguin 1975)

Cassese A, *International Law* (2nd edn, Oxford University Press 2005)

Charlesworth H and Chinkin C, *The Boundaries of International Law: A Feminist Analysis* (Manchester University Press 2000)

Chinkin C M and Kaldor M, *International Law and New Wars* (Cambridge University Press 2017)

Collins V, *State Crime, Women and Gender* (Routledge 2016)

Conaghan J, *Law and Gender* (Oxford University Press 2013)

Crawley H, *Refugees and Gender: Law and Process* (Jordans 2001)

Cullen A, *The Concept of Non-International Armed Conflict in International Humanitarian Law* (Cambridge University Press 2010)

Dörr O and Schmalenbach K, *Vienna Convention on the Law of Treaties: A Commentary* (Springer 2012)

Edwards A, *Violence against Women under International Human Rights Law* (Cambridge University Press 2011)

Enloe C, *The Morning After: Sexual Politics at the End of the Cold War* (University of California Press 1993)

Foster M, *International Refugee Law and Socio-Economic Rights: Refuge from Deprivation* (Cambridge Studies in International and Comparative Law, Cambridge University Press 2007)

Freedman J, *Gendering the International Asylum and Refugee Debate* (2nd edn, Palgrave Macmillan 2015)

Goodwin-Gill G and McAdam J, *The Refugee in International Law* (3rd edn, Oxford University Press 2007)

Grahl-Madsen A, *The Status of Refugees in International Law*, vol 1 (A. W. Sijthoff 1966)

Haslam J, *No Virtue Like Necessity: Realist Thought in International Relations since Machiavelli* (Yale University Press 2002)

Hathaway J and Foster M, *The Law of Refugee Status* (2nd edn, Cambridge University Press 2014)

Hathaway J C, *The Law of Refugee Status* (1st edn, Butterworths 1991)

Holzer V, *Refugees from Armed Conflict: The 1951 Refugee Convention and International Humanitarian Law* (Intersentia 2015)

Jackson I C, *The Refugee Concept in Group Situations* (Martinus Nijhoff Publishers 1999)

Janis M W, *International Law* (6th edn, Wolters Kluwer 2012)

Kaldor M, *New and Old Wars: Organized Violence in a Global Era* (3rd edn, Polity Press 2012)
Kalyvas S N, *The Logic of Violence in Civil War* (Cambridge University Press 2006)
Koskenniemi M, *International Law Aspects of the European Union* (Kluwer Law International 1998)
Lindholm J, *Danske Asylafgørelser: Baggrund, Kontekst, Analyse* (Jurist- og Økonomforbundets Forlag 2014)
Lülf C, *Conflict Displacement and Legal Protection: Understanding Asylum, Human Rights and Refugee Law* (Routledge 2019)
Macdonald I and Toal R, *Immigration Law and Practice in the United Kingdom* (9th edn, LexisNexis 2014)
MacKinnon C A, *Only Words* (Harper Collins 1994)
Martin S, *Refugee Women* (2nd edn, Lexington Books 2004)
McAdam J, *Complementary Protection in International Refugee Law* (Oxford University Press 2007)
Meger S, *Rape Loot Pillage: The Political Economy of Sexual Violence in Armed Conflict* (Oxford University Press 2016)
Mole N, *Asylum and the European Convention on Human Rights* (4th edn, Council of Europe 2007)
Peterson V S and Runyan A S, *Global Gender Issues* (Westview Press 1993)
Shaw M, *The Dialectics of War: An Essay in the Social Theory of Total War and Peace* (Pluto 1988)
Shaw M N, *International Law* (8th edn, Cambridge University Press 2017)
Sinclair I M, *The Vienna Convention on the Law of Treaties* (2nd edn, Manchester University Press 1984)
Sjoberg L, *Gendering Global Conflict: Toward a Feminist Theory of War* (Columbia University Press 2013)
Smart C, *Feminism and the Power of Law* (Routledge 1989)
Spijkerboer T, *Gender and Refugee Status* (Ashgate 2000)
Thomas R, *Administrative Justice and Asylum Appeals: A Study of Tribunal Adjudication* (Hart Publishing 2011)
Wallace R M M and Martin-Ortega O, *International Law* (7th edn, Sweet & Maxwell/Thomson Reuters 2013)
Wouters J, Nollkaemper A and De Wet E, *The Europeanisation of International Law: The Status of International Law in the EU and its Member States* (Cambridge University Press 2008)
Yuval-Davis N, *Gender & Nation* (Thousand Oaks 1997)

Contributions to Edited Books

Abi-Saab G, 'The Proper Role of International Law in Combatting Terrorism' in Bianchi A (ed), *Enforcing International Law Norms against Terrorism* (Hart Publishing 2004)
Arbel E, Dauvergne C and Millbank J, 'Introduction: Gender in Refugee Law – from the Margins to the Centre' in Arbel E, Dauvergne C and Millbank J (eds), *Gender in Refugee Law: From the Margins to the Centre* (Routledge 2014)
Banks W, 'Toward an Adaptive International Humanitarian Law: New Norms for New Battlefields' in Banks W (ed), *New Battlefields/Old Laws, Critical Debates on Asymmetric Warfare* (Columbia University Press 2011)
Bauloz C and Ruiz G, 'Refugee Status and Subdiary Protection: Towards a Uniform Content of International Protection?' in Chetail V, Bruycker P D and Maiani F (eds), *Reforming the Common European Asylum System: The New European Refugee Law* (Brill Nijhoff 2016)
Bell J, 'Legal Research and the Distinctiveness of Comparative Law' in Hoecke M V (ed), *Methodologies of Legal Research: What Kind of Method for What Kind of Discipline?* (Hart Publishing 2011)
Cantor D J and Durieux J-F, 'Refuge from Inhumanity? Canvassing the Issues' in Cantor D J and Durieux J-F (eds), *Refuge from Inhumanity? War Refugees and International Humanitarian Law* (Brill Nijhoff 2014)

Cantor D J and Trimiño Mora D, 'A Simple Solution to War Refugees? The Latin American Expanded Definition and Its Relationship to IHL' in Cantor D J and Durieux J-F (eds), *Refuge from Inhumanity? War Refugees and International Humanitarian Law* (Brill Nijhoff 2014)

Chetail V, 'Are Refugee Rights Human Rights? An Unorthodox Questioning of the Relations between Refugee Law and Human Rights Law' in Rubio-Marín R (ed), *Human Rights and Immigration* (Oxford University Press 2014)

Chetail V, 'Armed Conflict and Forced Migration: A Systematic Approach to International Humanitarian Law, Refugee Law, and International Human Rights Law' in Clapham A and Gaeta P (eds), *The Oxford Handbook of International Law in Armed Conflict* (Oxford University Press 2014)

Cockburn C, 'The Gendered Dynamics of Armed Conflict and Political Violence' in Moser C O N and Clark F C (eds), *Victims, Perpetrators or Actors? Gender, Armed Conflict and Political Violence* (Zed Books 2001)

Cockburn C, 'The Continuum of Violence: A Gender Perspective on War and Peace' in Giles W and Hyndman J (eds), *Sites of Violence: Gender and Conflict Zones* (University of California Press 2004)

Cooke M, 'Wo-man, Retelling the War Myth' in Cooke M and Woollacott A (eds), *Gendering War Talk* (Princeton University Press 1993)

Cooke M and Woollacott A, 'Introduction' in Cooke M and Woollacott A (eds), *Gendering War Talk* (Princeton University Press 1993)

Cownie F and Bradney A, 'Socio-Legal Studies: A Challenge to the Doctrinal Approach' in Watkins D and Burton M (eds), *Research Methods in Law* (Routledge 2013)

Crawley H, 'Engendering the State in Refugee Women's Claims for Asylum' in Jacobs S, Jacobson R and Marchbank J (eds), *States of Conflict: Gender, Violence and Resistance* (Zed Books Ltd 2000)

Crawley H, '[En]gendering International Refugee Protection: Are We There Yet?' in Burson B and Cantor D (eds), *Human Rights and the Refugee Definition: Comparative Legal Practice and Theory* (Brill Nijhoff 2016)

Distefano G, 'Use of Force' in Clapham A and Gaeta P (eds), *The Oxford Handbook of International Law in Armed Conflict* (Oxford University Press 2015)

Einarsen T, 'Drafting History of the 1951 Convention and the 1967 Protocol' in Zimmermann A (ed), *The 1951 Convention Relating to the Status of Refugees and Its 1967 Protocol: A Commentary* (Oxford University Press 2011)

El-Bushra J, 'Transforming Conflict: Some Thoughts on a Gendered Understanding of Conflict Processes' in Jacobson R, Jacobs S and Marchbank J (eds), *States of Conflict: Gender, Violence and Resistance* (Zed Books Ltd 2000)

Farrell T and Schmitt O, 'The Causes, Character and Conduct of Internal Armed Conflict and the Effects on Civilian Populations, 1990–2010' in Türk V, Edwards A and Wouters C (eds), *In Flight from Conflict and Violence: UNHCR's Consultations on Refugee Status and Other Forms of International Protection* (Cambridge University Press 2017)

Feller E, 'Foreword' in Zimmermann A (ed), *The 1951 Convention Relating to the Status of Refugees and Its 1967 Protocol: A Commentary* (Oxford University Press 2011)

Fiddian-Qasmiyeh E, 'Gender and Forced Migration' in Fiddian-Qasmiyeh E, Loescher G, Long K and Sigona N (eds), *The Oxford Handbook of Refugee and Forced Migration Studies* (Oxford University Press 2014)

Garlick M, 'Protection in the European Union for People Fleeing Indiscriminate Violence in Armed Conflict' in Turk V, Edwards A and Wouters C (eds), *In Flight from Conflict and Violence: UNHCR's Consultations on Refugee Status and Other Forms of International Protection* (Cambridge University Press 2017)

Gilbert G and Rüsch A M, 'International Refugee and Migration Law' in Evans M D (ed), *International Law* (5th edn, Oxford University Press 2018)

Giles W and Hyndman J, 'Introduction' in Giles W and Hyndman J (eds), *Sites of Violence: Gender and Conflict Zones* (University of California Press 2004)

Goodwin-Gill G, 'The Search for the One, True Meaning' in Goodwin-Gill G and Lambert H (eds), *The Limits of Transnational Law: Refugee Law, Policy Harmonisation and Judicial Dialogue in the European Union* (Cambridge University Press 2010)

Goodwin-Gill G, 'The International Law of Refugee Protection' in Fiddian-Qasmiyeh E Loescher G, Long K and Sigona N (eds), *The Oxford Handbook of Refugee and Forced Migration Studies* (Oxford University Press 2014)

Grandi P, 'Foreword' in Türk V, Edwards A and Wouters C (eds), *In Flight from Conflict and Violence: UNHCR's Consultations on Refugee Status and Other Forms of International Protection* (Cambridge University Press 2017)

Hans A, 'Escaping Conflict: Afghan Women in Transit' in Giles W and Hyndman J (eds), *Sites of Violence: Gender and Conflict Zones* (University of California Press 2004)

Harvey C, 'Engendering Asylum Law: Feminism, Process and Practice' in Millns S and Whitty N (eds), *Feminist Perspectives on Public Law* (Cavendish 1999)

Hathaway J, 'Refugee Status Arising from Generalized Oppression' in Alfredsson G and Macalister-Smith P (eds), *The Living Law of Nations: Essays on Refugees, Minorities, Indigenous Peoples and the Human Rights of Other Vulnerable Groups* (N. P. Engel 1996)

Husa J, 'Comparative Law, Legal Linguistics and Methodology of Legal Doctrine' in Van Hoecke M (ed), *Methodologies of Legal Research: What Kind of Method for What Kind of Discipline?* (Hart Publishing 2011)

Jacobson R, Jacobs S and Marchbank J, 'Introduction: States of Conflict' in Jacobs S, Jacobson R and Marchbank J (eds), *States of Conflict: Gender, Violence and Resistance* (Zed Books Ltd 2000)

Jain R B, 'Sampling Method in Legal Research' in Verma S K and Wani M A (eds), *Legal Research and Methodology* (Indian Law Institute 2001)

Jaquemet S, 'Expanding Refugee Protection through International Humanitarian Law: Driving on a Highway or Walking near the Edge of the Abyss?' in Cantor D J and Durieux J-F (eds), *Refugee from Inhumanity? War Refugees and International Humanitarian Law* (Brill Nijhoff 2014)

Juss S, 'Exodus after Conflict' in Westra L, Juss S and Scovazzi T (eds), *Towards a Refugee Oriented Right of Asylum* (Ashgate 2015)

Justesen P L, 'Denmark' in Carlier J-Y and others (eds), *Who Is a Refugee? A Comparative Case Law Study* (Kluwer Law International 1997)

Karp A, 'The Changing Ownership of War: States, Insurgencies and Technology' in Krause K (ed), *Armed groups and Contemporary Conflicts: Challenging the Weberian State* (Routledge 2010)

Kasfir N, 'Rebel Governance – Constructing a Field of Inquiry: Definitions, Scope, Patterns, Order, Causes' in Arjona A, Kasfir N and Mampilly Z (eds), *Rebel Governance in Civil War* (Cambridge University Press 2015)

Kelly L, 'Wars against Women: Sexual Violence, Sexual Politics and the Militarised State' in Jacobson R, Jacobs S and Marchbank J (eds), *States of Conflict: Gender, Violence and Resistance* (Zed Books Ltd 2000)

Kennedy D, 'Lawfare and Warfare' in Crawford J, Koskenniemi M and Ranganathan S (eds), *The Cambridge Companion to International Law* (Cambridge University Press 2012)

Lambert H, 'Transnational Law, Judges and Refugees in the European Union' in Lambert H and Goodwin-Gill G S (eds), *The Limits of Transnational Law: Refugee Law, Policy Harmonization and Judicial Dialogue in the European Union* (Cambridge University Press 2010)

Lambert H, 'Causation in International Protection from Armed Conflict' in Cantor D and Durieux J-F (eds), *Refuge from Inhumanity: War refugees and International Humanitarian Law* (Martinus Nijhoff Publisher 2014)

Lawson F H, 'Syria' in Angrist M P (ed), *Politics & Society in the Contemporary Middle East* (Lynne Rienner Publishers 2010)

McAdam J, 'Individual Risk, Armed Conflict and the Standard of Proof in Complementary Protection Claims: The European Union and Canada Compared' in Simeon J C (ed), *Critical Issues in International Refugee Law: Strategies toward Interpretative Harmony* (Cambridge University Press 2010)

McAdam J, 'Interpretation of the 1951 Convention' in Zimmermann A (ed), *The 1951 Convention Relating to the Status of Refugees and its 1967 Protocol: A Commentary* (Oxford University Press 2011)

Moreno-Lax V, 'Of Autonomy, Autarky, Purposiveness and Fragmentation' in Cantor D J and Durieux J-F (eds), *Refuge from Inhumanity?: War Refugees and International Humanitarian Law* (Brill Nijhoff 2014)

Moser C O N and Clark F, 'The Gendered Continuum of Violence and Conflict' in Moser C O N and Clark F C (eds), *Victims, Perpetrators or Actors? Gender, Armed Conflict and Political Violence* (Zed Books 2001)

Neff S C, 'A Short History of International Law' in Evans M D (ed), *International Law* (5th edn, Oxford University Press 2018)

Oktav Ö Z, Parlar Dal E and Kurşun A M, 'Reframing and Reassessing the VNSAs in Syrian Conflict: An Introduction' in Oktav Ö Z, Parlar Dal E and Kurşun A M (eds), *Violent Non-state Actors and the Syrian Civil War: The ISIS and YPG Cases* (Springer International Publishing 2018)

Oosterveld V, 'Women and Girls Fleeing Conflict: Gender and the Interpretation and Application of the 1951 Refugee Convention' in Turk V, Edwards A and Wouters C (eds), *In Flight from Conflict and Violence: UNHCR's Consultations on Refugee Status and Other Forms of International Protection* (Cambridge University Press 2017)

Pusane Ö K, 'How to Profile PYD/YPG as an Actor in the Syrian Civil War: Policy Implications for the Region and Beyond' in Oktav Ö Z, Parlar Dal E and Kurşun A M (eds), *Violent Non-state Actors and the Syrian Civil War: The ISIS and YPG Cases* (Springer International Publishing 2018)

Querton C, 'Women Fleeing Armed Conflict: Seeking International Protection in the United Kingdom' in Arbel E, Dauvergne C and Millbank J (eds), *Gender in Refugee Law: From the Margins to the Centre* (Routledge 2014)

Reed-Hurtado M, 'The Cartagena Declaration on Refugees and the Protection of People Fleeing Armed Conflict and Other Situations of Violence in Latin America' in Volker T, Edwards A and Wouters C W (eds), *In Flight from Conflict and Violence: UNHCR's Consultations on Refugee Status and Other Forms of International Protection* (Cambridge University Press 2017)

Rutinwa B, 'Relationship between the 1951 Refugee Convention and the 1969 OAU Convention on Refugees: A Historical Perspective' in Volker T, Edwards A and Wouters C W (eds), *In Flight from Conflict and Violence: UNHCR's Consultations on Refugee Status and Other Forms of International Protection* (Cambrdige University Press 2017)

Sharpe M, 'The 1969 OAU Convention in the Context of Individual Refugee Status Determination' in Volker T, Edwards A and Wouters C W (eds), *In Flight from Conflict and Violence: UNHCR's Consultations on Refugee Status and Other Forms of International Protection* (Cambridge University Press 2017)

Simma B and Müller A T, 'Exercise and Limits of Jurisdiction' in Crawford J, Koskenniemi M and Ranganathan S (eds), *The Cambridge Companion to International Law* (Cambridge University Press 2012)

Singerman D, 'Gender and Politics' in Angrist M P (ed), *Politics & Society in the Contemporary Middle East* (Lynne Rienner Publishers 2010)

Sjoberg L and Via S, 'Introduction' in Sjoberg L and Via S (eds), *Gender, War, and Militarism: Feminist Perspectives* (Praeger 2010)

Storey H, 'Persecution: Towards a Working Definition' in Chetail V and Bauloz C (eds), *Research Handbook on International Law and Migration* (Edward Elgar 2014)

Tsourdi E, 'What Protection for Persons Fleeing Indiscriminate Violence? The Impact of the European Courts on the EU Subsidiary Protection Regime' in Cantor D J and Durieux J-Fo (eds), *Refuge from Inhumanity?: War Refugees and International Humanitarian Law* (Brill Nijhoff 2014)

Türk V and Dowd R, 'Protection Gaps' in Fiddian-Qasmiyeh E, Loescher G, Long K and Sigona N (eds), *The Oxford Handbook of of Refugee and Forced Migration Studies* (Oxford University Press 2014)

Türk V, Edwards A and Wouters C W, 'Introduction' in Türk V, Edwards A and Wouters C W (eds), *In Flight from Conflict and Violence: UNHCR's Consultations on Refugee Status and Other Forms of International Protection* (Cambridge University Press 2017)

Vedsted-Hansen J, '"Konkret og individuelt": Et Kriteriums forvandling fra Kvalifikation til Eksklusion' in Møller-Sørensen A and Storgaard A (eds), *Jurist uden Omsvøb: Festskrift til Gorm Toftegaard Nielsen* (Christian Ejlers 2007)

Wallace R, 'Internal Relocation Alternative in Refugee Status Determination: Is the Risk/Protection Dichotomy Reality or Myth? A Gendered Analysis' in Juss S S and Harvey C (eds), *Contemporary Issues in Refugee Law* (Edward Elgar Publishing Limited 2013)

Wouters C, 'Protecting People Fleeing Conflict and Generalized Violence' in United Nations High Commissioner for Refugees and Council of Europe (eds), *Joint UNHCR / Council of Europe Colloquium on the Role of Regional Human Rights Courts in Interpreting and Enforcing Legal Standards for the Protection of Forcibly Displaced Persons: Conference Report* (Council of Europe 2011)

Wouters C, 'Conflict Refugees' in Costello C, Foster M and McAdam J (eds), *The Oxford Handbook of International Refugee Law* (Oxford University Press 2021)

Zimmermann A and Mahler C, 'Article 1A, para. 2 (Definition of the Term Refugee)' in Zimmermann A (ed), *The 1951 Convention Relating to the Status of Refugees and its 1967 Protocol: A Commentary* (Oxford University Press 2010)

Edited Books

Cantor D J and Durieux J-Fo (eds), *Refuge from Inhumanity?: War Refugees and International Humanitarian Law* (Brill Nijhoff 2014)

Gaeta P (eds), *The Oxford Handbook of International Law in Armed Conflict* (Oxford University Press 2014)

Gill N and Good A (eds), *Asylum Determination in Europe: Ethnographic Perspectives* (Palgrave Macmillan 2019)

Goodwin-Gill G and Lambert H (eds), *The Limits of Transnational Law: Refugee Law, Policy Harmonisation and Judicial Dialogue in the European Union* (Cambridge University Press 2010)

Türk V, Edwards A and Wouters C (eds), *In Flight from Conflict and Violence: UNHCR's Consultations on Refugee Status and Other Forms of International Protection* (Cambridge University Press 2017)

Williams W S and Ford C M (eds), *Complex Battlespaces: The Law of Armed Conflict and The Dynamics of Modern Warfare* (Oxford University Press 2018)

Journal Articles

Alsaba K and Kapilashrami A, 'Understanding Women's Experience of Violence and the Political Economy of Gender in Conflict: The Case of Syria' (2016) 24 *Reproductive Health Matters* 5

Altınay A G and Pető A, 'Europe and the Century of Genocides: New Directions in the Feminist Theorizing of Genocide' (2015) 22 *European Journal of Women's Studies* 379

Anker D, 'Refugee Law, Gender, and the Human Rights Paradigm' (2002) 15 *Harvard Human Rights Journal* 133

Annan J and Brier M, 'The Risk of Return: Intimate Partner Violence in Northern Uganda's Armed Conflict' (2010) 70 *Social Science & Medicine* 152

Arboleda E, 'Refugee Definition in Africa and Latin America: The Lessons of Pragmatism' (1991) 3 *International Journal of Refugee Law* 185

Atak I and Simeon J C, 'Human Trafficking: Mapping the Legal Boundaries of International Refugee Law and Criminal Justice' (2014) 12 *Journal of International Criminal Justice* 1019

Bacon R and Booth K, 'Persecution by Omission: Violence by Non-State Actors and the Role of the State under the Refugees Convention in Minister for Immigration and Multicultural Affairs v Khawar' (2002) 24 *Sydney Law Review* 584

Barrow A, 'UN Security Council Resolutions 1325 and 1820: Constructing Gender in Armed Conflict and International Humanitarian Law' (2010) 92 *International Review of the Red Cross* 221

Bauloz C, 'The Definition of Internal Armed Conflict in Asylum Law: The 2014 Diakité Judgment of the EU Court of Justice' (2014) 12 *Journal of International Criminal Justice* 835

Ben-Yehuda H, 'Territoriality and War in International Crises: Theory and Findings 1918–2001' (2004) 6 *International Studies Review* 85

Berna I-B, 'Gender Politics and Post-Conflict Reconstruction in the Western Balkans' (2013) 3 *Journal of Research in Gender Studies* 128

Bethlehem D, 'The End of Geography: The Changing Nature of the International System and the Challenge to International Law' (2014) 25 *European Journal Of International Law* 9

Betts A, 'Survival Migration: A New Protection Framework' (2010) 16 *Global Governance* 361

Bhabha J, 'Legal Problems of Women Refugees' (1993) 4 *Women: A Cultural Review* 240

Blake J N, 'Gang and Cartel Violence: A Reason to Grant Political Asylum from Mexico and Central America' (2012) 38 *Yale Journal of International Law Online* 31

Caprioli M, 'Primed for Violence: The Role of Gender Inequality in Predicting Internal Conflict' (2005) 49 *International Studies Quarterly* 161

Chaney P, 'Civil Society and Gender Mainstreaming: Empirical Evidence and Theory-Building from Twelve Post-Conflict Countries 2005–15' (2016) 83 *World Development* 280

Charlesworth H, Chinkin C and Wright S, 'Feminist Approaches to International Law' (1991) 85 *American Journal of International Law* 613

Cheeseman G, 'Review: The European Rupture: The Defence Sector in Transition / Restructuring the Global Military Sector Volume I: New Wars / Restructuring the Global Military Sector Volume II: The End' (1999) 53 *Australian Journal of International Affairs* 212

Chimni B S, 'The Geopolitics of Refugee Studies: A View from the South' (1998) 11(4) *Journal of Refugee Studies* 350

Chinkin C and Kaldor M, 'Gender and New Wars' (2013) 67 *Journal of International Affairs* 167

Chinkin C M, 'A Gendered Perspective to the International Use of Force' (1992) 12 *Australian Yearbook of International Law* 279

Chivers C J, 'Small Arms, Big Problems: The Fallout of the Global Gun Trade' (2011) 90 *Foreign Affairs* 110

Clark T and Simeon J C, 'War, Armed Conflict, and Refugees: The United Nations' Endless Battle for Peace' (2016) 35 *Refugee Studies Quarterly* 35

Crawford J and Hyndman P, 'Three Heresies in the Application of the Refugee Convention' (1989) 1 *International Journal of Refugee Law* 155

Crawley H, 'Gender, Persecution and the Concept of Politics in the Asylum Determination Process' (2000) 9 *Forced Migration Review* 17

Crenshaw K, 'Mapping the Margins: Intersectionality, Identity Politics, and Violence against Women of Color' (1991) 43 *Stanford Law Review* 1241

Cunningham D E, Gleditsch K S and Salehyan I, 'Non-state Actors in Civil Wars: A New Dataset' (2013) 30 *Conflict Management and Peace Science* 516

Dakkak H, 'Tackling Sexual Violence, Abuse and Exploitation' (2007) Special Issue: Iraq's Displacement Crisis: The Search for Solutions, *Forced Migration Review* 39

Danczuk J, 'The Global Spread of Arms: The Link between State Collapse, Small Arms Proliferation, and Global Conflict' (2016) 96 *Military Review* 42

Davis A, 'Intersectionality and International Law: Recognizing Complex Identities on the Global Stage' (2015) 28 *Harvard Human Rights Journal* 205

Durham H and O'Byrne K, 'The Dialogue of Difference: Gender Perspectives on International Humanitarian Law' (2010) 92 *International Review of the Red Cross* 31

Durieux J-F, 'Of War, Flows, Laws and Flaws: A Reply to Hugo Storey' (2012) 31 *Refugee Survey Quarterly* 161

Edwards A, 'Refugee Status Determination in Africa' (2006) 14 *African Journal of International and Comparative Law* 204

Edwards A, 'Transitioning Gender: Feminist Engagement with International Refugee Law and Policy 1950–2010' (2010) 29 *Refugee Survey Quarterly* 21

El-Bushra J, 'Fused in Combat: Gender Relations and Armed Conflict' (2003) 13 *Development in Practice* 252

Errera R, 'The CJEU and Subsidiary Protection: Reflections on Elgafaji – and After' (2011) 23 *International Journal of Refugee Law* 93

Farrag H H, 'Engendering Forced Migration: Victimization, Masculinity and the Forgotten Voice' (2009) 2 *Surfacing: Gender and Conflict* 1

Farrell T and Giustozzi A, 'The Taliban at War: Inside the Helmand Insurgency, 2004–2012' (2013) 89 *International Affairs* 845

Fearon J D and Laitin D D, 'Ethnicity, Insurgency, and Civil War' (2003) 97 *American Political Science Review* 75

Feijen L, 'Filling the Gaps? Subsidiary Protection and Non-EU Harmonized Protection Status(es) in the Nordic Countries' (2014) 26 *International Journal of Refugee Law* 173

Frederick B A, Hensel P R and Macaulay C, 'The Issue Correlates of War Territorial Claims Data, 1816–20011' (2017) 54 *Journal of Peace Research* 99

Freedman J, 'Mainstreaming Gender in Refugee Protection' (2010) 23 *Cambridge Review of International Affairs* 589

Freedman J, 'Protecting Women Asylum Seekers and Refugees: From International Norms to National Protection?' (2010) 48 *International Migration* 175

Friedman L, 'Legal Consequences of the Construction of a Wall in the Occupied Palestinian Territory (Advisory Opinion), International Court of Justice, 9 July 2004' (2005) 27 *Sydney Law Review* 715

Gardam J, 'A Feminist Analysis of Certain Aspects of International Humanitarian Law' (1992) 12 *Australian Yearbook of International Law* 265

Gardam J and Charlesworth H, 'Protection of Women in Armed Conflict' (2000) 22 *Human Rights Quarterly* 148

Garlick M, 'International Protection in Court: The Asylum Jurisprudence of the Court of Justice of the EU and UNHCR' (2015) 34 *Refugee Survey Quarterly* 107

Gil-Bazo M-T, 'Introduction: The Role of International Organizations and Human Rights Monitoring Bodies in Refugee Protection' (2015) 34 *Refugee Survey Quarterly* 1

Gil-Bazo M-T, 'Refugee Protection under International Human Rights Law: From Non-Refoulement to Residence and Citizenship' (2015) 34 *Refugee Survey Quarterly* 11

Gilbert G, 'UNHCR and Courts: Amicus Curiae … Sed Curia Amica Est?' (2016) 28 *International Journal of Refugee Law* 623

Giustozzi A, 'Counterinsurgency Challenge in Post-2001 Afghanistan' (2017) 28 *Small Wars & Insurgencies* 12

Goldberg P, 'Women and Refugee Status: A Review Essay' (1995) 7 *International Journal of Refugee Law* 756

Goodwin-Gill G S, 'The Dynamic of International Refugee Law' (2013) 25 *International Journal of Refugee Law* 651

Gorlick B, 'Human Rights and Refugees: Enhancing Protection through International Human Rights Law' (2000) 69 *Nordic Journal of International Law* 117

Gorris E A P, 'Invisible Victims? Where Are Male Victims of Conflict-Related Sexual Violence in International Law and Policy?' (2015) 22 *European Journal of Women's Studies* 412

Greatbatch J, 'The Gender Difference: Feminist Critiques of Refugee Discourse' (1989) 1 *International Journal of Refugee Law* 518

Grey R and Shepherd L J, '"Stop Rape Now?": Masculinity, Responsibility, and Conflict-Related Sexual Violence' (2013) 16 *Men and Masculinities* 115

Gunter M M, 'Iraq, Syria, Isis and the Kurds: Geostrategic Concerns for the U.S. and Turkey' (2015) 22 *Middle East Policy* 102
Harvey C, 'Time for Reform? Refugees, Asylum-seekers, and Protection Under International Human Rights Law' (2015) 34 *Refugee Survey Quarterly* 43
Hathaway J C, 'The Evolution of Refugee Status in International Law: 1920–1950' (1984) 33 *International and Comparative Law Quarterly* 348
Hathaway J C and Foster M, 'The Causal Connection ("Nexus") to a Convention Ground: Discussion Paper No. 3 Advanced Refugee Law Workshop International Association of Refugee Law Judges Auckland, New Zealand, October 2002' (2003) 15 *International Journal of Refugee Law* 461
Henderson T, 'Protecting Women in Peace and Conflict: International Humanitarian and Human Rights Law at Work' (2011) 71 *Peace and Freedom* 17
Henry N, 'Theorizing Wartime Rape' (2016) 30 *Gender & Society* 44
Henshaw A, 'Masculinity and New War: The Gendered Dynamics of Contemporary Armed Conflict' (2017) 25 *Gender & Development* 343
Hunt K, 'The Strategic Co-optation of Women's Rights' (2002) 4 *International Feminist Journal of Politics* 116
Hutchinson T, 'The Doctrinal Method: Incorporating Interdisciplinary Methods in Reforming the Law' (2015) 3 *Erasmus Law Review* 130
Indra D, 'Gender: A Key Dimension of the Refugee Experience' (1987) 6 *Refuge* 3
International Law Commission, 'Draft Articles on the Law of Treaties with Commentaries' (1966) *II Yearbook of the International Law Commission* 219
Isaac J C, 'Gender and Politics' (2014) 12 *Perspectives on Politics* 1
Jakuleviciene L, 'Lessons of the First EU Court of Justice Judgments in Asylum Cases' (2012) 19 *Jurisprudencija* 477
James C S, 'A New Protection Orientation and Framework for Refugees and Other Forced Migrants' (2017) 6 *Laws* 30
Johnsson A B, 'The International Protection of Women Refugees: A Summary of Principal Problems and Issues' (1989) 1 *International Journal of Refugee Law* 221
Juss S, 'Problematizing the Protection of "War Refugees": A Rejoinder to Hugo Storey and Jean-François Durieux' (2013) 32 *Refugee Survey Quarterly* 122
Kaldor M, 'Identity and War' (2013) 4 *Global Policy* 336
Kalin W, 'Refugees and Civil Wars: Only a Matter of Interpretation?' (1991) 3 *International Journal of Refugee Law* 435
Kalyvas S N, '"New" and "Old" Civil Wars: A Valid Distinction?' (2001) 54 *World Politics* 99
Kalyvas S N and Balcells L, 'International System and Technologies of Rebellion: How the End of the Cold War Shaped Internal Conflict' (2010) 104 *The American Political Science Review* 415
Klug A, 'Harmonization of Asylum in the European Union: Emergence of an EU Refugee System' (2004) 47 *German Yearbook of International Law* 594
Kumar S, 'Small Arms and Light Weapons: A Global Threat to Human Security and Development' (2008) 69 *The Indian Journal of Political Science* 787
Lacina B, 'Explaining the Severity of Civil Wars' (2006) 50 *Journal of Conflict Resolution* 276
Lambert H, 'The EU Asylum Qualification Directive, Its Impact on the Jurisprudence of the United Kingdom and International Law' (2006) 55 *International and Comparative Law Quarterly* 161
Lambert H, 'The Next Frontier: Expanding Protection in Europe for Victims of Armed Conflict and Indiscriminate Violence' (2013) 25 *International Journal of Refugee Law* 207
Lambert H and Farrell T, 'The Changing Character of Armed Conflict and the Implications for Refugee Protection Jurisprudence' (2010) 22 *International Journal of Refugee Law* 237
Lawson F H, 'Syria's Mutating Civil War and Its Impact on Turkey, Iraq and Iran' (2014) 90 *International Affairs* 1351
Lenaerts K, 'The Contribution of the European Court of Justice to the Area of Freedom, Security and Justice' (2010) 59 *International and Comparative Law Quarterly* 255

Lenaerts K and Gutierrez-Fons J A, 'To Say What the Law of the EU Is: Methods of Interpretation and the European Court of Justice' (2014) 20 *Columbia Journal of European Law* 3

Linke U, 'Gendered Difference, Violent Imagination Blood, Race, Nation' (1997) 99 *American Anthropologist* 559

Magner T, 'Does a Failed State Country of Origin Result in a Failure of International Protection? A Review of Policies toward Asylum-Seekers in Leading Asylum Nations' (2001) 15 *Georgetown Immigration Law Journal* 703

Mariño Menéndez F M, 'Recent Jurisprudence of the United Nations Committee against Torture and the International Protection of Refugees' (2015) 34 *Refugee Survey Quarterly* 61

Maystre M, 'The Interaction between International Refugee Law and International Criminal Law with Respect to Child Soldiers' (2014) 12 *Journal of International Criminal Justice* 975

McAdam J, 'The European Union Qualification Directive: The Creation of a Subsidiary Protection Regime' (2005) 17 *International Journal of Refugee Law* 461

McAdam J, 'Australian Complementary Protection: A Step-by-Step Approach' (2011) 33 *Sydney Law Review* 687

McAdam J, 'The Enduring Relevance of the 1951 Refugee Convention' (2017) 29 *International Journal of Refugee Law* 1

McFerson H, 'Women and Post-Conflict Society in Sierra Leone' (2011) 12 *Journal of International Women's Studies* 127

Meger S, 'Gender and Politics: A Discussion of Laura Sjoberg's Gendering Global Conflict: Toward a Feminist Theory of War' (2014) 12 *Perspectives on Politics* 168

Meger S, 'Toward a Feminist Political Economy of Wartime Sexual Violence: The Case of the Democratic Republic of the Congo' (2015) 17 *International Feminist Journal of Politics* 416

Melander E, 'Gender Equality and Intrastate Armed Conflict' (2005) 49 *International Studies Quarterly* 695

Melander E and Bjarnegård E, 'Revisiting Representation: Communism, Women in Politics, and the Decline of Armed Conflict in East Asia' (2013) 39 (4) *International Interactions 558*

Miakinkov E, 'The Agency of Force in Asymmetrical Warfare and Counterinsurgency: The Case of Chechnya' (2011) 34 *Journal of Strategic Studies* 647

Milne A T C, 'Prosecuting Cases of Gender Violence in the International Criminal Tribunal for Rwanda' (2005) 11 *Buffalo Human Rights Law Review* 107

Mullally S, 'Domestic Violence Asylum Claims and Recent Developments in International Human Rights Law: A Progress Narrative?' (2011) 60 *International and Comparative Law Quarterly* 459

Murphy J F, 'International Law in Crisis: Challenges Posed by the New Terrorism and the Changing Nature of War' (2011) 44 *Case Western Reserve Journal of International Law* 59

O'Sullivan M, 'Acting the Part: Can Non-state Entities Provide Protection under International Refugee Law?' (2012) 24 *International Journal of Refugee Law* 85

Oosterveld V, 'Gender at the Intersection of International Refugee Law and International Criminal Law' (2014) 12 *Journal of International Criminal Justice* 953

Peterson V S, 'Political Identities/Nationalism as Heterosexism' (1999) 1 *International Feminist Journal of Politics* 34

Phuong C, 'Persecution by Non-state Agents: Comparative Judicial Interpretations of the 1951 Refugee Convention' (2002) 4 *European Journal of Migration and Law* 521

Pierman G, 'The Grand Strategy of Nonstate Actors: Theory and Implications' (2015) 8 *Journal of Strategic Security* 69

Pittaway E and Bartolomei L, 'Refugees, Race, and Gender: The Multiple Discrimination against Refugee Women' (2001) 19 *Refuge* 21

Querton C, 'The Role of the European Court of Human Rights in the Protection of Women Fleeing Gender-Based Violence in their Home Countries' (2017) 7 (2) *Feminists @ Law* <https://journals.kent.ac.uk/index.php/feministsatlaw/article/view/425> accessed 18 March 2023

Querton C, 'Gender and the Boundaries of International Refugee Law: Beyond the Category of 'Gender-Related Asylum Claims'' (2019) 37 *Netherlands Quarterly of Human Rights* 379

Querton C, 'Non-state Actors of Protection and the Sliding Scale of Protection for Refugee Women' (2022) 41(3) *Refugee Survey Quarterly* 444

Querton C, 'Country Guidance, Country of Origin Information, and the International Protection Needs of Persons Fleeing Armed Conflicts' (2023) 42(3) *Refugee Survey Quarterly*, see https://academic.oup.com/rsq/advance-article/doi/10.1093/rsq/hdad003/7091824

Regan P M, 'Civil War and Territory? Drawing Linkages between Interstate and Intrastate War' (2009) 35 *International Interactions* 321

Riddell C, 'Review: Susan Brownmiller – Against Our Will: Men, Women and Rape' (1977) 11 *Sociology* 389

Rodriguez Serna N, 'Fleeing Cartels and Maras: International Protection Considerations and Profiles from the Northern Triangle' (2016) 28 *International Journal of Refugee Law* 25

Schmitt M N, '21st Century Conflict: Can the Law Survive?' (2007) 8 *Melbourne Journal of International Law* 443

Shacknove A E, 'Who Is a Refugee?' (1985) 95 *Ethics* 274

Shaw J, 'Importing Gender: The Challenge of Feminism and the Analysis of the EU Legal Order' (2000) 7 *Journal of European Public Policy* 406

Simeon J C, 'A New Protection Orientation and Framework for Refugees and Other Forced Migrants' (2017) 6 *Laws* 30

Sivakumaran S, 'Male/Male Rape and the "Taint" of Homosexuality' (2005) 27 *Human Rights Quarterly* 1274

Sivakumaran S, 'Sexual Violence against Men in Armed Conflict' (2007) 18 *European Journal of International Law* 253

Sjoberg L, 'Gender/Violence in a Gendered/Violent World' (2014) 42 *Journal of International Studies* 532

Stabile C and Kumar D, 'Unveiling Imperialism: Media, Gender and the War on Afghanistan' (2005) 27 *Media Culture and Society* 765

Storey H, 'Armed Conflict in Asylum Law: The "War-Flaw"' (2012) 31 *Refugee Survey Quarterly* 1

Storey H and Wallace R, 'War and Peace in Refugee Law Jurisprudence' (2001) 95 *American Journal of International Law* 349

Swaine A, 'Beyond Strategic Rape and between the Public and Private: Violence against Women in Armed Conflict' (2015) 37 *Human Rights Quarterly* 755

Tachou-Sipowo A-G, 'The Security Council on Women in War: Between Peacebuilding and Humanitarian Protection' (2010) 92 *International Review of the Red Cross* 197

Tax B, 'Refugee by Association' (2014) (47) *Forced Migration Review* 26

Thompson M, 'Women, Gender, and Conflict: Making the Connections' (2006) 16 *Development in Practice* 342

Toft M, 'Territory and War' (2014) 51 *Journal of Peace Research* 185

Touquet H and Gorris E, 'Out of the Shadows? The Inclusion of Men and Boys in Conceptualisations of Wartime Sexual Violence' (2016) 24 *Reproductive Health Matters* 36

UNHCR, 'Gender-Related Persecution: An Analysis of Recent Trends' (1997) 9 *International Journal of Refugee Law* 79

Vedsted-Hansen J, 'European Non-refoulement Revisited' (2010) 55 *Scandinavian Studies In Law* 269

Walby S, Armstrong J and Strid S, 'Intersectionality: Multiple Inequalities in Social Theory' (2012) 46 *Sociology* 224

Wallace R M M, 'Making the Refugee Convention Gender Sensitive: The Canadian Guidelines' (1996) 45 *International and Comparative Law Quarterly* 702

Wallach Scott J, 'Gender: Still a Useful Category of Analysis?' (2010) 57 *Diogenes* 7

Wankel M, 'Obscuring the Realities of Gender-Based Violence: European Policies on Iraqi Asylum Claims' (2009) 2 *Surfacing: Gender and Conflict* 18

Weber C, 'Review – Gendering Global Conflict: Toward a Feminist Theory of War' (2015) 29 *Gender & Society* 448

Wilsher D, 'Non-state Actors and the Definition of a Refugee in the United Kingdom: Protection, Accountability or Culpability?' (2003) 15 *International Journal of Refugee Law* 68

Yun M, 'Insurgency Warfare as an Emerging New Mode of Warfare and the New Enemy' (2010) 22 *Korean Journal of Defense Analysis* 111

Zalar B, 'Comments on the Court of Justice of the EU's Developing Case Law on Asylum' (2013) 25 *International Journal of Refugee Law* 377

Websites and Blogs

Amnesty International, 'Syria: Armed opposition groups committing war crimes in Aleppo city' (13 May 2016) <www.amnesty.org/en/latest/news/2016/05/syria-armed-opposition-groups-committing-war-crimes-in-aleppo-city/> accessed 12 July 2021

Cambridge Advanced Learner's Dictionary & Thesaurus, CUP, <https://dictionary.cambridge.org/dictionary/english/concrete> accessed 12 July 2021

CCE/RvV 'Politique de Publication' (1 November 2010) <www.rvv-cce.be/fr/arr/politique-publication> accessed 12 July 2021

CNDA, 'Recueils de jurisprudence' (undated) <www.cnda.fr/Ressources-juridiques-et-geopolitiques/Recueils-de-jurisprudence> accessed 12 July 2021

Consejo General del Poder Judicial, 'Centro de Documentación Judicial' (undated) <www.poderjudicial.es/search/indexAN.jsp> accessed 12 July 2021

DRAB, 'Praksis' (undated) <www.fln.dk/da/Praksis.aspx> accessed 12 July 2021

DRAB, 'Beretninger' (undated) <www.fln.dk/da/Publikationer/Publikationer/Beretninger.aspx> accessed 12 July 2021

EU External Action, 'The EU and the Crisis in Syria' (20 September 2019) <https://eeas.europa.eu/headquarters/headquarters-Homepage/59417/eu-and-crisis-syria_en> accessed 12 July 2021

Eurostat, 'Asylum Decisions in the EU – EU Member States Granted Protection to More than 700 000 Asylum Seekers in 2016: Over Half of the Beneficiaries Were Syrians (26 April 2017) <www.europeanmigrationlaw.eu/documents/Eurostat-AsylumDecisions-2016.pdf> accessed 12 July 2021

Eurostat, 'Asylum and First Time Asylum Applicants by Citizenship, Age and Sex Annual Aggregated Data' (Rounded) (migr_asyappctza) <http://appsso.eurostat.ec.europa.eu/nui/show.do?dataset=migr_asyappctza&lang=en> accessed 4 May 2017

Eurostat, 'Asylum in the EU Member States – 650 000 First-Time Asylum Seekers Registered in 2017: Syrians, Iraqis and Afghans Continued to Be Top Citizenships' (20 March 2018) <http://ec.europa.eu/eurostat/documents/2995521/8754388/3-20032018-AP-EN.pdf/50c2b5a5-3e6a-4732-82d0-1caf244549e3> accessed 12 July 2021

Eurostat, 'Asylum in the EU Member States – 580 800 First-Time Asylum Seekers Registered in 2018, Down by 11% Compared with 2017: Syrians, Afghans and Iraqis Continued to Be the Top Citizenships' (14 March 2019) <https://ec.europa.eu/eurostat/documents/2995521/9665546/3-14032019-AP-EN.pdf/eca81dc5-89c7-4a9d-97ad-444b6bd32790> accessed 12 July 2021

Eurostat, 'First Instance Decisions on Applications by Citizenship, Age and Sex Annual Aggregated Data (Rounded) [migr_asydcfsta]' <https://ec.europa.eu/eurostat/web/asylum-and-managed-migration/data/database> accessed 1 April 2019

Eurostat, 'First Instance Decisions on Applications by Citizenship, Age and Sex – Annual Aggregated Data (Rounded)', <https://ec.europa.eu/eurostat/databrowser/view/MIGR_ASYDCFSTA__custom_3117264/default/table?lang=en>last updated 15 July 2022, accessed 26 July 2022

Eurostat, 'First Instance Decisions on Asylum Applications by Type of Decision – Annual Aggregated Data TPS00192' (11 July 2019) <https://ec.europa.eu/eurostat/databrowser/view/tps00192/default/table?lang=en> accessed 17 August 2019

Eurostat, 'Asylum and First Time Asylum Applicants – Annual Aggregated Data (Rounded) (tps00191)' (6 February 2020) <https://ec.europa.eu/eurostat/databrowser/view/tps00191/default/table?lang=en> accessed 9 February 2020

Eurostat, 'Asylum Applicants by Type of Applicant, Citizenship, Age and Sex – Annual Aggregated Data (Rounded)' <https://ec.europa.eu/eurostat/databrowser/view/MIGR_ASYAPPCTZA__custom_1616346/default/bar?lang=en>last updated 18 November 2021, accessed 21 November 2021

Eurostat Metadata, 'Decisions on Applications and Resettlement (migr_asydec)' <https://ec.europa.eu/eurostat/cache/metadata/fr/migr_asydec_esms.htm> accessed 2 February 2020

Flood M and Duriesmith D, 'Gender, War, and Male Disadvantage' (2017) <www.xyonline.net/content/gender-war-and-male-disadvantage> accessed 12 July 2021

Flygtningenævnet, 'Information om nævnets offentliggørelse af praksis på fln.dk' (27 May 2010) <www.fln.dk/da/Information_til/Advokater/Naevnets_praksis> accessed 12 July 2021

Melander G, 'International Refugee Organization (IRO)', Max Planck Encyclopaedia of Public International Law (June 2007) <https://opil.ouplaw.com/view/10.1093/law:epil/9780199231690/law-9780199231690-e512#> accessed 12 July 2021

NGO Coordination Committee for Iraq, 'Iraqi Governorate Profiles' (undated) <www.ncciraq.org/en/about/about-iraq/iraqi-governorate-profiles> accessed 12 July 2021

Oficina de Asilo y Refugio, 'Asilo en Cifras 2013' (September 2014) <www.interior.gob.es/opencms/pdf/servicios-al-ciudadano/oficina-de-asilo-y-refugio/datos-e-informacion-estadistica/Asilo_en_cifras_2013_126140719.pdf> accessed 12 July 2021

Oficina de Asilo y Refugio, 'Asilo en Cifras 2014' (September 2015) <www.interior.gob.es/opencms/pdf/servicios-al-ciudadano/oficina-de-asilo-y-refugio/datos-e-informacion-estadistica/Asilo_en_cifras_2014_126150899.pdf> accessed 12 July 2021

Oficina de Asilo y Refugio, 'Asilo en Cifras 2015' (undated) <www.interior.gob.es/opencms/pdf/servicios-al-ciudadano/oficina-de-asilo-y-refugio/datos-e-informacion-estadistica/Asilo_en_cifras_2015_126150899.pdf> accessed 12 July 2021

Oficina de Asilo y Refugio, 'Asilo en Cifras 2016' (October 2017) <www.interior.gob.es/opencms/pdf/servicios-al-ciudadano/oficina-de-asilo-y-refugio/datos-e-informacion-estadistica/Asilo_en_cifras_2016_126150899.pdf> accessed 12 July 2021

Querton C, 'The Fall of Kabul: International Protection in the Context of the Armed Conflict and Violence in Afghanistan' (Refugee Law Initiative, 1 September 2021) <https://rli.blogs.sas.ac.uk/2021/09/01/the-fall-of-kabul-international-protection-in-the-context-of-the-armed-conflict-and-violence-in-afghanistan/> accessed 26 July 2022

Rechtspraak, 'Selectiecriteria' (26 March 2012) <www.rechtspraak.nl/Uitspraken/Paginas/Selectiecriteria.aspx> accessed 12 July 2021

Rechtspraak, 'Uitspraken' (undated) <https://uitspraken.rechtspraak.nl/> accessed 12 July 2021

RvV/CCE, 'Arrêts' (undated) <www.rvv-cce.be/fr/arr> accessed 12 July 2021

Ruttig T, 'More Violent, More Widespread: Trends in Afghan Security in 2017', Afghanistan Analysts Network (29 January 2018) <www.afghanistan-analysts.org/more-violent-more-widespread-trends-in-afghan-security-in-2017/> accessed 12 July 2021

UNAMA Press Release, 'UNAMA Special Report on Increasing Harm to Civilians from IEDs' (October 2018) <https://unama.unmissions.org/sites/default/files/7_october_2018_-_unama_special_report_on_increasing_harm_to_civilians_from_ieds_english.pdf> accessed 12 July 2021

Worsnop A, 'From Guerrilla to Maneuver Warfare: A Look at the Taliban's Growing Combat Capability' (Modern War Institute, 6 June 2019) <https://mwi.usma.edu/guerrilla-maneuver-warfare-look-talibans-growing-combat-capability/> accessed 12 July 2021

Research Papers and Reports

Asylum Aid, Migrants Resource Centre and NatCen Social Research, 'Through Her Eyes: Enabling Women's Best Evidence in UK Asylum Appeals' (November 2017) <www.natcen.ac.uk/media/1499615/through-her-eyes_full-report_nov17.pdf> accessed 12 July 2021

Bodea C and Elbadawi I A, Riots, Coups and Civil War: Revisiting the Greed and Grievance Debate (World Bank 2007)

Cheikh Ali H, Querton C and Soulard E, Gender Related Asylum Claims in Europe: A Comparative Analysis of Law, Policy and Practice focusing on Women in Nine EU Member States (European Parliament 2012)
Collier P and Hoeffler A, 'Greed and Grievance in Civil War' (2004) 56 Oxford Economic Papers 563
Collier P, Hoeffler A and Rohner D, 'Beyond Greed and Grievance: Feasibility and Civil War' (2009) 61 Oxford Economic Papers 1
d'État C, 'Les Dossiers Thématiques du Conseil d'État: Le Judge Administratif et le Droit d'Asile' (January 2016)
Crawley H and Lester T, Comparative Analysis of Gender-Related Persecution in National Asylum Legislation and Practice in Europe (EPAU/2004/05, May 2004)
de Neef C E J and de Ruiter S J, Sexual Violence against Women Refugees: Report on the Nature and Consequences of Sexual Violence Suffered Elsewhere (Ministry of Social Affairs and Labour 1984)
Durieux J-F, 'Salah Sheekh Is a Refugee: New Insights into Primary and Subsidiary Forms of Protection' (2008) 49 Refugee Studies Centre Working Paper Series
EASO, 'Article 15(c) Qualification Directive (2011/95/EU): A Judicial Analysis' (December 2014) <www.easo.europa.eu/sites/default/files/public/Article-15c-Qualification-Directive-201195EU-A-judicial-analysis.pdf> accessed 12 July 2021
ECRE/ELENA, 'The Impact of the EU Qualification Directive on International Protection' (October 2008) <www.ecre.org/wp-content/uploads/2016/07/ECRE-The-Impact-of-the-EU-Qualification-Directive-on-International-Protection_October-2008.pdf> accessed 12 July 2021
ECRE, 'No Reason for Returns to Afghanistan' (February 2019) <www.ecre.org/wp-content/uploads/2019/02/Policy-Note-17.pdf> accessed 12 July 2021
European Union Agency for Asylum, 'Analysis on Asylum and Temporary Protection in the EU+ in the Context of the Ukraine Crisis Week 28 (11–17 July) 2022' (20 July 2022) <https://euaa.europa.eu/publications/analysis-asylum-and-temporary-protection-eu-context-ukraine-crisis-14> accessed 26 July 2022
Farrell T and Schmitt O, The Causes, Character and Conduct of Armed Conflict, and the Effects on Civilian Populations, 1990–2010 (UNHCR 2012)
Flygtningenævnet, 'Formandskabet: Beretning 2016' (October 2017) <www.fln.dk/~/media/FLN/Publikationer%20og%20notater/Publikationer/Beretninger/Beretning%202016%20WEB.ashx> accessed 12 July 2021
Good A and Kelly T, Best Practice Guide: Expert Country Evidence in Asylum and Immigration Cases in the United Kingdom (The University of Edinburgh, July 2013) <www.ein.org.uk/sites/default/files/Expert%20Country%20Evidence%20BPG.pdf> accessed 2 February 2020
Gil-Bazo M-T, 'Refugee Status, Subsidiary Protection, and the Right to be Granted Asylum under EC Law' (20 November 2006), UNHCR Research Paper No 136
Guild E and Moreno-Lax V, Current Challenges for International Refugee Law, with a Focus on EU Policies and EU Co-operation with the UNHCR (European Parliament December 2013)
Holzer V, The 1951 Refugee Convention and the Protection of People Fleeing Armed Conflict and Other Situations of Violence (UNHCR, PPLA/2012/05, September 2012)
House of Lords Select Committee on Sexual Violence in Conflict, 'Sexual Violence in Conflict: A War Crime' (12 April 2016, HL123) <https://publications.parliament.uk/pa/ld201516/ldselect/ldsvc/123/123.pdf> accessed 12 July 2021
Human Rights Watch, '"We'll Kill You If You Cry": Sexual Violence in the Sierra Leone Conflict' (January 2003) Vol 15(1A) <www.hrw.org/reports/2003/sierraleone/sierleon0103.pdf> accessed 12 July 2021
Immigration and Refugee Board of Canada, Afghanistan: Whether the Taliban Has the Capacity to Pursue Individuals after They Relocate to Another Region; Their Capacity to Track Individuals over the Long Term; Taliban Capacity to Carry out Targeted Killings (2012–January 2016) (Immigration and Refugee Board of Canada, 2016)
International Committee of the Red Cross (ICRC), Addressing the Needs of Women Affected by Armed Conflict (International Committee of the Red Cross 2004)
Médecins Sans Frontières, Shattered Lives: Immediate Medical Care Vital for Sexual Violence Victims (MSF June 2009)

Murray W, Military Adaptation in War (Institute for Defence Analyses 2009) <www.ida.org/-/media/feature/publications/m/mi/military-adaptation-in-war/ida-paper-p-4452.ashx> accessed 12 July 2021

Nicholson F, 'The "Essential Rights" to Family Unity of Refugees and Others in Need of International Protection in the Context of Family Reunification' (UNHCR, Legal and Protection Policy Research Series PPLA/2018/02, January 2018) <www.refworld.org/docid/5a902a9b4.html> accessed 12 July 2021

Oosterveld V, Women and Girls Fleeing Conflict: Gender and the Interpretation and Application of the 1951 Refugee Convention (UNHCR, PPLA/2012/06, September 2012)

Ormhaug C, Armed Conflict Deaths Disaggregated by Gender (International Peace Research Institute 2009)

Querton C, 'I Feel Like as a Woman I'm Not Welcome': A Gender Analysis of UK Asylum Law, Policy and Practice (Asylum Aid 2012)

The Fund for Peace, 'Fragile States Index 2021' <https://fragilestatesindex.org/wp-content/uploads/2021/05/fsi2021-report.pdf> accessed 12 July 2021

Türk V, Protection Gaps in Europe? Persons Fleeing the Indiscriminate Effects of Generalized Violence (United Nations High Commissioner for Refugees 2011) <www.refworld.org/publisher,UNHCR,4d37d8402,0.html> accessed 12 July 2021

United Nations Assistance Mission in Afghanistan, 'Fact Sheet 2017' (February 2018) <https://unama.unmissions.org/sites/default/files/unama_poc_ar_2017_data_visualisation_final.pdf> accessed 12 July 2021

United Nations Assistance Mission in Afghanistan, 'Afghanistan Protection of Civilians in Armed Conflict: Annual Report 2017' (February 2018) <https://unama.unmissions.org/sites/default/files/afghanistan_protection_of_civilians_annual_report_2017_final_6_march.pdf> accessed 12 July 2021

UNHCR, 'Global Trends: Forced Displacement in 2014' (18 June 2015) <www.unhcr.org/556725e69.pdf> accessed 12 July 2021

UNHCR, 'Global Trends: Forced Displacement in 2015' (20 June 2016) <www.unhcr.org/576408cd7.pdf> accessed 12 July 2021

UNHCR, 'Global Trends: Forced Displacement in 2016' (19 June 2017) <www.unhcr.org/5943e8a34.pdf> accessed 12 July 2021

UNHCR, 'Global Trends: Forced Displacement in 2017' (19 June 2018) <www.unhcr.org/5b27be547.pdf> accessed 12 July 2021

UNHCR, 'Global Trends: Forced Displacement in 2018' (19 June 2019) <www.unhcr.org/5d08d7ee7.pdf> accessed 12 July 2021

UNHCR, 'Global Trends: Forced Displacement in 2020' (18 June 2021) <www.unhcr.org/uk/statistics/unhcrstats/60b638e37/global-trends-forced-displacement-2020.html> accessed 12 July 2021

UNHCR, 'Global Trends 2021' (16 June 2022) <www.unhcr.org/62a9d1494/global-trends-report-2021> accessed 26 July 2022

Newspaper Articles

Allegra C, 'Revealed: Male Rape Used Systematically in Libya as Instrument of War' *The Guardian* (London, 3 November 2017) <www.theguardian.com/world/2017/nov/03/revealed-male-used-systematically-in-libya-as-instrument-of-war> accessed 12 July 2021

Cockburn P, 'War against ISIS: US Strategy in Tatters as Militants March On' *Independent on Sunday* (London, 12 October 2014) <www.independent.co.uk/voices/comment/war-against-isis-us-strategy-in-tatters-as-militants-march-on-9789230.html> accessed 12 July 2021

Editorial, 'The Guardian View on Afghanistan: War Quickens as Politicians Falter' *The Guardian* (London, 30 January 2015) <www.theguardian.com/commentisfree/2015/jan/30/guardian-view-afghanistan-war-quickens-politicians-falter> accessed 12 July 2021

Kurdistan 24, 'Baghdad Rejects Efforts by European Nations to Forcibly Deport Iraqi Refugees' (29 January 2018) <www.kurdistan24.net/en/news/ce115375-001b-46ea-810e-65e5c480267a> accessed 12 July 2021

International Law

United Nations, 'Conférence de Plénipotentiaires sur le Statut des Réfugiés et des Apatrides: Compte Rendu Analytique de la Cinquième Séance' (Geneva, 19 November 1951) (4 July 1951) UN Doc A/CONF.2/SR.5

United Nations, 'Conférence de Plénipotentiaires sur le Statut des Réfugiés et des Apatrides: Compte Rendu Analytique de la Quatrième Séance' (Geneva, 19 November 1951) (3 July 1951) UN Doc A/CONF.2/SR.4

UN Committee on the Elimination of All Forms of Discrimination against Women, 'General Recommendation No 19' in 'Note by the Secretariat, Compilation of General Comments and General Recommendations Adopted by Human Rights Treaty Bodies' (29 July 1994) UN Doc HRI/GEN/1/Rev.1

UN Committee on the Elimination of All Forms of Discrimination against Women, 'General Recommendation No 25, on Article 4, Paragraph 1, of the Convention on the Elimination of All Forms of Discrimination against Women, on temporary Special Measures' in 'Compilation of General Comments and General Recommendations Adopted by Human Rights Treaty Bodies' (2004) UN Doc HRI/GEN/1//Rev.7

UN Committee on the Elimination of All Forms of Discrimination against Women, 'General Recommendation No 35 on Gender-Based Violence against Women, updating General Recommendation No. 19' (2017) UN Doc CEDAW/C/GC/35

UN Committee on the Elimination of All Forms of Discrimination against Women, Concept Note: General Discussion on the Protection of Women's Human Rights in Conflict and Post-Conflict Contexts (United Nations 2011)

UN Committee on the Elimination of All Forms of Racial Discrimination, 'General Recommendation No 25: Gender Related Dimensions of Racial Discrimination' (20 March 2000) UN Doc A/55/18

UN Commission on the Status of Women (54th Session), 'High-level Round Table on the Implementation of the Beijing Declaration and Platform for Action and the Outcomes of the Twenty-third Special Session of the General Assembly and Its Contribution to Shaping a Gender Perspective in the Realization of the Millennium Development Goals' (10 March 2010) UN Doc E/CN.6/2010/CRP.5

UN Division for the Advancement of Women, 'Gender and Racial Discrimination: Report of the Expert Group Meeting' (21–24 November 2000)

United Nations Fourth World Conference on Women, Platform for Action: Women and Armed Conflict (United Nations 1995)

United Nations General Assembly, 'Conference of Plenipotentiaries on the Status of Refugees and Stateless Persons: Summary Record of the Nineteenth Meeting' (26 November 1951), <www.unhcr.org/protection/travaux/3ae68cda4/conference-plenipotentiaries-status-refugees-stateless-persons-summary.html> accessed 12 July 2021

United Nations General Assembly, Note on International Protection: International Protection in Mass Influx (submitted by the High Commissioner) (A/AC.96/850, 1 September 1995)

UN General Assembly, Human Rights Council Report of the Independent International Commission of Inquiry on the Syrian Arab Republic A/HRC/23/58, 18 July 2013

UN Human Rights Committee, 'General Comment No 29 – Article 4: Derogations during a State of Emergency' (31 August 2001) UN Doc. CCPR/C/21/Rev.1/Add.11

UN Human Rights Council, 'Report of the Special Rapporteur on torture and other cruel, inhuman or degrading treatment or punishment, Manfred Nowak' (15 January 2008) UN Doc A/HRC/7/3

UN Human Rights Council, 'Report of the Special Rapporteur on Torture and Other Cruel, Inhuman or Degrading Treatment or Punishment, Juan E. Méndez' (5 January 2016) UN Doc A/HRC/31/57

UN Office for the Coordination of Humanitarian Affairs (OCHA), Security Council Norms and Practice on the Protection of Civilians in Armed Conflict: Analysis of Normative Developments in Security Council Resolutions 2009–2013 (OCHA Policy and Studies Series 008, May 2014)

United Nations Secretary-General, 'Report to the Security Council on the Protection of Civilians in Armed Conflict' (8 September 1999) UN Doc S/1999/957

United Nations Secretary-General, Women, Peace and Security: Study Submitted by the Secretary-General Pursuant to Security Council Resolution 1325 (2000) (United Nations 2002)

UN Security Council, 'Conflict-related Sexual Violence: Report of the Secretary-General' (23 March 2015) UN Doc S/2015/203

United Nations Security Council, 'Resolution 1265' (17 September 1999) UN Doc S/RES/1265

United Nations Security Council, 'Resolution 1296' (12 April 2000) UN Doc S/RES/1296

United Nations Security Council, 'Resolution 1325' (31 October 2000) UN Doc S/RES/1325

United Nations Security Council, 'Resolution 1674 on Protection of Civilians in Armed Conflict' (2006)

United Nations Security Council, 'Resolution 1738' (23 December 2006) UN Doc S/RES/1738

United Nations Security Council, 'Resolution 1820' (19 June 2008) UN Doc S/RES/1820

United Nations Security Council, 'Resolution 1888' (30 September 2009) UN Doc S/RES/1888

United Nations Security Council, 'Resolution 1894' (11 November 2009) UN Doc S/RES/1894

United Nations Special Rapporteur on Violence against Women Its Causes and Consequences, 15 Years of the United Nations Special Rapporteur on Violence against Women Its Causes and Consequences (United Nations 2009)

UN World Conference on Human Rights, 'Vienna Declaration and Programme of Action', Adopted on 25 June 1993, Endorsed in UNGA Resolution 48/121 (20 December 1993) UN Doc A/RES/48/121

UNHCR Guidelines and Documents

UNHCR Executive Committee, 'Conclusion on the Provisions of International Protection Including through Complementary Forms of Protection' No. 103 (LVI) 2005, <www.unhcr.org/uk/excom/exconc/43576e292/conclusion-provision-international-protection-including-complementary-forms.html> accessed 12 July 2021

UNHCR, Note on Burden and Standard of Proof in Refugee Claims, 16 December 1998

UNHCR, Interpreting Article 1 of the 1951 Convention Relating to the Status of Refugees, April 2001

UNHCR, Guidelines on International Protection No. 1: Gender-Related Persecution within the Context of Article 1A(2) of the 1951 Convention and/or Its 1967 Protocol Relating to the Status of Refugees (HCR/GIP/02/01, 2002)

UNHCR, Annotated Comments on the EC Council Directive 2004/83/EC on Minimum Standards for the Qualification and Status of Third Country Nationals or Stateless Persons as Refugees or as Persons who otherwise need International Protection and the Content of the Protection granted (OJ L 304/12 of 30.9.2004) (January 2005) <www.unhcr.org/protect/PROTECTION/43661eee2.pdf> accessed 12 July 2021

UNHCR, 'Eligibility Guidelines for Assessing the International Protection Needs of Iraqi Asylum-Seekers', August 2007

UNHCR, 'Statement on Subsidiary Protection Under the EC Qualification Directive for People Threatened by Indiscriminate Violence' (January 2008) <www.refworld.org/pdfid/479df7472.pdf> accessed 12 July 2021

UNHCR, 'Guidance Note on Refugee Claims Relating to Victims of Organized Gangs' (31 March 2010) <www.refworld.org/docid/4bb21fa02.html> accessed 12 July 2021

UNHCR, International Protection Considerations with regard to people fleeing the Syrian Arab Republic, Update I, December 2012

UNHCR, 'International Protection Considerations with regard to people fleeing the Syrian Arab Republic, Update II' 22 October 2013

UNHCR, 'Key Considerations of the Court: BE: RvV 122 129 04.04.2014 (Syria)' <www.refworld.org/cgi-bin/texis/vtx/rwmain/opendocpdf.pdf?reldoc=y&docid=582068d64> accessed 12 July 2021

UNHCR, Guidelines on International Protection No. 11: Prima Facie Recognition of Refugee Status (HCR/GIP/15/11, 24 June 2015)

UNHCR, International Protection Considerations with Regard to People Fleeing the Syrian Arab Republic Update IV (HCR/PC/SYR/01, November 2015)

UNHCR, Guidelines on International Protection No. 12: Claims for Refugee Status Related to Situations of Armed Conflict and Violence under Article 1A(2) of the 1951 Convention and/or 1967 Protocol Relating to the Status of Refugees and the Regional Refugee Definitions (HCR/GIP/16/12, 2 December 2016)

UNHCR, Expert Meeting on Complementarities between International Refugee Law, International Criminal Law and International Human Rights Law (UNHCR 2011)

UNHCR, Summary Conclusions on International Protection of Persons Fleeing Armed Conflict and Other Situations of Violence; Roundtable 13 and 14 September 2012, Cape Town, South Africa (UNHCR 2012)

UNHCR, Handbook and Guidelines on Procedures and Criteria for Determining Refugee Status under the 1951 Convention and the 1967 Protocol Relating to the Status of Refugees (UNHCR 2019 (re-issue))

EU Law

Consolidated versions of the Treaty on European Union and the Treaty on the Functioning of the European Union 2012/C 326/01, Official Journal C 326, 26/10/2012 P. 0001–0390

Consolidated version of the Treaty on the Functioning of the European Union [2012] OJ C326/47

Council Directive 2001/55/EC of 20 July 2001 on Minimum Standards for Giving Temporary Protection in the Event of a Mass Influx of Displaced Persons and on Measures promoting a balance of efforts between Member States in receiving such persons and bearing the consequences thereof

Council Directive 2004/83/EC of 29 April 2004 on Minimum Standards for the Qualification and Status of Third Country Nationals or Stateless Persons as Refugees or as Persons Who Otherwise Need International Protection and the Content of the Protection Granted [2004] OJ L304/12

Council Implementing Decision (EU) 2022/382 of 4 March 2022 Establishing the Existence of a Mass Influx of Displaced Persons from Ukraine within the Meaning of Article 5 of Directive 2001/55/EC, and Having the Effect of Introducing Temporary Protection [2022] OJ L 71/1

Directive 2011/95/EU of the European Parliament and of the Council of 13 December 2011 on Standards for the Qualification of Third-Country Nationals or Stateless Persons as Beneficiaries of International Protection, for a Uniform Status for Refugees or for Persons Eligible for Subsidiary Protection, and for the Content of the Protection Granted (recast) [2011] OJ L337/9

Directive 2013/32/EU of the European Parliament and of the Council of 26 June 2013 on Common Procedures for Granting and Withdrawing International Protection OJ L 180

European Commission, Proposal for a Council Directive on Minimum Standards for Giving Temporary Protection in the Event of a Mass Influx of Displaced Persons and on Measures Promoting a Balance of Efforts between Member States in Receiving Such Persons and Bearing the Consequences Thereof (COM(2000) 303 final, 24 May 2000)

European Commission, Proposal for a Council Directive on Minimum Standards for the Qualification and Status of Third Country Nationals and Stateless Persons as Refugees or as Persons Who Otherwise Need International Protection (COM(2001) 510 final, 12 September 2001)

European Commission, Proposal for a Directive of the European Parliament and of the Council on Minimum Standards for the Qualification and Status of Third Country Nationals or Stateless Persons as Beneficiaries of International Protection and the Content of the Protection Granted (COM(2009) 551 final, 21 October 2009)

European Commission, Report from the Commission to the European Parliament and the Council on the Application of Directive 2004/83/EC of 29 April 2004 on the Minimum Standards for the

Qualification and Status of Third Country Nationals or Stateless Persons as Refugees or as Persons Who Otherwise Need International Protection and the Content of the Protection (COM(2010) 314 final, 2010)

European Commission, Communication from the Commission to the European Parliament, the Council, the European Economic and Social Committee and the Committee of the Regions: A European Agenda on Migration (COM(2015) 240 final, 13 May 2015)

European Commission, Proposal for a Regulation of the European Parliament and of the Council on Standards for the Qualification of Third-country Nationals or Stateless Persons as Beneficiaries of International Protection, for a Uniform Status for Refugees or for Persons Eligible for Subsidiary Protection and for the Content of the Protection Granted and Amending Council Directive 2003/109/EC of 25 November 2003 Concerning the Status of Third-country Nationals Who Are Long-term Residents (COM(2016) 466 final, 2016)

European Commission, Proposal for a Regulation of the European Parliament and of the Council Addressing Situations of Crisis and Force Majeure in the Field of Migration and Asylum (COM(2020) 613 final)

European Union, 'Common EU Guidelines for Processing Country of Origin Information (COI)' (ARGO project JLS/2005/ARGO/GC/03, April 2008) <www.refworld.org/docid/48493f7f2.html> accessed 12 July 2021

Joint Position of 4 March 1996 Defined by the Council on the Basis of Article K.3 of the Treaty on European Union on the Harmonized Application of the Definition of the Term 'Refugee' in Article 1 of the Geneva Convention of 28 July 1951 Relating to the Status of Refugees ((96/196/JHA) [1996] OJ L63/2)

Protocol (No) 22 on the Position of Denmark Annexed to the Treaty on the Functioning of the European Union

Regulation (EU) 2021/2303 of the European Parliament and of the Council of 15 December 2021 on the European Union Agency for Asylum and Repealing Regulation (EU) No 439/2010

National Law

Belgium

Loi du 15 décembre 1980 sur l'accès au territoire, le séjour, l'établissement et l'éloignement des étrangers / Wet van 15 december 1980 betreffende de toegang tot het grondgebied, het verblijf, de vestiging en de verwijdering van vreemdelingen <www.ejustice.just.fgov.be/cgi_loi/change_lg.pl?language=fr&la=F&cn=1980121530&table_name=loi> accessed 12 July 2021

Denmark

Udlændingeloven: Lov nr. 226 af 8 juni 1983, Lovtidende A 1983, S. 549–550 as amended by Lov om ændring af udlændingeloven: Lov nr. 239 af 10 marts 2019, Lovtidende A 2019 <www.retsinformation.dk/eli/lta/2021/1910> accessed 12 July 2021

Justitsministeriet Udlændingeafdelingen, Svar på spørgsmål nr. 342 (Alm.del) fra Folketingets Udvalg for Udlændinge- og Integrationspolitik (26 June 2013) <www.ft.dk/samling/20121/almdel/uui/spm/342/svar/1063917/1265343/index.htm> accessed 12 July 2021

Forslag til Lov om ændring af udlændingeloven, Folketingstidende A, Lovforslag nr. L 72 (14 November 2014)

Lov om ændring af udlændingeloven: Lov nr. 153 af 18 februar 2015, Lovtidende A 2015

Lov om ændring af udlændingeloven: Lov nr. 102 af 3 februar 2016, Lovtidende A 2016

France

Code de l'Entrée et du Séjour des Etrangers et du Droit d'Asile (CESEDA) <www.legifrance.gouv.fr/affichCode.do?cidTexte=LEGITEXT000006070158&dateTexte=20130416> accessed 12 July 2021

Law n. 2018–778 of 10 September 2018

Spain

Ley 29/1998, de 13 de julio, reguladora de la Jurisdicción Contencioso-administrativa

Ley 12/2009, de 30 de octubre, reguladora del derecho de asilo y de la protección subsidiaria BOE núm. 263, de 31 de octubre <www.interior.gob.es/web/servicios-al-ciudadano/normativa/leyes-ordinarias/ley-12-2009-de-30-de-octubre> accessed 12 July 2021

Real Decreto 557/2011, de 20 de abril, por el que se aprueba el Reglamento de la Ley Orgánica 4/2000, sobre derechos y libertades de los extranjeros en España y su integración social, tras su reforma por Ley Orgánica 2/2009

The Netherlands

Vreemdelingenwet 2000 (Vw 2000) <https://wetten.overheid.nl/BWBR0011823/2013-01-01> accessed 12 July 2021

United Kingdom

European Union (Withdrawal Agreement) Act 2020

Nationality and Borders Act 2022 <www.legislation.gov.uk/ukpga/2022/36/contents/enacted> accessed 26 July 2022

Statement of Changes in Immigration Rules (HC395) May 1994 (as amended) <www.gov.uk/guidance/immigration-rules/immigration-rules-part-11-asylum> accessed 12 July 2021

The Refugee or Person in Need of International Protection (Qualification) Regulations 2006 <www.legislation.gov.uk/uksi/2006/2525/made> accessed 12 July 2021

INDEX

For EU product safety concerns, contact us at Calle de José Abascal, 56–1°, 28003 Madrid, Spain or eugpsr@cambridge.org.

www.ingramcontent.com/pod-product-compliance
Lightning Source LLC
LaVergne TN
LVHW081933200926
848484LV00009B/2421

* 9 7 8 1 0 0 9 3 5 9 3 9 9 *